DATE DUE

From paddy field
to ski slope

日本 研究 Japanese Studies

Japanese Studies

Ceremony and symbolism in the Japanese home
Michael Jeremy and M. E. Robinson

Becoming Japanese   *Joy Hendry*

Language and popular culture in Japan   *Brian Moeran*

Further titles in preparation

Okpyo Moon

From paddy field
to ski slope

The revitalisation of tradition
in Japanese village life

Manchester University Press
Manchester and New York
Distributed exclusively in the USA and Canada by St. Martin's Press

Copyright © Okpyo Moon 1989

Published by Manchester University Press
  Oxford Road, Manchester M13 9PL, UK
and Room 400, 175 Fifth Avenue,
  New York, NY 10010, USA

Distributed exclusively in the USA and Canada
by St. Martins Press, Inc.,
  175 Fifth Avenue, New York, NY 10010, USA

British Library cataloguing in publication data
Moon, Okpyo
  From paddy field to ski slope: the
  revitalisation of tradition in Japanese
  village life. – (Japanese studies)
  1. Japan. Villages. Social change
  I. Title   II. Series
  307.7'2'0952

Library of Congress cataloging in publication data applied for

ISBN 0 7190 2957 0 *hardback*

Printed in Great Britain
by Billings and Sons Ltd., Worcester

Contents

Contents

Illustrations

Maps

Tables

Figures

Introduction

The prosperity enjoyed by modern Japan is perhaps most vividly felt in her villages. Up until the beginning of the 1950s, most of them were at a barely subsistent level with very limited cash income and with hardly any modern living facilities. Within some thirty years, most farm families in Japan have come to live in spacious new houses with such modern facilities as a gas cooker, refrigerator and washing machine. Most families also own one or two cars with which they plan a retirement trip somewhere in Japan or abroad, in addition to the regular coach trips organised jointly by the villagers. Furthermore, they are now entitled to government pensions and for once they don't seem to have to worry about the future when they are old and not able to work any longer. Indeed, the present material affluence is so conspicuous compared to the dilapidated conditions of the immediate post-war years that at times villagers themselves find it hard to believe and many express a genuine concern for whether this will continue.

This complete transformation of lifestyle is even more stark in a remote, hitherto predominantly agricultural, mountain village like Hanasaku which has developed into an ultra-modern ski resort. The ski resort opened in 1964 and other subsequently developed tourist attractions now bring in thousands of tourists every year with their cash and urban influence to this previously isolated area. To describe and analyse the political, economic and social implications of this development in the context of the everyday lives of Hanasaku people is the main purpose of this book. In doing so, however, it becomes inevitable to touch upon some theoretical questions concerning economic development and social change in general.

One of these concerns what has become known as 'the modernisation approach', a major macrotheoretical framework put forward to explain the process of economic development and social change in general. At its crudest, advocates of this view assume that one can describe the general features of 'traditional' and 'modern' societies and treat development as the transformation of the one type into the other entailing the eventual modification or elimination of 'traditional' pattern variables.[1] Smelser's more elaborate model depicts this process of transformation in terms of structural differentiation, i.e. 'the evolution from a multi-functional role structure to several more specialized structures'.[2] He argues, for example, that as the economy develops, several kinds of economic activity are removed from family and community; consumption and production activities are separated; and wage-labour undermines the family production unit. Along with these developments, he further maintains that demands for 'economic rationality' bring pressures against the recruitment of labour along kinship lines, thereby gradually dissolving the control of extended family and village. Similarly, multi-functional religious and political roles are replaced by more specialised structures, and recruitment to various occupational, political, and religious positions tends to become more dependent on achievement criteria than on ascription.

Although it is true that Smelser and other modernisation theorists are dealing with more macro-level and long-term changes than those considered here, Hanasaku nevertheless seems to provide a useful case for testing the concept of 'structural differentiation', since many aspects of the post-war economic changes in Hanasaku match the elements which Smelser describes as affecting rural social transformation: mechanisation of cultivation techniques, introduction of cash crops, greater involvement in wage-earning activities and increased individual mobility. To examine systematically whether this economic development has brought the kind of unilineal and inter-related structural differentiation suggested by Smelser and others may therefore provide us with a good opportunity to assess the utility of such a model for understanding short-term changes and adaptations.

Another theoretical proposition concerns the so-called 'community' model which is in many ways ideologically related to the preceding one. Since Embree and Suzuki, many western and Japanese social scientists working on rural Japan have placed great emphasis on the traditional hamlet (*buraku*) or 'natural village' (*shizenson*) in Suzuki's terminology.[3] Based on the household as constituent unit, a hamlet often possesses a distinct structure and regulations, owns property and acts as a collective on the basis of territorial bonds. These bonds are often symbolically reinforced by the existence of a shrine where residents regularly worship their common guardian god. Within a hamlet, we may also find elaborate mechanisms for co-operation based on kinship or territorial ties such as *dōzoku*, *kumi* or *kō*, and these provide the basis for the high degree of cohesive solidarity often displayed by its constitutent members.

2

One notable recent trend in the studies of these units is the greater emphasis given to the dynamics of change they are undergoing in the face of rapid economic growth in the country as a whole. This reflects a major shift of interest from the static and descriptive emphasis of earlier analysis, concentrating largely on the clarification of different organising principles within the units. One interpretation of possible change in Japanese village communities in the future can be found in the following statement by Fukutake, a leading Japanese rural sociologist.

Japanese villages have been interpreted until recently as being 'village communities' in the technical sense of *Dorfgemeinde*. This concept belongs to a theoretical scheme in which the 'village community' is one stage beyond a 'primitive communal society'. In the latter the communal system is continued and maintained because the level of productivity is too low for an individualistic system of independent production. A 'village community', by contrast, is typically found where, even though individualistic production becomes predominant, a certain amount of cooperation based on communal ownership is an essential supplementary element of productive activity. Thus, the constraints of the whole community limit the individual's private activity and these restrictions are reinforced by the fact that the village community is usually isolated and exclusive, a microcosm of its own.[4]

The above statement seems to represent a succinct version of the view of many Japanese social scientists adhering to the so-called *sonraku kyōdō-tairon*, or 'community theories'.[5] By assuming that the solidary and co-operative nature of rural communities in Japan has been a consequence of a less developed economy, the argument implies that, as the economy develops and the people become economically less dependent upon each other for survival, this co-operation and solidarity will eventually disappear and people will become more 'individualistic'. This view thus exhibits an ideological kinship to the 'modernisation approach' discussed above.

Highly 'functionalist' though it may be, this view has been in some ways confirmed by a number of recent studies. While not explicitly recognising a tie with Fukutake's view, Moeran has observed the following changes in the social organisation of a pottery making village in Kyushu.[6] In the past, when its residents were engaged mainly in farming with pottery making supplementing agricultural income, they co-operated closely with each other. The cultivation of paddy rice and the existence of a communal kiln for part-time pottery making necessitated such co-operation. After the Second World War, however, the demand for 'folk craft' pottery rapidly increased, and people became involved full-time in pottery making, with a concomitant decline in agriculture. These developments have led to the breakdown of certain forms of co-operation as the residents began to build individual kilns and to adopt new technology for pottery making to meet

3

the increasing demand. Furthermore, the specific kind of marketing developed to sell pottery produced in this village has placed an emphasis on individual talent and thus contributed toward the weakening of community solidarity which was based on relative equality in terms of wealth and status. On the basis of these observations, Moeran remarks: 'Much of what has been written concerning the household (*ie*), extended household (*dōzoku*) and hamlet (*buraku*) expresses an ideal that may have been true in the past, but is no longer strictly adhered to in practice'.[7]

Itō has noted a similar tendency in a different context.[8] In the village he studied, the development of two new cash crops after the war, silkworms and tobacco, has led to the emergence of two factional groups pursuing the cultivation of each crop and fiercely competing with each other within the community. According to him, the specialisation of different crops, penetration of cash economy and commercialism, and people's greater involvement with a social and economic network outside the community have effectively diversified the interests of the hamlet residents and consequently undermined its traditional solidarity which was based on the closed nature of the community and relative homogeneity of its members.

Of another Kyushu village, however, Matsunaga reports a slightly different phenomenon.[9] According to him, despite the shift from paddy rice to chrysanthemum cultivation as year-round cash crop and despite a gradual increase in the number of commuters and immigrants in the village resulting from the growth of urban centres nearby, a remarkable degree of continuity has been maintained in the social and religious life of the village. Not only has the content of the village festival centering on old agricultural practices not changed, but also many of the newcomers and non-farmers have been incorporated into the traditional co-operative system of the community without much disruption. This contrary evidence notwithstanding, Matsunaga also implicitly suggests that the community system will eventually disappear, by interpreting the phenomenon he observed in the village as a 'cultural lag', i.e. a phenomenon which shows the changes in cultural practices lagging behind the changes in the economic sphere.[10]

It is in the light of these studies that I will examine the process of social change the people in the village of Hanasaku have experienced as a consequence of the development of a tourism industry. Hanasaku is no longer an isolated and exclusive community of its own. Its economy is far removed from the subsistence level and its people now live in almost constant contact with outsiders. Nevertheless, as will be shown in the following chapters, a fair number of co-operative mechanisms and a con-

4

siderable degree of interdependency are still maintained in the village. It is of course true that the village has witnessed the breakdown of certain specific forms of co-operation, especially those that had been intertwined with the old practices of agriculture and forestry. In other aspects of social and religious life, however, new forms of co-operation and communal activity are also appearing, which apparently function in the direction of intensifying and strengthening existing hamlet and village solidarity. Is this simply a phenomenon of 'cultural lag', or are there other underlying reasons? This is one of the main questions this study will try to answer and in doing so I hope it will also shed some light on the more general issue of the future of the Japanese 'village community' in the face of drastic economic changes.

Fieldwork

The materials discussed in this book were mostly collected during fieldwork carried out between February 1981 and October 1982. Of this period, the sixteen months from June 1981 to September 1982 were spent in the village. As in much other anthropological research, the period in the village was mostly spent on informal interviews, participant observation and a survey of locally available historical and statistical sources including family and land registries. In addition, literary sources were referred to in order to place the data collected in the village in a wider context.

The selection of the research site
The site was chosen with the following considerations. First, a village in Kantō area, an area surrounding Tokyo to the east and north, was considered desirable. While it is often assumed that significant regional variations exist in Japan in the patterns of village organisation,[11] few intensive ethnographic investigations have yet been published about villages in this area. Some information can be found in *Sanson Seikatsu no Kenkyū* (Studies of Life in Mountain Villages) published in 1938 by *Nihon Minzokugaku Kenyūsho* (Institute for Japanese Folklore) under the editorship of a leading Japanese folklorist, Yanagita Kunio (1875–1962); and more recently in *Shinshu no Sonraku Seikatsu* (Village Life in Shinshu) by Takeuchi, a detailed ethnographic report published in three volumes about a village in the present Nagano prefecture.[12] However, compared to the south-western Inland Sea region studied intensively by the Michigan team of American anthropologists during the early 1950s,[13] Kyushu[14] and

5

north-eastern Japan,[15] only scanty information is available in the English language about the Kantō area, in central-northern Japan. It was therefore thought that any descriptive account of village life in this region would be of some comparative value, especially in terms of the organisational pattern of the extended household groups.[16]

Secondly, I wanted to avoid a village near a major city where commuters were prevalent. There would be value in studying such a village to understand the phenomenon of commuting *per se*[17] or that of so-called U-turn or J-turn migration. After a period of continuous emigration, some villages in Japan, especially those that lie within relatively easy commuting distance of cities, seem to be gaining population slightly as some of the youngsters who once migrated to cities have decided to return to their home villages when they have difficulties in adapting to urban life. Although people mention as reasons for this reverse migration pollution in the cities, lack of living space or decent jobs, etc., the more important aspect of this phenomenon seems to be that some, though not all, Japanese villages have now become sufficiently well-off to be able to attract their offspring back.[18]

A study of commuter villages is also of some interest to see how community life is organised, or disorganised, by the absence of those employed elsewhere. While focusing on change, I was more interested in an area where local industry has developed than in an area where the local population has been absorbed into cities as commuters. Although there have been suggestions that all Japanese villages will eventually become commuter villages,[19] such a possibility is very remote in a village like Hanasaku, which does not lie within easy commuting distance of a town or a city despite recent improvements in transportation. Under these circumstances, people often endeavour to develop a local industry as Hanasaku did to meet the increasing demand for cash income, and patterns of community life in these locally developed villages may differ considerably from those of commuter villages.

Finally, a special effort was made to avoid a village inhabited by such minority groups as *Burakumin* or Korean Japanese. There are of course some practical difficulties in carrying out research in those communities in terms of possible reaction of the residents concerned as well as in terms of securing financial support from Japanese sources, since minority problems in general are considered to be a 'national shame' by most Japanese authorities. In addition, from my earlier work[20] I concluded that the study of a *Burakumin* community constitutes quite a separate problem which I do not particularly wish to pursue here. In fact, as it turned out, there are few such outcaste villages in this region at the northern end of Gunma prefecture.[21]

In addition to these considerations, however, one of the vital elements in choosing a research site is of course whether one can find a place to stay in the village for one year or more either as a lodger or by renting a house. Personally, I had to visit some twenty villages in the Kantō region alone before I was able to find a village which meets all these basic requirements and which also has a family that was willing to accept me as a lodger. Interestingly, the best introduction that enabled me to find such a place was neither a letter from a Tokyo University professor nor even his personal presence, but that of a primary school teacher who once worked in the village school. The teacher, whom I met only once, did not even write a formal introductory letter for me, but at the mere mention of her name, a farm family which has a daughter who was taught by the teacher some six years ago agreed without much difficulty to provide me with room and board in return for some compensation.

Although it was not a factor considered beforehand, the development of a tourism industry nonetheless seems to be a topic that deserves serious consideration in relation to rural development in Japan, since it has appeared in many parts of the country where the existing agricultural resources are too meagre to satisfy the people's increasing need for additional cash income. Hanasaku was one such example. Though there may be a number of ways of approaching the subject from an anthropological perspective,[22] I shall confine myself in this study to only one aspect: in what ways the development of a tourism industry has transformed the social and economic life of the host society.

The unit under study

Literally, it is the word *mura* that should be translated as 'village'. In Japan, however, the word refers to a political unit that corresponds to an amalgamation of several 'natural villages'. Before the administrative change in 1888, Hanasaku was officially Hanasaku *mura* like many other 'natural villages' at the time. These *mura* belonged to a larger administrative unit, the *gun* (county). The *gun* was abolished in the 1920s, and enlarged *mura* were placed directly under the prefectural government. Under this new administrative system, therefore, a *mura* is the smallest political division with a government and an assembly of its own.

In everyday usage, however, the term *mura* means three different things depending on the context.[23] For example, when Hanasaku people say 'Every household in the village should be called upon and asked to come at

7

the time of funeral' (*Sōshiki no toki wa mura chū yobi da*), the word *mura* is used to refer only to one's own hamlet, i.e. the *buraku*. If people say 'All the people in the village used to gather at the time of the village festival' (*Omatsuri no toki wa mura no hitobito ga zenbu atsumatta*), it is the old village unit, the Hanasaku *mura*, that they are referring to. Again they may say, '*Mura ni chūgakkō ga hitotsu arimasu*', meaning that there is one middle school in the new administrative village, Katashina *mura*. Indeed, people apply the same term freely to designate three totally different units according to the context, a situation which reminds us of the Nuer concept of *cieng* discussed by Evans-Pritchard.[24]

For the purpose of consistency, however, I shall in this study use the English word 'village' only to designate traditional villages like Hanasaku, and apply the Japanese term *mura* to new administrative units like Katashina of which Hanasaku comprises a part. The word 'hamlet' will be reserved for the sub-units of Hanasaku village, such as Yamazaki, Noboto or Kajiya. Although most community studies on Japan have dealt with *buraku* or hamlet units, to consider the hamlets as more or less independent units of their own seemed to me unreasonable in the case of Hanasaku. Not only do the people in the village refer to the hamlets as *kumi*, thus indicating that they are parts of a larger unit, but also there are a number of political and religious roots which unite the six hamlets in Hanasaku into one unit. While the hamlets are clearly divided and tend to compete with each other within the village, as will become clear in the following chapters, much that happened in one of the hamlets can be adequately understood only in the context of the whole village. It is for this reason that I shall deal with the six hamlets or *buraku* together in this study.

Hanasaku village is now the third *ku* or district of Katashina *mura*. When the thirteen villages in this area were placed under the new political division of Katashina *mura*, they were divided into eight districts according to their respective size and location. Hanasaku, being one of the largest of the villages and situated well into the mountain area considerably separated from the major highway and from other villages, was made a district of its own. This clear geographical demarcation makes the village a good site for anthropological research, despite its relatively large size of over two hundred households. Perhaps owing to its geographical isolation and to the fact that it had been an independent village unit during the Tokugawa period (1603–1868), the people in Hanasaku seem to display a strong sense of belonging to the village unit, which in this case is identical with the district division. The identification of the village unit with the new administrative division also contributes toward the relative political strength of Hanasaku as compared to other districts made up of several former villages, where loyalty tends to divide.

Notes

1 See, for example, Hoselitz 1960; Moore 1963; Eisenstadt 1966, 1970; Dalton 1971; Bennett 1967.
2 Smelser 1966: 35.
3 According to Suzuki 1940: chapter one, a 'natural village' is neither a cluster of houses nor an administrative village which he distinguishes from the former as *gyōseison*, but a unit which has an autonomous force of its own over and above individual members, which in turn regulates the behaviour of its members.
4 Fukutake 1967: 84.
5 For further discussions on *sonraku kyōdōtai*, see *Sonrakushakai kenkyūkai* 1954, 1959; Matsubara 1957; Shimazaki 1967; Nakano 1967; Yoden and Matsubara 1968; Nakamura 1971; Iwamoto 1970a; Takeuchi 1976.
6 Moeran 1981; 1984.
7 Moeran 1981; 42.
8 Itō 1982.
9 Matsunaga 1981.
10 Cf. Ogburn 1966.
11 Cf. Izumi and Gamō 1952; Ishino and Bennett 1953.
12 Takeuchi *op. cit.*
13 Beardsley, Hall and Ward 1959; Cornell and Smith 1956; Norbeck 1954.
14 Embree 1939; Hendry 1981; Moeran 1984.
15 Ariga 1943; Brown 1966.
16 It is generally assumed that there exists a sort of dichotomy in the patterns of village organisation between north-eastern Japan where the archetypal *dōzoku* have developed and the south-western region where villages are organised around neighbourhood groups and thus on a more egalitarian principle as opposed to the hierarchical principle of *dōzoku*. See Izumi and Gamō *op. cit.*; Johnson 1967; Fukutake 1967; chapter five; Nakane 1967: chapter three; T. Smith 1959: chapter one. Given the dichotomy, Professor Suenari Michio has suggested to me that the northern Kantō area may be considered a dividing line.
17 Cf. Kinoshita, Yamamoto and Sasaki 1978.
18 A similar tendency of return migration has been observed in other post-industrial societies like England or the United States. See Nalson 1982. However, while the return migrants in those societies mostly consist of 'hobby farmers' recruited from a relatively well-off urban population seeking a different way of life, in Japan, the phenomenon can be literally considered U-turn or J-turn migration in that the migrants are mostly the returning children of old time residents.
19 Bennett 1967.
20 Moon Kim 1979; see also De Vos and Wagatsuma 1966; Donoghue 1977, Yoshino and Murakoshi 1977.
21 Moon Kim 1984: 17–18.
22 Cf. Nash 1981; see also Tamao 1980; Moeran 1983; Graburn 1977, 1983.
23 According to Nakane 1970: 59, the term *mura* is also used in the sense of 'primary

community'. For instance, when used as jargon among professional lawyers and politicians, *mura* indicates an internal faction within a larger association or a political party to which one belongs.

24 Evans-Pritchard 1940: 136.

The village and its hamlets

Communication

The village of Hanasaku is located at the north-eastern end of Gunma prefecture, an area some two and a half hours by train from Tokyo (see Map 1). For the first two hours, the journey takes one through rice fields dotted with mulberry bushes. Then the scenery suddenly changes and mountains covered with thick forests begin to appear. The train passes enormous, garish billboards advertising hot springs, ski grounds, wild mushroom fields and artificial fish farms. The traveller soon realises that he has entered a tourist region. To get to Hanasaku requires a one hour bus journey from the station at Numata along steep mountain passes with dark green forests on one side and steep valleys on the other, and then another local bus which runs only four times a day since Hanasaku is not on the main road. Unless one carefully plans the journey from Numata or walks to the village, which takes about one and a half hours, one may end up waiting for two or three hours.

About three miles from the major highway the road divides, and this marks the beginning of Hanasaku village. On the right lie three hamlets – Kajiya, Tochikubo and Noboto. Passing Noboto, the road leads after about five minutes on foot to the Olympia ski ground. On the left lies Yamazaki *buraku*, and after another twenty-minute walk the road reaches Kuryu. Before reaching Kuryu from Yamazaki, a road forks off to the right towards another small settlement called Hariyama. The six hamlets together constitute Hanasaku village.

On the whole, however, the scanty bus service does not bother the villagers very much, since most of them now possess a car or a *toraku* (a small four-wheeled lorry). The first and last services are, however, vital for the people in Hanasaku as well as those in Hataya and Surubuchi, the two neighbouring villages that constitute the second *ku* (district) of Katashina *mura*. All children from the three villages between the ages of twelve and

1. Kagoshima
2. Miyazaki
3. Kumamoto
4. Ōita
5. Fukuoka
6. Saga
7. Nagasaki
8. Kōchi
9. Tokushima
10. Kagawa
11. Ehime
12. Yamaguchi
13. Hiroshima
14. Shimane
15. Okayama
16. Tottori
17. Hyōgo
18. Kyoto
19. Wakayama
20. Osaka
21. Mie
22. Nara
23. Shiga
24. Fukui
25. Ishikawa
26. Gifu
27. Aichi
28. Shizuoka
29. Nagano
30. Toyama

31. Niigata
32. Yamanashi
33. Gunma
34. Kanagawa
35. Tokyo
36. Chiba
37. Saitama
38. Ibaraki
39. Tochigi
40. Fukushima
41. Yamagata
42. Miyagi
43. Akita
44. Iwate
45. Aomori

HOKKAIDŌ

TŌHOKU

KANTŌ

CHŪGOKU

CHŪBU

KINKI

SHIKOKU

KYŪSHŪ

0   300 km

Map 1: Japan: regions

12

fifteen use the bus to commute to the middle school in Kamada, the administrative centre of Katashina *mura* (see Map 2).

The major highway, the *Kokudō* (National Highway) 120, and the prefectural road that connects Hanasaku to it are virtually the only roads that link the village to the outside world, leading primarily to Numata, the nearest urban and marketing centre, but eventually to Tokyo and its surrounding employment centres where most of the younger sons of the village hope to find work. Before automobile transport became as common as it is now, there was another road leading out of the village toward Numata through Kawaba *mura* to the south and Tone to the west (see Map 3). This second road fell into neglect when the prefectural road connecting Hanasaku to the major highway was widened and paved in the early 1960s. The same happened to the two mountain paths that connected the village to Kamada. In some ways, therefore, Hanasaku has become more isolated in recent years with the development of automobile transportation. Even among the villages in Katashina *mura*. Hanasaku is considered the most remote and most unfavourably located. In order to change this, the village is now campaigning to revive the old road leading to Kawaba and Numata, but has been opposed by the authorities in Kawaba who intend to develop their own tourism industry and fear competition from Hanasaku.

Historical background

The genealogical record available in the village in the form of ancestral tablets (*ihai*) kept in each household indicates only a little over three hundred years of history even for the oldest families. Other available evidence, however, suggests a much longer history of settlement in the area. A number of Jōmon and Yayoi sites,[1] for instance, are found throughout Katashina *mura*, and one of the three local tombs believed to belong to the subsequent 'Tomb Period' is situated in Hanasaku, where a small shrine marks it as an object of reverence.[2]

Another reference can be found in a document purportedly written in the Kamakura period (1185–1333).[3] This is the record of a hunting expedition carried out by Minamoto Yoritomo in 1192 which talks of four people from Hanasaku called upon to serve in the expedition. It also records that two *koku* of rice (a *koku* is about five bushels or 150 kilograms of brown rice) was supplied by the village for the occasion. At that time, the area was ruled by the Ōtomo family based in a castle in

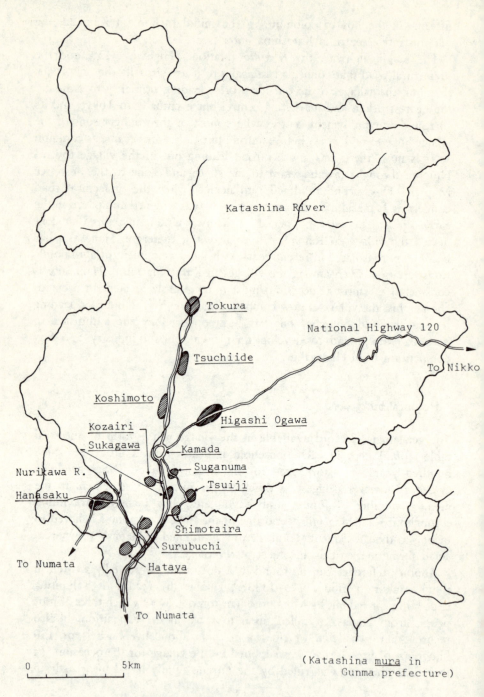

Katashina River

Tokura

National Highway 120

Tsuchiide

To Nikko

Koshimoto

Kozairi
Sukagawa

Higashi Ogawa

Kamada

Suganuma

Tsuiji

Nurikawa R.

Hanasaku

Shimotaira

Surubuchi

To Numata

Hataya

To Numata

0   5km

(Katashina mura in
Gunma prefecture)

Map 2: Villages in Katashina *mura*

14

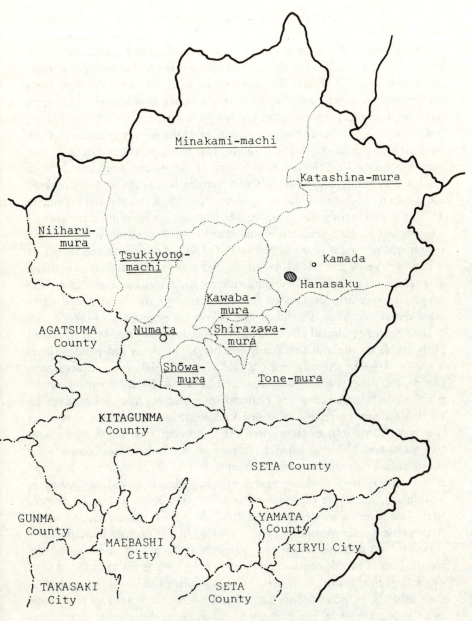

Map 3: Tone county

Takasaki. Sometime in the early fourteenth century, however, the present area of Tone county was taken over by the Numata family based in a castle located in the present Numata city, who retained power for nearly two hundred years. During this period, Tone was divided into three shires (*shō*) of which one, Tsuchiide,[4] covered an area not much different from the present Katashina *mura* although the number of settlements is said to have been smaller, especially on the northern frontier.

For about sixty years from the beginning of the sixteenth century, Tone became a centre of continuous conflict like many places in Japan at that time. Four local lords including the Numata family competed for the area until it was finally consolidated under Sanada Masayuki who, by making allegiance to Toyotomi Hideyoshi, was successful in establishing his rule in 1590. On conquering the area, Sanada returned to his old fief in Shinshū (the present Nagano prefecture) and sent his son Nobuyuki to be the first feudal lord in the fief (*han*) of Numata. The Sanada period lasted for about a hundred years until 1681 when the fief was confiscated by the ruling Tokugawa shogunate, thus ending rule by local lords in the region. The shogunate regularly dispatched its representatives to Numata and exercised direct rule until the end of the Tokugawa period (1603–1868).

Despite these political changes, old village units like Hanasaku remained fairly stable throughout the Tokugawa period, enjoying independent legal status and being directly responsible to the feudal (*han*) government. During the early years of the Meiji period (1868–1912), however, larger political units subsuming the hitherto independent villages began to be created for more effective centralised administration. Katashina *mura*, as it is now, came into existence in 1888 following a series of administrative measures. Thirteen villages situated in northern Tone County were incorporated into this new political unit. At first, there were two administrative offices in Katashina *mura*, one in Sukagawa and the other in Koshimoto, in charge of southern and northern Katashina *mura* respectively (see Map 2). It was not until 1897 that a new administrative centre responsible for the whole *mura* was created in the present Kamada.

Nowadays, administration for all residents of the *mura* including the registration of births, deaths and marriages as well as the transfer of land ownership and so forth is carried out at the offices in Kamada.[5] Although the county (*gun*) was abolished as an official political division, it survives as an important social and economic unit as far as those living in Hanasaku and Katashina *mura* are concerned. Most local associations, for example, have their immediate headquarters at county level in Numata, for whose offices local representatives at the *ku* or *mura* level sometimes aspire. Also winners of local annual *mura* athletic meetings, baseball matches and dancing competitions are sent to compete with those from other *mura* or *machi* (towns)[6] that belong to the old county. Even for cattle auctions, there is only one market, in Niiharu *mura*, for the whole of Tone county.

Compared to the county unit, the significance of the prefectural division to people in Hanasaku seems to be minimal. Once in every four years, they vote for candidates to the prefectural assembly, but few have yet aspired to the office from Katashina *mura*. Similarly, although school teachers are appointed and circulated within the prefectural boundary, they have little influence nowadays on community life in general, except for those with children at school who thereby become directly involved. The incidence of marriage alliances also drops sharply outside the county boundary, as do opportunities for travel. Big cities are concentrated in the south-eastern part of Gunma prefecture (see Map 4), where a number of the villagers' second and third sons are employed. Except for these urban centres, knowledge of and interaction with other parts of the prefecture is surprisingly limited beyond the county boundary.

Topography and climate

The Kantō region includes the largest plain in Japan and the two metropolises of Tokyo and Yokohama. The average population of 800 or more per square kilometre is the most dense in Japan.[7] Being located at its northernmost end, however, in many respects Katashina *mura* resembles the rural Tōhoku region to the north rather than the very urban southern part of Kantō.

The composition of the almost 400 square kilometres that constitute Katashina *mura* can be seen in Table 1: only three per cent of the land is cultivatable and most of the rest is covered by forests, coarse grass and marshes. There are more than twenty mountains over 2,000 metres above sea level, numerous hills and slopes, and many volcanic lakes and hot springs. Thus, though unfavourably situated for agricultural purposes, the *mura* possesses many potential tourist attractions which local people have begun to exploit.

The area is drained by the Katashina River which runs through the *mura* from north to south and continues into Tone *mura* where it joins the Tone River. The Tone River, which continues through Shōwa *mura* west of Tone and eventually into the Pacific, drains the vast Kantō Plain. Settle-

17

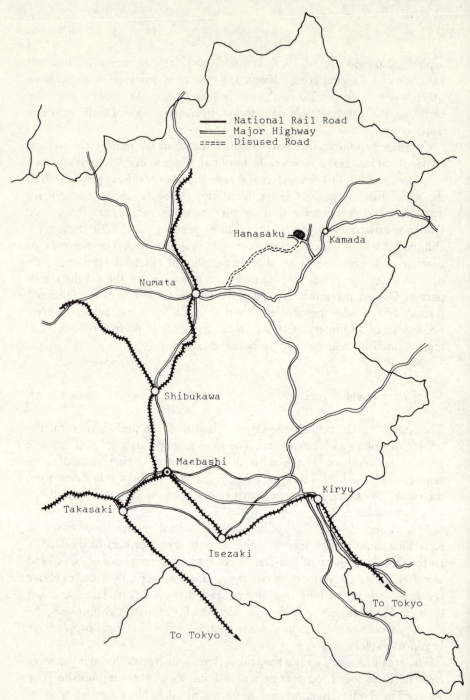

Map 4: Wider communication

Table 1: Land composition of Katashina *mura*

Types of land	Area (sq. km.)	Percentage (%)
House sites	0.79	0.2
Paddy and dry fields	11.93	0.3
Forest and grass land	143.86	36.8
Marsh land and other	234.63	60.0
Total	391.21	100.0

Source: Katashinasonshi 1963: 2

ments in the *mura* have developed on the southern foothills of the mountains near the Katashina River. Hanasaku itself lies in the foothills of the Maehotaka range (2,039 metres above sea level) to the north and Akakura (1,256 metres above sea level) to the south. In between the mountains, the village site forms a kind of hollow, with a branch of the Katashina River, the Nurikawa, running through its centre (see Map 2).

The fairly small stretches of land available are mostly hilly and thus unsuitable for irrigated rice. What paddy fields there are were mainly built in the immediate post-war period. Even with these, though, the average crop yields in the area have not been high, chiefly owing to unpredictable weather conditions and the unfertile nature of the volcanic ash which covers most of the area. For this reason, the district has always been considered as a fairly undesirable place to live. People often say that they constantly face the prospect of starvation, while believing much less labour provides a better life in the plains. A local saying runs, 'Better to descend to the plains than remain in an isolated mountain valley' (*Setchin yori toma e teru*).

The climate in the region is characterised by cool summers and relatively harsh winters, again unfavourable for agriculture but ideal for summer camping and winter skiing. The coldest month is January with an average temperature of 25°F. On colder days, however, the temperature often drops below 10°F. Snow falls on average sixty days a year, mostly in December, January and February.

Demography

According to the 1980 census, Hanasaku village has a population of 888 residing in 214 households, a figure considerably lower than the 1,160 recorded in 1960, when there were 205 households (see Table 2 below). A similar decline can be observed in the population of Katashina *mura* as a whole.

The decline may be attributable to a number of factors, one being modern birth control methods introduced to the village after the war. Before the Meiji Restoration, the most common form of population control was a method known as *mabiki*,[8] literally meaning 'to thin out', or more bluntly put, infanticide. In this area, strangulation is said to have been the commonest method of *mabiki*.[9] After the Meiji Restoration, however, all such methods were strictly prohibited, resulting in a constant population increase thereafter. For the country as a whole, the population almost trebled between early Meiji and the mid-1950s, boosted by the so-called post-war baby boom. To halt this increase, the national government initiated a Family Planning Programme introducing various modern contraceptives, which reached the village during the early 1950s. Women in their late fifties or early sixties talk of their first experiences of the new methods occurring as they had their last child. Some women in their early fifties were indeed successful in limiting the number of children to about three, while others continued having more. For young couples nowadays, the commonest number is two to three. The sharp decline in infant and childhood mortality in the post-war period may have been another factor in the decision by married couples to limit the number of children through legal abortion or the use of contraceptives.[10] In fact, the Family Planning Programme was so effectively carried out that by the early 1970s the government reversed its policy and started granting child benefits for the third child on to encourage people to have more children, although this policy was withdrawn not long afterwards owing to financial difficulties on the part of the government.

Another important factor in the population decline is migration. As Vogel has already noted, the Japanese family system, by requiring inheritance by a single child, has been conducive to regular migration from rural areas to the cities.[11] However, certain changes are taking place in this pattern. There is, for instance, a change in the age at which children leave home. While children who do not take over the house are expected to leave and become independent, in Hanasaku they do not appear to have left home in their early adolescence as Vogel seems to argue.[12] Girls often remained at home until their marriage, unless their families were so poor that they had to send them to other farming households as babysitters or farm hands. Cases of girls sent to factories at a very early age were rare in the village. Inheriting sons also rarely left home. Nowadays, however, not

Table 2: Population changes

	Households	Male	Female	Total
Hanasaku				
1686	69	–	–	–
1838	130	290	268	558
1875	119	243	229	472
1888	117	–	–	541
1960	205	569	591	1160
1965	207	554	550	1104
1970	202	493	492	985
1975	207	441	440	881
1980	214	440	448	888
Katashina mura				
1877	–	–	–	2899
1903	–	–	–	3960
1912	–	–	–	4452
1920	910	2143	2220	4363
1925	974	2472	2371	4843
1930	–	3081	2722	5803
1935	1156	3319	2960	6279
1940	1382	4172	3528	7700
1947	–	3970	3919	7889
1950	1456	4141	3976	8117
1955	1542	4317	4244	8561
1960	1634	4279	4212	8491
1965	1629	3748	3822	7570
1970	1596	3310	3444	6754
1975	1583	3045	3183	6228
1980	1611	2985	3149	6134

	Population	Population density
Gunma prefecture (area: 6349.96 sq. km.)		
1960	1,578,476	248.6
1965	1,605,584	252.8
1970	1,658,909	261.2
1975	1,756,480	276.4
1980	1,848,562	290.9
Tone county (area: 1629.89 sq. km.)		
1960	69,835	42.8
1965	66,658	40.9
1970	59,084	36.3
1975	56,917	34.9
1980	56,103	34.4

only girls but also many inheriting sons go to the city after leaving school at the age of sixteen or eighteen. Sons who do not inherit almost without exception leave home as soon as they finish school, either for further education or training in the city or for employment. The difference between the successor of the house and the non-succeeding children is that the former mostly return while the latter do not. Thus, as will be seen later, twenty-one households out of forty in Yamazaki provide cases where the would-be successor left home and later returned, while in nine cases the successor is still not at home, some employed in the city while others are receiving further education. In two families, the children are still of school age. In only the remaining eight cases (20%) has the successor never left home.

According to villagers, this phenomenon of short-term migration for first sons (or succeeding children)[13] and daughters is quite new to Hanasaku, applying only to those in their twenties and early thirties. This combined with the effects of birth control may explain the gradual decline in the village population since 1960. The trend towards an urban concentration of the population may also be partly understood through comparing changes in the figures for Tone County and Gunma Prefecture as a whole shown in Table 2. The latter, which includes eleven major cities, has witnessed a steady increase over the past twenty years, while Tone county, which covers mostly rural areas since Numata became an independent city in the 1950s, has experienced a constant decline. The population of Numata city alone has increased from 42,919 in 1960 to 47,150 in 1980, reaching a population density of 324.5 per sq. km. compared to 15.7 in Katashina *mura*.

Migration to the cities, however, has always taken place on an individual basis and not on the basis of household units. Thus, as can be seen in Table 3 below, the number of households in Hanasaku has remained fairly stable despite the continuous decline in the total number of individuals residing in them. This means that, despite migration to the cities, a large measure of continuity has been maintained as far as the functioning of the hamlet structure is concerned, since the basic unit of the hamlet is the household (*ie*) and not the individual. There are some cases in which the children who were to inherit migrated to the cities and never came back. Thus in Kuryu two households have disappeared since 1960, having been unable to persuade their would-be successors to return. Even in such cases, the parents do not follow their children to the cities, but remain in the village.

The increase in the number of households results either from the divi-

Table 3: Households and (population) in six hamlets of Hanasaku

	Noboto	Tochikubo	Kajiya	Yamazaki	Kuryu	Hariyama
1960	45 (258)	29 (283)	48 (256)	48 (245)	21 (121)	14 (97)
1965	44 (232)	29 (189)	50 (242)	50 (237)	20 (109)	14 (95)
1970	43 (215)	29 (158)	47 (220)	49 (211)	20 (94)	14 (87)
1975	46 (206)	29 (149)	46 (202)	52 (176)	20 (81)	14 (67)
1980	55 (244)	30 (141)	48 (207)	48 (168)	19 (69)	14 (59)

sion of existing households or from immigration. Short-term households such as those of retired parents (*inkyoya*), or of temporary residents such as school teachers and officials who work for the regional forestry office, all show up in the fluctuations in the total number of households in the village. The nature of these changes will be discussed in detail in Chapter 5. Though limited in scale, signs of reverse migration from cities are also notable in Hanasaku as some of the young villagers came back. A number of unrelated urban people have moved in as well in the hope of starting a tourist business in the village. The slight increase in the village population from 881 in 1975 to 888 in 1980 has in fact been chiefly due to this reverse migration, one of the major consequences of the development of the tourism industry as will be shown later. This phenomenon is particularly noteworthy in view of the many other mountain villages in Japan which have been almost abandoned through large scale emigration to urban centres.[14]

Internal divisions

The six hamlets making up Hanasaku village can be divided into two groups and characterised as 'agricultural' and '*minshuku*' (country inn) hamlets. This of course does not mean that people in the former all practise agriculture, nor that those in the latter all run a country inn. There are, as of 1981, about sixty inns and hotels in the three hamlets comprising the latter group, but some of the innkeepers are also partly engaged in agriculture. Similarly, most of the agricultural households in the former group are only 'part-time' farmers in the sense that they also have income from non-agricultural sources.

There are, however, certain grounds for dividing the hamlets into two groups. One of these is the geographical proximity of the three *minshuku*

23

hamlets, Noboto, Tochikubo and Kajiya. Being located close to each other, the three hamlets share the same irrigation system, based on a common reservoir of water drawn from the Nurikawa, the large stream skirting the village to the north-east (see Map 5). The arrangement seems to work well, since the three hamlets and their fields are situated on different levels with Noboto the highest and Kajiya the lowest and the water reservoir is situated up on the hill not far from Noboto. This ecological situation has therefore required close co-operation in paddy farming among the residents of the three hamlets.

Although Yamazaki is situated not far from these hamlets as the crow flies, there is a small mountain ridge dividing it from Tochikubo and Noboto, and for this reason, people in Yamazaki sometimes refer to those in the latter two hamlets as the 'people over the mountain'. Yamazaki shares water resources with Kuryu and Hariyma, the other two agricultural hamlets, although each hamlet has its own reservoir constructed independently near their settlement. Although they all draw water from the Katsurazawa, the smaller stream skirting the southern boundary of the village, a common irrigation system is impractical due to the relatively long distance between the three hamlets.

The three *minshuku* hamlets also share one silk worm raising farm house where all the silkworms from the three hamlets are taken and raised during the first stages of the two-yearly silkworm cycle. Those with silkworms in the house take turns in providing mulberry leaves daily for all the silkworms. This ensures another occasion for close co-operation between the residents of the three hamlets. This house, with its special heating system, was built early in the 1970s with the help of a government subsidy. When the same subsidy was made available to them, however, people in the three agricultural hamlets decided to build a separate small house for each household.

Ecological divisions match divisions in other spheres as well. With regard to religion, for example, the three *minshuku* hamlets are linked in their worship of the local mountain god, Jūnisama. When people in the village were still engaged in charcoal burning and timbering in the mountains, the worship of this god was one of their primary religious concerns. Though its importance has somewhat diminished with the decline of traditional mountain industries, a ceremony is still held to revere the god, and the three *minshuku* hamlets have a common shrine where their representatives jointly hold the ceremony on the eighth of April each year. As in the case of the irrigation system, each of the agricultural hamlets, Yamazaki, Kuryu and Hariyama, has a separate shrine of its own where they worship on different days of the year.

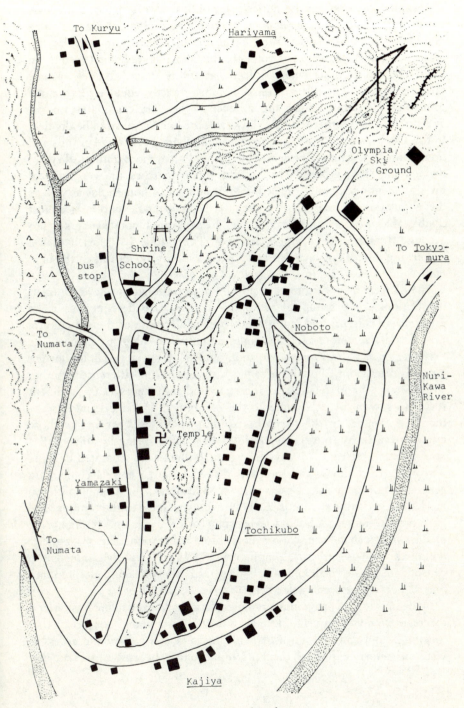

Map 5: **The hamlets**

A similar division can be noticed in political affairs. Every four years when there is an election of *mura* assemblymen, Hanasaku as a whole nominates three candidates, three being the maximum number who can attain seats in the assembly if voters in the village unite behind them.[15] In the election of all other village officials, as will be described later, each of the six hamlets, regardless of size, assumes strictly equal rights on the principle of rotation. Since the number of possible candidates for the assembly is three rather than six, however, the hamlets have to be divided. In this case, instead of the six hamlets being divided into three groups and nominating one candidate each, which would seem more natural, they are divided into two groups. The division again matches the geographical division mentioned above. Since the total number of households as well as the population of one group, Kajiya, Tochikubo and Noboto, is almost double that of the other group, the division does not even take into account their respective voting strength. Every four years, each of the groups nominates one and two candidates respectively, and when the next term comes, the position is reversed.

The hamlets belonging to each group are also thought to have contrasting outlooks: the group of *minshuku* hamlets are described as more progressive, enterprising and adventurous, while those of the agricultural group as always more cautious, timid and slow to adapt to change. The existence of numerous *minshuku*, shops and small businesses in the former group is often pointed out by villagers as a sign of this difference. Another story often told in relation to the supposed differences is the different reactions shown by each hamlet to the government-initiated Land Replanning Programme. In the past, the paddies in the area were, like those elsewhere in Japan, mostly small plots, the smallest being less than half a *tan* (one *tan* is about 0.25 acre). These small plots were separated by high, narrow earth mounds, and the plots owned by any one household were generally not adjacent. Under these conditions, it was impossible to mechanise agriculture, even if machines were available to the farmers. The government, hence, initiated a programme of enlarging and re-organising paddies into a shape suitable for mechanised cultivation. The programme, literally known as 'Structural Improvement' (*Kōzōkaisen*), was intended to consolidate all the small and widely dispersed plots of each household into one or two larger rectangular fields.

By definition, the programme required farmers to exchange plots of land to create compact parcels. Farmers were understandably concerned that they might not end up with fields with the same soil quality and access to water as before. Partly for this reason and partly because of the expense

26

involved, people on the whole initially opposed the change. With substantial financial subsidies from the government and other encouragements, people began to be persuaded, but still the response differed greatly among the hamlets. While almost all the paddies owned by the residents of Tochikubo have now been reorganised and while the programme has been partially implemented in Kajiya and Noboto, people in Yamazaki have resisted the innovations until the end. Although the programme was initiated more than ten years ago, the reorganisation of paddies owned by Yamazaki residents has not even begun.

The real reason behind this unusually strong resistance in Yamazaki is not simply the personality of its residents. The fields owned by Yamazaki residents are on the whole smaller and those that belong to one household tend to be more widely dispersed than in other hamlets. As a result, it is much more difficult to reach a consensus among the residents of Yamazaki about exchanges of paddy. The fact that all hamlet decisions should be reached not by majority vote but by a consensus of all those concerned infinitely delays any action that can be taken by the *buraku* as a whole.

Yet, despite this real obstacle, people like to explain the situation in different terms. Yamazaki residents who favour the programme and hamlet officials who are anxious for their own reasons, all express with some bitterness that, 'We, Yamazaki people, have always been like this. There is no way out.' On the other hand, 'those over the mountain' have always been more progressive and hence have had no problems with the programme, although such claims are not always true.

One can observe the separation into two groupings on numerous other occasions, either co-operative or competitive. In the volleyball tournaments of the Wives Association or in the baseball matches of the Youth Group, competing teams are often grouped in this fashion. Similarly, in numerous village labour pools, work teams are often made up in this way. Some of the Hoshino lineages in Noboto in fact openly recognise that they are off-shoots of those in Kajiya, while those in Yamazaki strongly deny it even though the possibility has been suggested by several local historians. More recently, the fact that *minshuku* have developed only in the hamlets 'over the mountain' intensifies the separation, as the interests of the residents of these hamlets are often in conflict with those of the other three.

Chiefly due to the fact that the three hamlets Yamazaki, Kuryu and Hariyama, still remain predominantly agricultural while there have developed country inns in the other three, Noboto, Tochikubo and Kajiya, the two groups of hamlets are nowadays clearly distinguishable in their outlook. The hamlets in the latter group, especially Noboto which has

27

literally become a *'minshuku mura'* (country inn village) as it appears in many of the nationally circulated tourist guidebooks, have a much more urbane look compared to those in the former group, with their numerous country inns, 'pensions',[16] shops and restaurants. Some of the larger inns and hotels are three or four storeyed buildings with such exotic names as *Fuoshizunsu* (Four Seasons) or *Supesushatoru* (Space Shuttle). There are also a brand-new petrol station and a supermarket equipped with freezers, selling meat, fish and other groceries. In agricultural hamlets, on the other hand, there are only a couple of small conventional-style miscellaneous shops which largely cater for the needs of school children and postmen visiting the village from Kamada each day. Although, containing the shrine, school and temple, Yamazaki used to occupy a somewhat central position in village affairs, most of the more recently built village facilities are situated in the *minshuku* hamlets; the source of a small grudge on the part of Yamazaki people.

The different impact of the tourism industry on the hamlets in Hanasaku is more obvious when we compare their employment patterns. On the whole, most people in Yamazaki, Kuryu and Hariyama still regard themselves as farmers even when they have a larger income derived from non-agricultural sources. Of the forty households in Yamazaki, for example, thirty-one classify themselves as 'farming households' (*nōka*) although many of them are in fact part-time farmers in the sense that they have income sources outside agriculture. As Table 4 shows, non-farming occupations in this hamlet include construction work (eighteen), timbering and other forestry work (eleven), tourism-related work (nine), and public employment (six). Apart from these, one of the Yamazaki residents who is also the *mura* assemblyman works as a subcontractor for a Tokyo paper company that owns much of the forest land in the area. Another notable entrepreneur from an agricultural hamlet is one of the Hariyama residents who owns an apple orchard.

The employment patterns of the three *minshuku* hamlets manifest some notable differences from those of the agricultural hamlets. To start with, there are many more individually operated enterprises in these hamlets, supposedly reflecting the 'progressiveness' of the residents discussed above. Apart from the country inns, for example, there are in Kajiya alone two sawmill workers, two timbermen, one plasterer and one navvy. In Tochikubo and Noboto, there are two carpentry companies, one button factory subcontracting work from the intermediary office in Kamada, and one timber subcontractor. A *mura* assemblyman in Tochikubo also operates a vegetable-pickling factory. All of these are small-scale businesses em-

Table 4: Occupations in Yamazaki (age 18–65)

	H	W	S	S'w	F	M	Others	Total (%)
Agriculture	10	24	1	1	1	2	–	39 (37.1)
Construction work	9	3	6	–	–	–	–	18 (17.1)
Forestry	10	1	–	–	–	–	–	11 (10.5)
Tourism industry	2	3	3	–	–	–	1	9 (8.6)
Public employment	–	2	4	–	–	–	–	6 (5.7)
Self-employed	–	1	2	1	1	–	–	5 (4.8)
Carpenters	–	–	2	–	–	–	1	3 (2.9)
Commuters and factory workers	1	1	3	–	–	–	2	7 (6.7)
Not working	1	3	–	3	–	–	–	7 (6.7)
Total	33	38	21	5	2	2	4	105 (100)

Key: H, husband or household head; W, wife; S, inheriting son or adopted son-in-law; S'w, son's wife or inheriting daughter; F, household head's father; M, mother; Others, mostly collateral kin.

ploying three to eight people. Some of the employees come from outside the village, but most are Hanasaku people, largely from the same hamlet.

In addition to these, there are one Japanese-style restaurant, two western-style snack bars, two souvenir shops and several smaller shops. The restaurant is in Kajiya not far from the petrol station, and hosts most of the local primary school alumni meetings which have become more frequent recently. While the restaurant provides a meeting place mostly for the middle-aged or the old, young people more often gather in one of the snack bars which also provides the enormously popular *karaoke* music.[17] There are also two recently-opened hairdressers, one in Kajiya and the other in Noboto, where most of the village wives go to have perms every two or three months. The hairdressers together with the modern supermarket, western-style restaurants and petrol station reflect the rapidly changing lifestyle, changing perhaps more rapidly in this village as a consequence of the development of the tourism industry and the resultant economic prosperity.

The more diverse employment patterns also imply that agriculture has much less importance in the *minshuku* hamlets than in the other three, and this can be seen in the distribution of occupations of Noboto residents (see Table 5). A number of differences may be noted when they are compared with those of an agricultural hamlet, Yamazaki (see Table 4). Those engaged fully in agriculture comprise only 15.8% (twenty-four) of the

Table 5: Occupations in Noboto (age 18–85)

	H	W	S	S'W	F	M	Others	Total (%)
Agriculture	7	13	–	–	1	3	–	24 (15.8)
Tourism industry	19	34	5	4	–	4	2	68 (44.7)
Forestry	12	–	2	–	–	–	–	14 (9.2)
Construction work	6	1	2	–	–	–	–	9 (5.9)
Commuters	1	–	8	–	–	–	1	10 (6.6)
Factory workers	1	3	2	1	–	–	–	7 (4.6)
Carpenters	1	–	2	–	–	–	–	3 (2.0)
Plasterers	3	–	–	–	–	–	–	3 (2.0)
Public employment	–	–	1	–	–	–	2	3 (2.0)
Shop proprietors	–	2	–	1	–	–	–	3 (2.0)
Migrating labourers	1	–	–	–	–	–	–	1 (0.7)
Not working	–	3	–	2	–	2	–	7 (4.6)
Total	51	56	22	8	1	9	5	152 (100)

Key: H, husband or household head; W, wife; S, inheriting son or adopted son-in-law; S'W, son's wife or inheriting daughter; F, household head's father; M, mother; Others, mostly collateral kin.

total working population while those in the tourism industry number almost three times higher. The number of farming households in this hamlet has dropped from thirty-seven in the agricultural census of 1965 to twenty-eight in that of 1980. Other non-agricultural occupations are also more varied than in Yamazaki, including more commuters, factory workers and shop proprietors.

Apart from Tochikubo, two *minshuku* hamlets also have a much more heterogeneous population compared to the agricultural hamlets. For example, Kajiya, perhaps due to its location at the entrance of the village, used to have the largest immigrant population among its residents, some of whom settled in the village before the Second World War. The most remarkable of these pre-war immigrants may be the family running the petrol station. Not only operating the supermarket, a *minshuku* and the petrol station, the head of the family also works as a subcontractor for the regional forestry office. For this work, he employs more than twenty villagers. During the winter when there is not much work to be done in the mountains, all of his employees work in a cafeteria which he managed to lease from the local government, near another ski ground opened by the government a few years ago.

Noboto, on the other hand, has recently become more heterogeneous than Kajiya largely as a result of the reverse migration discussed above.

Altogether sixteen out of fifty-eight households in Noboto are those of recent immigrants from urban areas. Eight of them moved into the village in 1978. The move of these eight families, mostly young couples from the Tokyo area who were attracted by the idea of running a *minshuku* in a remote resort, was arranged, after some complications, by a land broker based in neighbouring Tone *mura*. The eight households comprise a residential quarter a little apart from the main hamlet, and four more families of immigrants have since joined them under similar circumstances. Another four families of immigrants settled in the village through an uxorilocal marriage during the present generation. Three of them run a *minshuku* and one works as a plasterer. Unlike the above twelve families of unrelated immigrants, however, these four families are almost completely integrated into community life.

Notes

1 The Jōmon period refers to the Japanese Mesolithic Age that lasted from roughly 3,000 BC to 300 BC, while the Yayoi indicates the subsequent cultural phase from approximately 300 BC to AD 300 Cf. Meyer 1976: 17.

2 *Katashina Sonshi* 1963: 27.

3 *Ibid.*: 53.

4 In some records, the same shire appears as Katashina *sho. Katashina Sonshi* 1963: 38–41.

5 On the workings of the *mura* offices, see Steiner 1956; Ward 1953; Dull 1954.

6 *Machi* is a unit equivalent to *mura* under the prefectural government but with a larger population. In addition to *mura* and *machi*, there is also *shi* which is conventionally translated as 'city' with a still larger population. Apart from small urban centres, both *machi* and *shi* cover, for administrative purposes, quite rural areas as well.

7 Trewartha 1965: 438.

8 Nakane 1967: 51.

9 Tauber 1960: 6 suggests, however, that infanticide could not have been widespread during the Tokugawa period since rates of death were almost as high as those for births.

10 Smith 1978: 41.

11 Vogel 1967: 93.

12 *Ibid.*: 94; In the country as a whole, there is evidence that boys of adolescent age did move to the cities during the pre-war period. Tauber 1951: 154–5.

13 The successor to the house is not always the first son. For further details, see Chapter 5.

14 This phenomenon of rural under-population, known as *kasogenshō*, became one of the important issues of rural sociology in Japan in the mid-1960s. Nōrinshō Nōseikyoku 1967; Kawamoto 1967; Nakayashu 1965; Kunimoto 1973; Smith 1978: 14–20.

15 In politics, especially in local elections, territorial bonds almost always take priority over other social ties, kinship or otherwise, which often extend beyond the village boundaries. This tendency of a local community to vote as a bloc in order to have its interests adquately represented in the *mura* assembly has been noted by others as well. See Smith and Reyes 1957: 468; Ward 1951: 1034–6, 1960: 157; Steiner 1956: 195.

16 The country inns which provide western-style accommodation are commonly called 'pensions' in Japan while those that provide Japanese-style accommodation are called *minshuku*. Food, especially breakfast, is also different and 'pensions' are usually a little more expensive than *minshuku*.

17 *Kara* is a Japanese word meaning 'empty' or 'vacant' and *oke* is an abbreviation of the English word 'orchestra' or 'orchestration'. Combining the two, *karaoke* means recorded music of popular songs to whose accompaniment people can sing. It has become so popular in the village that it frequently appears at village festivals or house-warming parties, and there is also a yearly *karaoke* singing competition both village-wide and *mura*-wide, organised by so-called *karaoke* maniacs.

Agriculture and change

Before the opening of the ski resort in the early 1960s, the economy of Hanasaku did not differ much from other mountain villages in Japan. It was a predominantly agricultural community with a cash income derived from contribution to the Japanese silk industry while timbering and charcoal-burning were pursued as regular winter-time occupations. A series of post-war developments at national level, however, had a serious impact on this general pattern of mountain village economy and resulted in the so-called *kasogenshō* or rural under-population in some parts of Japan. The development of the tourism industry in Hanasaku can also be adequately understood in the context of this general disintegration of the traditional mountain village economy.[1] This chapter will examine one aspect of this disintegration, namely the decline of agriculture and its effects on community life.

The data here are mostly drawn from a single hamlet in the village, Yamazaki, a hamlet which has remained predominantly agricultural even after nearly twenty years of tourist development in the village. As shown in the previous chapter, no *minshuku* have yet developed in this hamlet. Instead, the population superfluous to agriculture has mostly been absorbed into the wage-labour market. The consequences for household organisation differ in nature from those where *minshuku* have been increasingly replacing agriculture as in Noboto or where people have successfully combined both occupations into a corporate household business as in Tochikubo. Discussion in this and the following chapters will concentrate on these differences.

Land ownership

There are forty households in Yamazaki excluding those employed by the school. Of these, thirty-eight households own land of one type or another.[2] The remaining two, recent immigrant families, do not own any land but have houses built on rented land.

The 1,712,757 sq. km. of land owned by the residents of Yamazaki can be divided into six different categories: house sites (*takuchi*), paddy (*ta*), dry fields (*hatake*), forest (*sanrin*), grassland (*genya*) and small pieces of unworkable land classified as miscellaneous plots (*zatsuchi*). Forest land occupies 814,495 sq. km. or 47.6% of the total. Most of the forest land, however, was acquired only in the 1920s and the 1950s. During the Tokugawa period, forest land (68% of the area) was managed directly by local feudal lords, and apparently no clear-cut ownership had been established.[3] At the time of the Meiji Restoration (1868), however, the government began to take over much of the forest land while at the same time recognising private ownership where local people were able to submit proof of ownership.

Until then, mountains and slopes within the boundary of each hamlet were utilised freely by its residents as a common source of grass, firewood, thatch, etc. These mountains comprised an indispensable part of the subsistence economy of most Japanese villages. However, towards the end of the Meiji campaign, which took many decades,[4] the consolidation of state forest land was carried out to such an extent that the government had taken over a large part of the mountains which hitherto had been utilised by local people, and had deprived them of entry. The measure gave rise to strong resistance all over the country. Partly to appease public resentment, the government returned part of the consolidated land.

The task of retransferring ownership was a time-consuming one. In Hanasaku, it came about during the mid-1920s, when the mountain range that faces Yamazaki to the south was distributed among the residents of the hamlet at a nominal price.[5] In 1953 when more administrative reorganisation was implemented, there again arose many disputes over village or hamlet owned forest land and over land which had been conditionally leased to a hamlet by the government. As a result, the government divided and sold most of the hitherto communally owned forest land under dispute.[6]

The background to the villagers' acquisition of forest land is important because it indicates that, although forest land occupies the bulk of village land now, people only recently began to conceive of it as private property. Commercial-utilisation of individually owned forest land is still very limited. Agricultural land, on the other hand, has long been an important indicator of relative wealth in a village, and this seems to be especially true of the paddy fields in Yamazaki.[7]

According to my own data, thirty-two of the households in Yamazaki own one or more plots of paddy land and cultivate rice. In the land registry kept in the local government office, however, only eighteen households are reported to have any paddy. The figure for total paddy in the hamlet is also grossly misrepresented in this record, showing a little under three hectares, while agricultural census data kept in a different department in the same office indicates more than 8.5 hectares of paddy under cultivation. The discrepancy seems to arise from the fact that the land registry record does not include paddy converted from upland dry fields after the war, since the census data indicate a considerably smaller area of dry fields under cultivation than is shown in the land registry.

Most farmers in Yamazaki are owner-cultivators. One household headed by a widow has rented out most of its farmland to the household of which it is an offshoot (see Chapter 5) since the widow took a job in a button factory in Noboto. She owns a little over one hectare of dry fields,[8] generally of inferior quality, very far from the village. After her husband died, she stopped cultivating the most inconveniently situated parcels, but even with the remainder, she found it increasingly difficult to cope on her own, especially as she got older (she was fifty-six in 1981). Eventually, she decided to leave farming completely, but she claims that the decision was not a matter of preference. Now all her farmland has been rented out, partly to a family in Kawaba *mura* into which one of her husband's sisters married and partly to the main household in the same hamlet. The widow's two sons are both employed outside the village. The elder son is working not far from the village, in Tone *mura*. When he marries and comes back to the village to live with her, she hopes to get all the farmland back and to cultivate it herself, possibly with help from her daughter-in-law. For the time being she lends out her land because she thinks it has to be cultivated to prevent it from growing too coarse with wild grass and weeds. She claims that she does not receive anything from her tenant families. It is almost unheard of these days to find a tenant who is willing to pay rent. Most often, it is the landlord who asks tenants to cultivate his land.

Several similar kinds of free tenancy exist in the hamlet. There are two families that farm rice fields rented from a landlord in Hariyama. One of the two tenants in Yamazaki represents a branch household of the Hariyama one, which had been a substantial landlord family before the war, and still owns some fields in other hamlets. According to the villagers, the family had branched out in Yamazaki in order to take care of the main household's fields there.

Another family, consisting of an elderly couple and one unmarried son, has also rented out most of its dry fields. As a main household, this family has one of the largest holdings in the hamlet but, as the son was employed full time as the manager of the ski ground and did not lend even an occasional hand with the farming, the couple found it too difficult on their own and decided to rent out most of their dry fields. They kept for themselves the paddy and some of the dry fields to cultivate house vegetables. They will go on farming this land as long as they can. They hope that the woman their son marries will be a person who knows a little about farming so that she may continue the occupation. The couple's main tenant is one of their branch households in the hamlet which lost most of its farmland immediately after the war during long years of illness suffered by its previous head.

The overall effect of the post-war Land Reform is difficult to measure since people's memory of it began to fade long ago. What is apparent, however, is that there were no big landlords in the village even before the war. For Katashina *mura* as a whole, the total area of farmland involved in the Reform[9] was about 160 hectares, of which about thirty were owned by people or companies not resident in the *mura*. Of the forty-nine resident landlords who had some land bought by the government and sold to tenants, eleven were from Hanasaku and had about ten hectares. Of these, however, there were only three whose land exceeded one *chō*: the two village institutions – the shrine and the temple and the landlord in Hariyama already mentioned. Nearly seven hectares of land belonged to these three. The landlord family in Hariyama, it is said, used to be money-lenders and had been able to purchase land from those who had fallen into debt.

The biggest landlord in the *mura* was a Hoshino family in Surubuchi, a neighbouring village. According to the records available, the family appears to have lost more than sixteen hectares of farmland during the Reform, and there are several households in Yamazaki which benefited from the redistribution. Even before the war, however, there were not as many tenant farmers in this village as in other parts of the country.[10] Life for those who had to rely mainly on rented land certainly seems to have been very harsh. Stories told by the villagers about the methods of rent collection adopted by some landlords illustrate the situation. Instead of receiving rent at a fixed amount per unit area, some landlords fixed rent as a certain portion of the crop harvested each year. Then, just before the crops were to be harvested by the cultivators, the landlords would cut four or five rows out of every ten. With such a method of rent collection, there could be absolutely no deception on the part of the tenants. The landlords also believed that it would prevent their tenants from neglecting their fields, since the quality of not only the crops that were to be taken away as rent but also of those that would remain depended on how hard the tenants worked. Until just before the war, the sight of fields where only five alternate rows remained is said to have been common.

That situation is difficult to imagine now, only a little over thirty years after the war, when tenants are practically doing the landowner a favour by taking land he cannot farm himself. The Japanese expression *tsukute kureru*, literally 'take trouble (for the landowners) to farm', aptly describes the position of tenants today. The power enjoyed by the landlords before the war was possible because land was the only significant means of making a livelihood. With the development of cash income sources other than farming, villagers who do not own land are now more likely to turn to non-farming occupations than to become tenant farmers. Indeed, many families in Noboto which could not cultivate all of their farmland and were unable to find a tenant planted trees for timber. Land holdings can no longer be considered the sole indicator of relative wealth in the village. For example, the income level of a family in which the husband works as a labourer employed fulltime by the regional forestry office,[11] and the wife cultivates about one *chō* of farmland with occasional help from her husband, is much higher than that of a family where both husband and wife are full-time farmers cultivating more than two *chō* of paddy and dry fields. Nevertheless, farmland remains the most fundamental item of property for people in the village. Not only do families of large holdings still enjoy a relatively high social status, but few want to sell land for cash. There have been almost no land transactions in Yamazaki for the past fifteen years or so. Many people in the village think the material prosperity they are enjoying as a result of the economic growth of the country as a whole has already reached its peak. When hard times come, therefore, land is the only thing that they can rely on. For most people in Yamazaki, land is like life insurance. They would not give it up for cash, which might disappear. Many young people also think it is worth keeping.

Crops

One of the most striking features of the crops cultivated in this village is their wide variety, which is a post-war innovation. Table 6 shows the range of the crops cultivated by the residents of Yamazaki, Kajiya and Tochikubo in 1980. The first thing to be noted is the complete disappearance of two important pre-war crops, foxtail millet (*awa*) and barley

Table 6: Crops in Yamazaki, Kajiya and Tochikubo

	Yamazaki		Kajiya		Tochikubo	
	Households	Area	Households	Area	Households	Area
Paddy rice	29	645	27	735	26	684
Wheat	–	–	1	10	–	–
Millet	7	73	1	10	6	31
Potatoes	12	62	27	80	10	52
Sugar-cane	1	1	–	–	–	–
Soybeans	29	195	12	51	6	21
Adzuki beans	15	60	25	102	6	12
Green soybeans	23	635	20	339	24	364
Kidney beans	–	–	–	–	10	79
Tobacco	2	70	11	376	–	–
Tomatoes	1	20	7	60	15	240
Cucumbers	10	50	27	80	20	37
Egg-plants	6	11	27	30	18	28
Chinese cabbages	13	64	14	176	23	255
Cabbages	6	10	10	72	11	108
Spinach	4	2	9	47	3	7
Spring onions	8	9	21	20	8	5
Giant radishes	10	27	13	161	17	144
Carrots	3	1	9	12	4	3
Green peppers	3	2	1	1	3	2
Water melons	–	–	8	92	–	–
Strawberries	1	2	–	–	–	–
Other vegetables	21	435	27	445	23	324
Cut flowers	2	20	–	–	3	40
Seedling trees	1	10	–	–	–	–
Pasture	–	–	–	–	1	30
Mushrooms	–	–	6	2	9	259

Unit of area – *are* (100 sq. m.)

(*mugi*). Two other very important pre-war crops, soybeans and wheat, have also been greatly reduced.[12] The two changes are partly related. Unlike some warmer parts of the country, a double cropping of paddy rice and barley was never possible in this village. The transplanting of the paddy is done toward the end of May and in early June while the fields have to be flooded well before then so that the soil can absorb sufficient water. On the other hand, due to the cooler weather, the cutting of barley has to be delayed until the end of July in order to have the grain fully ripe, and the fields have to remain drained until then. This makes the double cropping of barley and wet rice impossible. Consequently barley used to be

38

double cropped with foxtail millet in this area, while wheat was double cropped with soybeans. Although foxtail millet and soybeans must be transplanted around mid-June,[13] the task can be done between the lines of fully grown barley and wheat, since both are dry crops. Barley and wheat are then harvested in late July and August, thus giving room for newly transplanted millet and soybeans to grow.

When people began to give up foxtail millet and wheat after the war, many gave up barley and soybeans as well.[14] Millet and barley were, however, the first to lose popularity. With other grain crops such as *kibi* and *hie*, the two once comprised the staple food of the people in this region. A large quantity of foxtail millet, for instance, would be eaten boiled with a tiny bit of rice or as pounded cakes on occasions when all now eat rice cakes. Rice used to be so scarce, an old lady told me, that when people had guests in the house they usually presented layers of pounded millet cakes with a piece of rice cake on each side. Also, people often jokingly mention that anybody who had fallen sick would be cured as soon as he was shown a handful of rice or if he could smell boiling rice. Barley and *hie* (barnyard grass) were eaten by men or given to animals. In the latter case, however, the grain was fed boiled but unhusked.

These food crops were grown in the village until some time after the war. As rice production grew, however, they all began to disapppear. Even before the war, there were several households that grew rice, but they usually exchanged it for cash rather than consuming it themselves, except on very special occasions such as the New Year. Therefore, for many people, it used to be a great pleasure to be invited to the main households, since it was mostly these which owned a plot or two of paddy fields before the war and had rice to serve. After the war, however, many paddy fields were created. In Katashina *mura* as a whole, for example, the total area of irrigated land more than trebled from about thirty-seven hectares in 1921 to nearly 145 hectares in 1956.[15] The six hamlets in Hanasaku have now among them about sixty-two hectares of paddy fields whereas the area was less than thirty hectares until just before the war.[16] As a result of this increase, people are now more than self-sufficient in rice. Everybody can now have rice every day, and many even sell rice.

The change is very dramatic for old people who experienced the worst periods of the war, when even the distasteful foxtail millet or barley had to be hidden from officials who would go round every house in the village with a stick, checking the amount of grain stored. The officials then took most of the grain to send to soldiers abroad, leaving only a minimum for the family. The amount the officials considered minimum was so small

39

that many people tricked them by making a false bottom in the wooden storage cases and hiding grain underneath it. An old lady from a main household also deplores the fact that people now often throw away boiled rice even though perfectly edible. In the past, not a grain of rice was thrown away. Even before the war, her household was fortunate enough to be able to offer a small spoonful of boiled rice to their ancestors and to the gods of the house. The rice thus offered would become covered with mould or would completely dry up, but even those bits of rice were never thrown away. Instead it was taken down, thoroughly washed, soaked in boiled water for about an hour and then eaten. It was, according to her, 'rather delicious' if one took it with three o'clock tea.

If we consider how strongly rice was desired and to what extent people had experienced its scarcity within living memory, it is much easier to understand the problems of the Crop Changing Movement (*tensaku undō*). In the early 1970s, the authorities in Katashina *mura* started a campaign to curtail rice production. The post-war government's efforts to increase rice production had borne fruit and by the end of the 1960s, Japan already had a surplus of rice sufficient to feed the nation for more than three years. At the national level, the curtailment campaign had started long before it was initiated by the local government. The Land Replanning Programme mentioned previously was partly geared to this end. If farmers agreed to have their fields reshaped into rectangular ones, seventy per cent of the construction expenses were to come from the state and only thirty per cent from the farmers. One advantage to the farmers was, as we have seen, that the total area of paddy could be considerably increased. The fields also became easier to work with machines. However, the farmers could receive the governmental subsidy for restructuring only on condition that they promised to grow other crops on half of each remade paddy field, for which effort they were also entitled to receive 'crop changing subsidies' (*tensaku shōreikin*) from the government. Thus, farmers could in effect have their fields reshaped at virtually no cost at all, since the amount of the crop changing subsidies often exceeded the thirty per cent share of the cost required for reconstruction.

Despite these obvious advantages, however, farmers in hamlets like Yamazaki and Kuryu have not accepted the Programme. Although it seems only rational from the viewpoint of the central authorities, facing serious long-term overproduction problems, that rice growing should be discouraged by all means, farmers for whom rice self-sufficiency was hard earned and only recently achieved can not readily agree to this new policy. The government wishes to encourage rice production only in areas where the best rice can be produced, and discourage it in all other areas, like Katashina *mura*, so that only good quality rice would be distributed throughout the country. For farmers, on the other hand, it only means that once again they have to buy rice even though they have paddy fields of their own.[17] For families who own a relatively large holding of paddy the problem may not be serious, since they can be self-sufficient in rice even if they cultivate only half of their holdings. In a hamlet like Yamazaki where there are many small holders, however, the opposition is strong.

The head of one household in Yamazaki is so against the Programme that he will not even participate in any of the hamlet meetings if the topic is discussed. He personally owns about 0.1 hectare of paddy, but he cultivates about 0.3 hectare of tenanted paddy field belonging to the Hariyama landlord mentioned before. If all the fields in Yamazaki belonging to the Hariyama owner were to be made into one large plot as a result of the Programme, the tenant fears he may lose the 0.3 hectare he is now working on, because the owner himself may want to cultivate the field or give the tenancy of the whole field to his branch household. Even with one household with a holding as small as 0.1 hectare opposing, there is no means of implementing the Programme.

In the face of persistent opposition, in 1978 the local government began to offer crop changing grants to all farmers whether they had agreed to the Programme or not, so they receive subsidies per unit area of paddy where they grow crops other than rice.[18] The total area for growing rice is assigned to each hamlet as a reduction quota just as hamlets were assigned an amount of rice to be paid in tax during the Tokugawa period. The hamlet then assumes a collective responsibility for its quota. Unlike the Tokugawa period, however, there is now no means of coercing the assignment if it is not fulfilled. Nevertheless, the government relies on the competitive spirit which the residents of each hamlet are supposed to have toward other hamlets in order to meet the goal. Each year, the officials of Katashina *mura* plan to divert at least seventy hectares of the total paddy area to other crops, but they are achieving only about sixty per cent of their target. Yamazaki is one of the least co-operative hamlets, fulfilling less than half of its qouta each year.

Another reason it is so difficult to persuade people to turn away from rice growing is that rice is one of the easiest crops to cultivate. In the past, weeding rice fields took much time. With the introduction of chemical herbicides, however, the task has become much easier. Rice is also believed to be one of the crops most resistant against diseases and insects. In other words, little sterilisation is needed for rice, while vegetables of any commercial value require disinfection quite often. Rice is also less vulnerable to animal attack.

One of the most popular new crops is a type of sweetcorn known as *bantamu*,[19] a crop which happens to be a favourite of local bears and foxes. During the *bantamu* harvest, which varies from late July to early September depending when the seeds were sown, the whole village goes into a state of alert against attack by bears. One adult bear can eat about one hundred and fifty *bantamu* in a single visit to a field. Once attacked, therefore, little of the crop remains to be sold. The bears usually appear during the night, although on a couple of occasions during my stay in the village, they appeared at about three o'clock in the afternoon.[20] To scare them off, farmers set a carbide fire in the middle of the *bantamu* fields, which gives regular explosive sounds of considerable noise every quarter of an hour or so. The explosions often continue throughout the day. Compared to the danger of bears, foxes present only a minor hazard. Setting up a fence of several iron strands adequately deters them.

One other advantage of rice growing is that it does not require constant attention. Once transplanting is over, by late May,[21] only occasional spreadings of weed killer and even less frequent spreadings of insecticide are required until harvesting in October. Even the task of letting in water every evening and out again the next morning has become much easier nowadays since everybody can get to the fields by motorbike or by the small lorries which some of them keep for agricultural use. Vegetable cropping, on the other hand, not only needs more sterilisation and weeding, but also preparing the produce in the form of a marketable commodity takes much time and labour.[22] Moreover, once fully grown, vegetables cannot be left in the field. Therefore, farmers sometimes have to hire extra labour to harvest vegetable crops.

One of the reasons why soybeans are no longer popular as a commercial crop is that they require much time and labour. Paddy rice production including transplanting, cutting, threshing, peeling, polishing, sterilisation and weeding is now completely mechanised, but for soybeans, most of the work is still done by hand using traditional tools. It is the same with vegetable crops, but their incomes are much higher than those from soybeans.[23] Unlike other staple food crops of pre-war years, however, soybeans are still cultivated for home consumption since they constitute the raw material for one of the basic food items in the village, bean paste (*miso*). Made from boiled and crushed soybeans mixed with chemical malt (*koji*), bean paste is one of the most important protein sources. The paste is often dissolved in water and boiled with seasonal vegetables, sometimes with beancurd or with mushrooms added, to make *misoshiru* soup. *Miso-shiru* was served almost every day during my stay in the village. Many people in the cities drink bean paste soup with rice for breakfast, but few in this village do. Instead, they eat bread made from plain flour with pinches of soda, salt and sugar, and baked with a small amount of seasoned bean paste spread on it. This homemade bread has been replaced for some families by factory produced bread, and during the winter it is often replaced with cakes made of rice. The electric oven used to bake the bread, the factory produced bread, and the rice cakes are all post-war innovations for the people in this villages. In the past most of them ate foxtail millet cakes (*awa mochi*) baked on an *irori*, a kind of open-pit hearth which has now almost disappeared even in this village.

One of the most popular vegetable crops in Yamazaki is the green soybean called *edamame*. These are soybeans picked when they are very young, green and soft and eaten boiled or steamed with a pinch of salt. The fact that such young soybeans can be eaten and sold was apparently not known to the people in this village until after the war, although they were long accustomed to the cultivation of the crop in its mature form. Some twenty-five years ago, however, a Tokyo merchant came to the village and offered an unconditional contract for cultivating *edamame*. Most of the cultivators can be said to have been more or less successful, even though it is grown on a small scale. Farmers in this village were less reluctant to adopt this than other new crops, since it is always possible to eat or sell the beans in their mature form (*taizu*) even if the right time for picking the *edamame* is missed. This may explain why the crop still enjoys the widest popularity in the village. On the other hand, for other vegetable crops, once the right harvest time is missed, the loss is much greater. Fluctuations in price are also greater for vegetable crops than for rice or other grains. They are also more vulnerable to natural disasters and animal hazards. These reasons together explain the wide variety of crops culti- vated in this area. In order to avoid failures resulting from labour shor- tage, unpredictable weather conditions, price fluctuations and so forth, farmers have chosen to allocate their farmland to a range of crops, rather than investing the whole area to one or two crops. They can avoid a total disaster and are also able to distribute the limited labour-force to different crops according to a well-planned agricultural cycle. The fact that the fields are mostly terraced on the hillside and widely dispersed, also makes this strategy workable.

Some crops such as tobacco, tomatoes, seed cucumbers and out flowers are cultivated only on a contractual basis. The majority, however, are cultivated individually and sold through the agricultural co-operative. Only two households in the hamlet sell their produce individually, even though they usually receive a better price for the same produce than the agricultural co-operative does, sometimes twice or three times the price. In order to market individually, however, one must drive for up to three hours during the night to the market and back. While night bidding markets for vegetables are open in most of the large cities in the prefecture including Numata, Shibukawa, Maebashi, Takasaki and Isezaki (see Map 4), a producer with transport usually makes a round of these night markets to find the best price. Thus the venture is only worthwhile when there is enough manpower within the family to do the driving and when the amount of one crop produced is sufficiently large. The two private marketing households in Yamazaki both have a husband and wife in their late thirties or early forties who are both full-time farmers. Other farmers, however, seem content with the moderate prices that the agricultural co-operative is able to offer. Some farmers complain that since people sort and grade their own produce there can be a considerable variety in quality, although commodities handled with greater care may receive a much better price when individually marketed. The advantage of marketing through the agricultural co-operative on the other hand is that they can sell their produce whenever they wish and can also borrow money whenever they need it on condition that they deliver their agricultural products later. Most of all, farmers in this area consider marketing through the co-op much easier and safer because they produce only a small amount of a wide variety of crops whose individual marketing involves much risk and trouble. In other villages in Katashina *mura* such as Sukagawa, Shimotaira and Tsuiji where extensive land stretches exist and where the average area cultivated by one household is much larger,[24] more people are said to be engaged in contractual farming and individual marketing, both of which are no doubt much more profitable than the method adopted by Yamazaki farmers, even though the risk involved may be greater.

Farm labour

As elsewhere in Japan, the agricultural population of Hanasaku has gradually but constantly decreased since the war. If we consider one household in particular, the process of change may be easier to understand. In 1950, Household A in Yamazaki consisted of six members:

44

The household head (aged 57)
His wife (52)
First son (21)
Third daughter (18)
Fourth daughter (16)
Second son (14)

The first two daughters had already married, the first during the war and the second in 1947. Of the six members left, the household head and his wife worked full time on family land which was then a little over one hectare and on some tenanted land. The first son also worked almost full time on the land, although he was also employed on a daily basis as a forestry worker when the farmwork was not too demanding. All the remaining children helped with farming and housework, although the last child was still at school.

The next year, the second son finished middle school at the age of fifteen and left home to be employed in a factory near Shibukawa. Shortly afterwards, in 1954, the first son married a woman from the same hamlet. Thus, by 1955, the household again had six full working members:

The household head (62)
His wife (57)
First son (26)
First son's wife (23)
Third daughter (23)
Fourth daughter (21)

All of these except the son, who had started working full time as a labourer for the regional forestry office since his marriage, worked the family land. Each morning, as soon as dawn broke, the household head called the family together and assigned them tasks such as weeding, ploughing, transplanting or harvesting. He was so strictly in control of the affairs of the whole family, and of the family purse, that it was very difficult to disobey his command. With five people and one horse working on the land, the family, which had owned no paddy before the war, was able to convert about six *tan* of paddy from its own dry fields in the period between 1955 and 1960 and to clear and reclaim about five *tan* of new upland dry fields in the state-owned mountains, as many families in this area had done.

The third daughter married in 1957 and the fourth in 1961, leaving the family with only three full-time farmers: the head, his wife and the son's wife. The son continued working as a forestry labourer. There were also two children in the family to be looked after: the son's first son was born in 1956 and the second in 1959. One of the two women, therefore, had to stay at home, although the children were sometimes brought to the field while the mother and the grandmother were working. The situation remained unchanged until 1970 when the household head died at the age of seventy-seven. He had not done much work in his final years, and the son's wife, who was mainly in charge of the family farming, found it increasingly difficult to carry on. Consequently, she bought a powered cultivator to save time and labour. This family acquired the machine some time in the late 1960s, although it had been available in the area since early in the decade.

In 1981, the family consisted of five members:

The former head's wife (83)

Her son, the present head (52)

His wife (49)

Their first son (25)

Their daughter (17)

After finishing high school at eighteen, their second son had left home in 1978 and studied to become a medical examiner in an evening school in Ōta-shi, a city in southern Gunma prefecture, while working part time in a hospital where his mother's sister worked as a nurse. He is now employed in a municipal hospital in Isezaki. The daughter is still at school. The first son who will succeed the house has been working in the ski ground since completing high school in 1974. Although the mother-in-law helped with the farming until the late 1970s, the children have never worked on the land. Thus, with her husband still working for the regional forestry office, the wife now carries on the occupation alone.

During the 1970s, however, she has been able to acquire most of the farm machinery that has become available in this area through cheap loan programmes provided by the agricultural co-operative and through government subsidies.[25] The family now has a thresher, a huller, a rice-mill, and a binder, in addition to the cultivator already mentioned and an electric motor to power some of the machines. It also owns a rice-transplanter jointly with two other households and belongs to one of the two groups that jointly possess a tractor. With the help of the machines, and assisted by her husband in the evenings and on Sundays, the wife cultivates about 3.5 *tan* of paddy and about nine *tan* of dry fields. The remainder of the family land has been left idle since it is impossible for her to cultivate it despite the machinery. The fields she gave up are mainly those where it is difficult to use the cultivator.

The machines are mostly designed to help with rice cultivation, but there have been other innovations such as chemical herbicides and fertilisers which have greatly reduced the time and labour required. She claims that without chemical herbicides she would be able to farm only one-third of the land she is now working on. Other aids such as *maruchi*[26] have also been introduced to increase production. In a village like Hanasaku where paddy occupies only a small portion of land under cultivation, the impact of herbicides, artificial fertilisers and aids like *maruchi* seems to be of greater importance in reducing total labour input than the machines.

Many households in Yamazaki are in a similar situation. There are eighteen households in which only wives are fully engaged in agriculture. In another three, only husbands work on the land, their wives being either dead or employed elsewhere. Thus, in all, twenty-one families in Yamazaki have only one member working on the land. Only in five families with relatively large holdings do both husband and wife still farm. Families with smaller holdings have either given up farming altogether or carry on only on a part-time basis while working full time in a non-agricultural occupation. This is the case with four families in the hamlet, each headed by a woman.

The twenty-six families in Yamazaki in which farming is still carried on have altogether thirty-two full-time farmers, whose distribution in terms of age and sex can be seen in Fig. 1. More than seventy per cent of the total are women and more than eighty per cent are over forty. The table clearly indicates that the agricultural population increasingly consists of women and the old. Why more men give up farming than women was once clearly explained to me by a farmer in the following calculation.

In the construction field in which many villagers who left farming are now employed, a man receives an average of 6,000 yen (approx. fourteen pounds in sterling) per day, and he usually works about twenty-five days a month. At this rate, a man can earn for the six month period of the agricultural season roughly 900,000 yen. On the other hand, if he cultivates the whole of his family holding, which is normally a little over one hectare in Yamazaki, he may earn at most 1,200,000 to 1,300,000 yen in sales income of which nearly half goes into herbicides, chemical fertilizers and other farm expenses. Thus, for a man, construction labour is clearly preferable in-terms of income.

A woman on the other hand receives only about 3,500 yen per day, and an average working month is also less for a woman for various reasons. As a result, six months of working in the construction field may bring a woman a little over 400,000 yen while she may earn as much as 500,000 to 600,000 yen if she works on farmland. Thus if one also takes into account

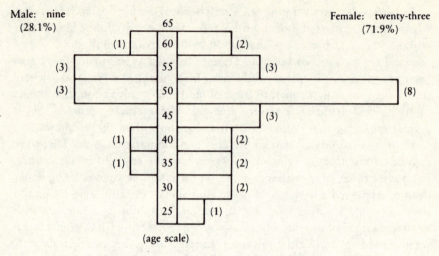

Fig. 1: Distribution of full-time farmers by age and sex

the rice and vegetables consumed at home, farming is still a more profitable occupation for a woman than construction labour. It is true that farming has no fixed working hours as such, but as it provides more freedom and flexibility, many women who have to take care of the house and the elderly, prefer it to other wage-earning occupations.

The fact that new employment opportunities have been more limited for women than for men also partly explains why more women still remain on the land. In addition to construction work, there are two watch component factories and several button factories in Katashina *mura*. Factories, however, not only pay no more than construction work but also often require an eye-tiring precision which many women over forty find difficult. Women may also be employed as forestry workers. Although the regional forestry office does not employ women due to the hazards of the work, a subcontractor does and he pays women only slightly less than men, but even this man employs only a small number of women.

For various reasons, therefore, it is more sensible for a woman to continue farming than for a man, unless the holdings are large enough to occupy more than two persons on the land. As more and more farm machinery and other facilities for reducing farm labour are made available by continuing government efforts to modernise Japanese agriculture, the present pattern of one-person farming is likely to continue.[27] Troubles lie ahead, however, when the next generation takes over. Many young people in the village have never learnt farming and they are not interested in becoming full-time farmers in the future. Lack of interest seems to be greatest among girls. Therefore, in a hamlet like Yamazaki where women work on the land while their husbands are employed elsewhere, the so-called 'successor problem' (kokeisha mondai) is even more serious than elsewhere. Perhaps for this reason, many farm households are having difficulties securing a spouse for those who will inherit and succeed to the house. Of seventeen men in the hamlet in the age group twenty-five to thirty-five, only five are married, and four of these got married to city girls and then came back to the village afterwards. Significantly, none of these four spouses came from Katashina mura or from Tone county, and three of them are from outside Gunma prefecture. By contrast, it is interesting to note that there are fourteen men of the same age group in Noboto, excluding the residents of Tokyo mura, and eleven of them are married.

The agricultural cycle

With the introduction of new crops and farm machinery, the agricultural cycle has undergone socially significant change. When crops cultivated by the villagers were largely identical, their working cycles also largely coincided, and they were able to carry out a number of communal activities at the beginning and end of each task. Many of these activities and forms of co-operation related to them have disappeared as household crops have diversified and as machines have replaced co-operative activities. These changes will be outlined here by comparing the agricultural cycle of the past with that of the present.

Before the war, farm work was scheduled by the lunar calendar, roughly a month later than the Gregorian solar calendar. When most households in the hamlet were still engaged in the cultivation of barley and wheat over the winter, the first springtime task of farmers was 'treading on the barley plants' (mugifumi), in early March by the lunar calendar. The earth starts thawing around this time of year and undermines the roots of barley (mugi) and wheat (komugi) that had been growing beneath the snow during the winter. The ground had to be trodden on in order to resettle the roots. Throughout the month of March, people including the old and children from every household in the village came to the fields and trod down the barley, weeding at the same time. Mugifumi no longer takes place since the villagers stopped growing barley and wheat after the war.

After the mugifumi, in late April (solar), people began 'the burning of

49

earth mounds' to prepare the rice fields. This task is called *kuromoshi* and its purpose is to kill weeds that have grown during the winter, but it is also said to have some sterilising effects. *Kuromoshi* is still carried out by a hamlet labour pool known as *kuromoshi-ninsoku*,[28] and it now marks the beginning of farm work in the village. At about 7:30 a.m., one person from every paddy-owning household gathers in the front yard of the 'management official' of the hamlet.[29] They are then divided into several teams which start setting fire to all earth mounds that divide the paddy. Although the total size of paddy land is not large in Yamazaki, it is divided into smaller parcels in this hamlet than in others and the parcels tend to be more widely dispersed. As a result the task requires more time. Moreover, since the task of widening and clearing agricultural paths for cultivators is also carried out by this *ninsoku*, it often becomes a whole day's work.

It is said, that this is better done on a hamlet-wide basis, as only then can sterilisation be effectively achieved.[30] The same reasoning applies to the biannual hamlet-wide sterilisations carried out by the *ninsoku*. The first one in April concentrates on houses and their surroundings, and is known as *yukashita shōdoku* (sterilisation of underneath the floor). Then, in late July or early August when it is very hot and the plants are prone to diseases, all paddy fields in the hamlet are jointly sterilised. On both occasions, the local government office sends the sterilisation equipment on a round of the houses and fields in each hamlet.

Formerly, when *kuromoshi-ninsoku* was over, people individually prepared for their rice transplantation. Rice seeds used to be sown in late April in seedbeds in one corner of a paddy field. The plants were left there for forty to fifty days before being transplanted. Therefore, transplanting of rice (*taue*) used to last well into June in this area. Under natural conditions, it took at least ten days before the first shoots came up. Nowadays, however, seeds are mostly sown in specially made seedboxes suitable for mechanised transplantation. Since these boxes are movable, they are placed in a specially heated room until the shoots appear, and this now takes only two or three days because of the heat. Once the shoots appear, the boxes are placed in a vinyl house which is much warmer than the fields. Transplantation is thus done about twenty-five days after the seeds are sown, about twenty days earlier than before.

Some time before the transplantation, however, there is another occasion that requires hamlet-wide cooperation, *mizukake-ninsoku*. During the winter, water is kept out of the fields by blocking the main entrance to the irrigation ditches, and *mizukake* signifies the first flooding in the spring. Since there has always been sufficient water in this area, there has been no organised method of hamlet-wide water control. The first flooding is important, however, since all the fields that have been left dry over the winter have to be sufficiently flooded for transplantation. As in *kuromoshi-ninsoku*, one person from every household gathers at the house of the 'management official', and they are divided into teams. Starting with those located on a higher level and working downwards, they flood the fields. It is essential for the participants to keep a close eye on the direction of water flow to make sure that no fields are missed.

After the first flooding, the fields need a thorough ploughing, known as *takaki*. In 1982, this was done exclusively by tractors, although until sometime after the Second World War most households in this area had employed a horse for the job.[31] It is said that using a horse for ploughing flooded fields was an arduous job requiring at least two people, usually a man and a woman. The woman's job was to lead the horse, while the man kept control of the wooden-framed ploughing tool behind the animal. Since most women were unable to keep control of the plough in the muddy fields, many households are said to have had extreme difficulties in carrying out the task when most men were away during the war. Even now, *takaki* is mostly done by a man using a tractor or a cultivator.

Transplantation shortly following *takaki* was one of the major co-operative occasions, but since the total area of paddy was not very large, the scale of co-operation did not involve more than two or three households. The most commonly adopted form of labour exchange on this occasion was known as *ē*. *Ē* of rice transplantation was usually a general exchange of labour between two households. Once two households agreed to perform *ē* for rice transplantating, the total labour-forces of their households were mobilised until the transplantation of their paddy area was complete. While the work was being carried out, there was no distinction in which fields were to be done first. The work schedule used to be arranged by what was convenient in terms of location and respective size, regardless of which household they belonged to. In this regard, the *ē* of rice transplantation as it was carried out in the past cannot be regarded as a balanced form of labour exchange, since the areas of paddy of the two households might not be equivalent to the labour-forces involved.

This kind of *ē* involved in rice transplantating has almost completely disappeared since the introduction of rice transplanting machines. A form of labour exchange in the name of *ē* is still carried out in different contexts, however. It is carried out for vegetable cutting, at one stage of silkworm raising, and in plucking off green soybeans (*mamemogi*). On these occasions, the form of *ē* is more balanced and reciprocal than the old

$\bar{e}$ of rice transplanting. Now the exchange of labour is more often done on the basis of individual manpower, rather than the whole household. Moreover, individual manpower is strictly calculated with regard to age and sex. For instance, if one household in the village needs extra labour for the cutting of *nozawana*,[32] they either hire somebody on a daily basis for cash wages, or they seek out another household which grows the same vegetable. They then inquire, 'Would you like to do it in money or shall we do it as $\bar{e}$?' (*Okane ni shimasuka, $\bar{e}$ ni shimasuka*). Since it is rather difficult to find labour for hire these days and since the cutting of *nozawana* is best done in the shortest possible period once the plants are fully grown, the household approached is very likely to agree to $\bar{e}$.

The labour offered in such cases is normally calculated in terms of a day's work. Thus, if a woman from household A works cutting the *nozawana* of household B for three and a half days, the latter is obliged to return $\bar{e}$ *kaeshi* (the same number of days' work) when it is time for A to cut their vegetables. A day's work by a man is considered equivalent to one and a half day's work by a woman, and a day's work by a youth under eighteen is returned by half a day's work by an adult man, etc. There is, however, little complication in this regard, since those who participate in $\bar{e}$ these days are almost exclusively women.

The stricter method for calculating manpower in doing $\bar{e}$ these days apparently results from the spread of a cash economy, as the present-day level of wage differentials is clearly reflected in giving and returning $\bar{e}$. Daily agricultural wages are slightly higher than those in other labour markets. A woman receives between 5,000 and 5,500 yen for a day's work in addition to the midday meal at about eleven o'clock in the morning and tea with pickles and sweets at about three o'clock in the afternoon.[33] When one hires a person with a machine for rice transplanting, however, the wages are decided by the area worked and not by the number of days. In 1981, the wage for the transplantation of one *tan* was 4,500 yen for the machine and manpower. The price was the same whether it was done within an hour or three hours. Such wages are decided early in the spring at hamlet meetings with reference to other hamlets and other villages in the *mura*. The wages within one village are often identical but there might be slight variations between villages.

When labour is hired or exchanged between kinsmen, the transaction becomes more diffused. When, for instance, one asks a cousin to do the transplanting, the payment is always a little more than the accepted amount, and it is not immediately given. This seems to signify that the faster any economic transaction is concluded, the more distant the social tie. Often some gift is presented in addition to the payment. The diffused and more general nature of the $\bar{e}$ of rice transplantation in the past may also be understood in this context, since it was often done between households closely related by kinship or affinal ties. Of the twenty households in Yamazaki whose past rice transplantation $\bar{e}$ partners I was able to trace, eighteen were related through sibling ties, of which fifteen were a brother/sister relationship, one between sisters and two between brothers. In only one case was it done between main and branch households.[34] The people in the village told me that only when there were no siblings living in the same village was it done between households related by main/branch household ties. The $\bar{e}$ partnership, therefore, sometimes crossed the hamlet boundary when siblings lived in different hamlets.

In this connection, it is interesting to note that the joint ownership of new agricultural machines manifests a similar pattern. Several households in Yamazaki, for instance, jointly own and share a rice-transplanter (*taueki*) with an affinally related household in a different hamlet, despite the fact that there are main or branch households in their own hamlet. Machine borrowings are also more often done between households related by blood ties rather than between the main and branch households, unless the latter ties have recently been intensified by a marriage.[35]

Nowadays, since households related by sibling ties do not always cultivate the same crop, the $\bar{e}$ partnership can only be established between a limited number of households. The $\bar{e}$ of silkworm raising or vegetable cutting are now often done with the closest possible neighbours for convenience.

A few households in Yamazaki still practise $\bar{e}$ of rice transplantation in a form very similar to that of the past, although they now use a machine. The event, however, is more a case of working together on a job which otherwise has to be done alone, than of exchanging labour. In one case, four households related as in Fig. 2, work jointly for the transplantation of the whole area of paddy belonging to them. All happen to be in the same hamlet, household C having branched off from household B during the present generation. Household B branched off from household D three generations ago. One can note, however, that the main/branch relationships between them have recently been strengthened by a marriage, household C contracting a first cousin marriage, as did household D in the previous generation.

In the cases of households A and D, both husband and wife work on the farm, while in the cases of B and C, only the husbands do so. Hence, six people worked together for the occasion, using two rice-transplanters

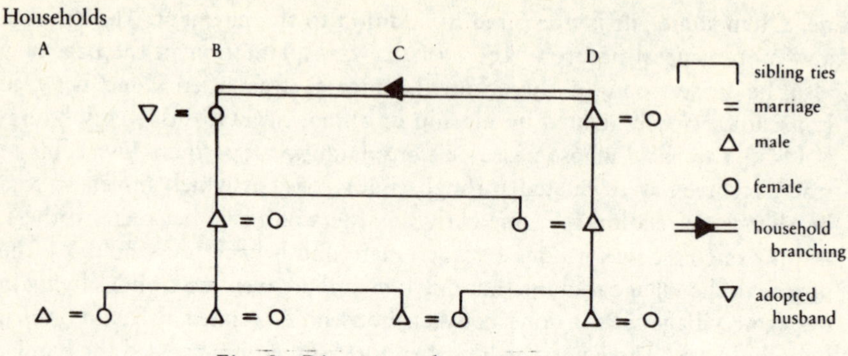

Households

Fig. 2: Rice transplanting *ē* group 1

owned by households B and D. In carrying out the joint enterprise, however, the area worked and the work-forces involved were not strictly calculated, and the sharing of food followed to celebrate the occasion. In the past, since rice used to be transplanted by hand, the *ē* usually lasted for about a week to ten days. During this period, the households used to take turns cooking for all members of the participating households, including the old and children who did not work at the enterprise but who had to be taken care of since everyone else participated in the *ē*. Nowadays, the *ē* is usually over within a couple of days, and the food is shared only among those who have participated, usually only with one meal at the end. To celebrate the occasion further and in hope of securing a good harvest, people in the village used to cook special ceremonial rice called *sekihan* and distribute it among their own neighbourhood group. This is no longer done either.

On the whole, the transplanting of rice has become a minor occasion. Those who still do *ē* seem to do so more for convenience and mutual fun than out of economic necessity. Therefore, if the exchanged labour becomes too unbalanced, there appear signs of strain. For example, the three households E, F, and G comprise another group still carrying out *ē* (see Fig. 3). Among them they own one machine jointly, and only the wife of household F can operate it. Therefore, during the transplantation, she is assisted by the husband of household E, and the wives of E and G transport the seedlings to the fields and plant them in corners where it is difficult to use the machine. The husbands of households F and G are employed elsewhere and do not participate.

In 1982, the quantity of rice seedlings transplanted was ninety boxes for household E, seventy for F and sixty for G. Although the three households

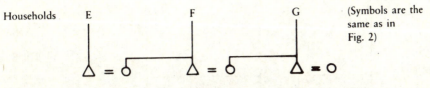

Households   E   F   G   (Symbols are the
                                                       same as in
                                                       Fig. 2)

Fig. 3: Rice transplanting *ē* group 2

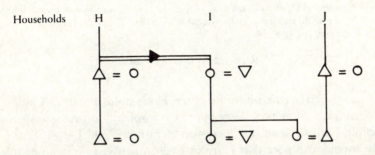

Fig. 4: Rice transplanting *ē* group 3

practised *ē* that year, the wife of household F said on several occasions that it would be much simpler if she did the work on her own. Not only can she use the machine herself, but she can also be assisted by her husband whenever she needs him. She still practises *ē* with households E and G because her family has done so for the past thirty years or so, when her father-in-law was alive. She does so also because she thinks household E, which is that of her husband's sister as well as their main household, will have great difficulty on its own if they stop co-operating. She believes, however, that the arrangement will only continue during the present generation.

Even in the past, most of the *ē* partnerships did not last more than one generation. Since the *ē* of rice transplantation is an unbalanced form of reciprocity, it cannot continue if one starts calculating gains and losses. People in the village told me that one is able to overlook such considerations only with households related by close kinship ties, such as between siblings. If the relationship extends beyond that boundary, friction soon develops. One solution to the problem is to change the partnership. The following example indicates such a situation (see Fig. 4). During the previous generation, household I had practised *ē* with household H, from which it had branched out and with which it is related by a sibling tie. However, it changed its *ē* partnership later to household J, since one of the

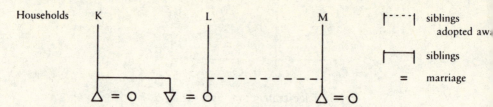

*The wife of household L in Yamazaki was adopted from household M in Kajiya to inherit the former, and her husband was later brought in from household K in Yamazaki as an 'adopted husband' (*mukoyōshi*).

Fig. 5: Rice transplanting *ē* group 4

wife's sisters had married into the latter. Households I and J no longer do *ē* between them. Now they carry out rice transplantation at separate times, household I with a machine borrowed from household J.

One should also note that *ē* are carried on between households related by brother/sister ties or between those of sisters much more frequently than between households of brothers. In fact one household in Yamazaki had done *ē* until a few years ago with a household in Kajiya from which the wife of the household had been adopted, despite the fact that one of her husband's natal brothers was living in the same hamlet (see Fig. 5). Cases such as this where men abandoned labour exchanges with their brothers living in close proximity had not been rare because the relationship between unrelated women, that is the brothers' two wives, is prone to friction. What is interesting, however, is the fact that the villagers explain specific situations with the general 'friction between women', even though the labour exchange relations are successfully established between the households of sisters.

This may partly explain why there have been so few *ē* partnerships established between the households of brothers, but at the same time one must remember that there have been fewer chances for two brothers to live in the same village than for a sister and a brother to do so. Brothers may live in the same village when one of the non-inheriting sons is allowed to establish a branch household, or when he has married into another household in the village as an adopted husband. As shall be shown later, however, chances for either have always been fewer than for a village girl to marry into the same village.

Village holidays have also disappeared with the changes in the agricultural cycle. Since there were no Sundays as such when most people in the village were still engaged in agriculture, they used to take self-imposed holidays whenever one stage of farm work was over. They took a day off, for instance, when the sowing of the soybeans and foxtail millet seeds was over in May, when the transplanting of rice was over in mid-June, or when the cocoons of the spring silkworms had been shipped in July. All the village-wide and hamlet-wide festivals were also conveniently situated during the course of the year for this purpose. At the end of August, after the barley and wheat had been harvested and threshed, and after the cocoons of the autumn silkworms had been shipped, there used to be a big summer festival. These occasions consisted of the summer village festival, the Gion festival and the repairing of the village and hamlet roads (*michi-bushin*), which was also almost like a village-wide feast since the end of the communal labour used to be celebrated by a big joint meal. These festivals were followed by the ancestral festival (*O-bon*),[36] and after the harvest there were the festival for the god of wealth (Ebisu-sama) and the autumn village festival in November (for further details about the village festivals, see chapter 8).

Unlike in the past when the weeding of the barley and wheat fields, the rice transplanting and the sowing of soybeans and foxtail millet seeds comprised the only major work in May and June, farmers in Hanasaku are now continuously busy throughout May, June and July with sowing different vegetable crops, transplanting, thinning out (*mabiki*), sterilisation, weeding, harvesting and so forth. Those who make several croppings of one vegetable are often kept busy from April to October. There is therefore simply no period in the present-day farming pattern when the whole village can relax at the same time. In fact, even individually, the farmers are unable to take time off.

Similarly, the end of August, which used to mark one of the biggest festive occasions in the past, has now become the busiest agricultural season. This is when the green soybeans have to be plucked from their branches and when various vegetable crops have to be prepared and shipped. Consequently, the summer village festival can no longer attract as many people as it once did. In 1981, the representatives of the six hamlets gathered together and performed the ceremony at the village shrine. I was the only other person in attendance. The villagers told me that most of them are just too busy and the youngsters and children are also busy either at work or at school.

Although the Gion festival still enjoys great popularity, its date (which used to come on the twenty-eighth of August each year, two days after the village summer festival) has had to be adjusted to the last Sunday of the month in order to attract young people. The summer festival now accordingly falls on the last Friday of the month. Similar changes have happened with other religious festivals and non-religious village-wide and hamlet-wide activities.

Notes

1 For a general description of mountain village economy and its changes in Japan, see Sugano 1976.
2 Although each plot of land is registered in individual names, no individual ownership is recognised within the household unit. Land plots that belong to the members of one household are always utilised corporately as household property. Also, individuals under whose name land plots are registered are often household members who have died.
3 Ushiomi 1968: 14.
4 For a detailed discussion on the origin of forest land ownership in Japan, see Ushiomi 1968, chapter one.
5 The mountain range was divided equally among those resident households of Yamazaki which at that time had full membership in the community, but, it is said, some families were unable to afford even the nominal price at which the land was offered, so their shares were bought up by more affluent members of the hamlet.
6 Some of it still remains a common asset of a hamlet or village. Recent methods of utilising these communally owned mountains will be discussed in the following chapter.
7 In 1926, paddy fields were reported to be nearly 2.4 times dearer than the same area of upland dry fields. *Katashina Sonshi* 1963: 329. Even today when, due to the development of cash cropping, dry fields may yield much more income than the same area of paddy fields, the estimated price of the latter is almost twice that of the former.
8 One hectare = 100 are = 10,000 sq. m. = approx. 2.45 acres. One *chō*, on the other hand, = approx. 9,917.36 sq. m., making the village measurement roughly equivalent to a hectare. In these rounded-off terms, one *tan* = 10 are = 1,000 sq. m.
9 There were three different categories of farmland involved in the Reform: (1) the total area of tenanted farmland owned by non-residents of the *mura* (2) that part of tenanted farmland owned by resident landlords that exceeded one *chō*, and (3) the total area of farmland exceeding three *chō* whose owners were farmers themselves. These lands were bought by the government and sold at a nominal price to those who were working on them. For a detailed analysis of the Land Reform, see Dore 1959.
10 The proportion of tenant houholds in Katashina *mura*, even if one includes part tenants, did not exceed two fifths of the total number of households before the war. *Katashina Sonshi* 1963: 357. It is said that there were villages in other parts of the country where tenant farmers comprised nearly two thirds of all farmers. Fukutake 1967: 8.
11 All those who work for the regional forestry office are now 'civil servants' receiving a monthly salary from the state and enjoying regular holidays and bonuses. Annual income ranges from £4,200 to £5,700 depending on age and years of service.
12 Until 1965, 157 households in Hanasaku cultivated soybeans on 56.85 hectares, while 158 cultivated wheat on 66.32 hectares. By 1975, however, only one household in the whole village cultivated wheat, and those cultivating soybeans were reduced to thirty-six on less than three hectares. The number of those cultivating barley and foxtail millet began to decrease more rapidly after the war, and by 1970, no one was cultivating any millet.

13 Transplanting is done for almost all of the crops cultivated in the village. Seeds are sown first in specially prepared square boxes filled with earth, and these boxes are kept in a vinyl house nearby until seedlings appear. They are then transplanted into the main fields. The method is supposed to be good for the plants and can also prevent loss of plants by birds, insects, or bad weather.

14 The sudden increase in the volume of imported grains especially from the USSR and the resultant fall in the prices of home-produced grains was one factor contributing to this decline. According to Sugano 1976:17, the proportion of Japanese supply of grain crops had decreased from fifty-three per cent in 1955 to only about one per cent in 1970.

15 *Katashina Sonshi* 1963: 329.

16 Part of this increase was made as a result of the Land Replanning Programme, and hence Noboto, Tochikubo and Kajiya show a greater increase than in hamlets like Yamazaki where the programme has not yet been implemented.

17 When sold, 60 kg or one *hyō* of rice brings farmers about 17,000 yen, but they have to pay at least 4,500 yen for 10 kg. of rice.

18 The amount of grant differs according to type of newly adopted crops. Farmers who grow vegetables may receive from 23,000 yen to 28,000 yen for ten ares, but those who grow soybeans, barley or any other kinds of grain crops which the government once again wishes to encourage in this region, may receive as much as 43,000 yen for ten ares.

19 This is a new type of sweetcorn introduced into the village during the early 1970s and whose seeds are said to be imported from California each year. People believe it to be easier to grow than other vegetable crops, and *bantamu* produced in this area is thought to be sweeter due to the cooler weather. The same claim is maintained about the beans grown in the area.

20 Most bears appearing in this area are about two metres tall. They can be a great hazard to men as well as to crops. A new 'hunting association' (*shuryō-kai*) has been formed in the *mura*. Whenever a bear appears within the territory of Katashina *mura*, all the members of this association are called through a broadcasting system known as *yūsen* that connects the government office with every house in the *mura*. The system is used for all emergency communication and also for broadcasting each day's bidding price for the crops.

21 Transplanting is now done about twenty days earlier than before as a result of a new heating system which enables farmers to grow rice seedlings more quickly.

22 Farmers who sell their products through the agricultural co-operative have to sort, grade and pack them in standardised envelopes and boxes provided by the co-op, and do all other preparation. Co-op personnel must also visit a designated place in every hamlet known as *shukkajo* where the products are taken.

23 By cultivating one *tan* of dry field, a farmer can produce two and a half to three *hyō* of soybeans. Since the selling price of one *hyō* of soybeans is slightly less than that of paddy rice at 15,000 yen, soybeans cultivated on one *tan* may bring 50,000 yen while if one cultivated vegetables on the same area it would usually bring about 150,000 yen of sales income. Excluding expenses for steriliser, chemical weedkiller, seeds and fertiliser, the net income is said to be about one third of the sales income.

24 In a village like Tsuiji, for instance, the average area of cultivation per household is said to be more than five hectares because many people in this village also cultivate farmland tenanted from the residents of Higashiogawa, which is a village to the north where many people have given up farming since the construction of National Highway 120 in the mid-1960s and have gone into tourism.

25 For instance, in 1981, if several families jointly purchase a tractor which costs about 1,600,000 yen (approx. £3,800), about three quarters of the price is covered by the government.

26 *Maruchi* are black vinyl sheets about one metre wide with small regular round holes at the centre. They are spread on the fields just before transplantation after the fields have been ploughed and a large amount of fertiliser has been added to the soil. The sheets help the plants grow faster and more safely, and prevent weeds from entering the covered area.

27 Although it would be wrong to say that mechanisation of Japanese agriculture has started only recently, it is true that most of the farm machinery in use in the village now has been bought since 1965. For instance, the agricultural census for 1965 records only two powered cultivators in Yamazaki, while the number had increased to twenty-nine in 1970. According to the data for 1980, there were thirty-three cultivators, twelve sprayers, nine rice-transplanters, sixteen binders and two tractors. The number of machines has increased since then. Thus, at the time of my research in 1981, there were six tractors in use of which four were owned individually. In 1982, ploughing, transplanting and reaping of rice was done exclusively by machines. Those who do not own machines either borrow them or hire villagers with the machines to do the work for them.

28 *Ninsoku* is the word used for all kinds of hamlet-wide and village-wide labour pools in this area.

29 The 'management official' (*unei-iin*) is in charge of all agricultural enterprises in the hamlet and acts as a liason official for the local agricultural co-operative. Agricultural activities have been so important in the past that this particular official is known as the 'management official of the hamlet'. For further details about hamlet officials, see Chapter 7.

30 In Noboto *kuromoshi* is no longer carried out as a hamlet-wide activity but is done individually by households which still farm.

31 Oxen replaced horses for a short while in the late 1950s and early 1960s, only to be gradually replaced by machines. For a brief account of the changes in animal husbandry in this area, see the following chapter.

32 *Nozawana* is a type of green vegetable which was introduced into the village in the early 1980s and is probably the only vegetable crop cultivated by Yamazaki farmers on a contractual basis. It enjoys a somewhat precarious popularity in the village. Being a short-lived crop (six to seven weeks), as many as five croppings a year are possible, and thus it can be quite profitable. On the other hand, as competition grows, the conditions of the contract have become more demanding and the price fluctuates a lot. There are two factories in Katashina *mura*, one in Tochikubo hamlet and the other in Tsuiji, which specialise in the pickling of this vegetable. Of the five households which grow the vegetable in Yamazaki, two grow it for the factory in Tsuiji.

33 Men are rarely hired for agricultural work these days except for rice transplanting with a machine.

34 For further discussion on the Japanese kinship system, especially on the significant difference between blood ties and the main/branch relationship, see Chapter 6.

35 In considering this phenomenon, one must remember that most agricultural machines were obtained recently, during the present generation, while the relationship between a main household and its branch is often several generations old and thus kinship ties can no longer be traced between their members. For details, see Chapter 6.

36 In this village, the *O-bon* festival used to be observed between the thirteenth and the fifteenth of July by the lunar calendar. As most city dwellers observe it by the Gregorian solar calendar nowadays and as the increasing number of descendants who have migrated to the cities can only come back to the village on those dates, the villagers felt that they had to adjust their own customs and recently changed the dates of the festival.

3

Supplementary occupations

Sericulture, charcoal making and animal husbandry were major sources of cash income in Hanasaku before the Second World War and continued to be the only substantial sources until the late 1950s. As wage-earning employment opportunities grew in the early 1960s and especially with the opening of the Olympia ski ground in 1964, the general employment pattern began to change. By 1981, charcoal making and animal husbandry had almost completely disappeared, and silkworm raising is carried out on a much reduced scale. Young people now work as salary earning commuters and, sometimes, as entrepreneurs.

Supplementary occupations in the past

Sericulture

During the Tokugawa period (1603–1868), sericulture comprised the largest source of cash income in many mountain villages in the region.[1] It especially flourished during the last years of the Tokugawa period, as the price of the cocoons began to increase rapidly as a result of new foreign trade.[2] The sudden expansion of the industry during these years coincided with a local event which seems to have had some significant consequences: the discovery of the revolutionary Nagai method of silkworm raising known as 'fumigatory raising' (*ibushikai*) or 'the high temperature method' (*kōonshiki*).

The outcome of silkworm rasing had not always been predictable or satisfactory due to the cooler weather and frequent rains from June to early August, coinciding with the local sericultural season. Because of the unfavourable climate, the worms could catch diseases at an early stage and produce empty cocoons. Furthermore, the local belief at the time was that silkworms dislike smoke and heat and hence the worms used to be kept under the coolest possible conditions. As soon as the spring silkworm season started in June, for example, people used to extinguish all fires within the house. The fire in the hearth was at once put out, and all meals and even the daily bath were taken outdoors.[3]

Some time during the early Meiji period (1868–1912), however, one Nagai family in Hariyama learned by chance that silkworms grow better under other conditions.[4] One day in late June, the family played host to several warrior guests from Numata who called in on their way to Tsuchiide to suppress anti-government violence. The weather that evening was rainy and rather chilly, as it tends to be at that time of year. Exhausted and chilled, the soldiers soon lit a fire. The family, who believed that a fire so near would kill all the silkworms then in the house, worried a great deal, but being peasants, they could not object. However, when the family looked into the room where the worms were, they found to their great surprise and delight that the worms had become much healthier and more lively. That year, it is said, the family produced the best cocoons in the whole village. Convinced that silkworms prefer warmth, the head of the family experimented further with the method the following year and was again very successful.

His new method soon spread to his neighbours and to other hamlets and villages in the *mura*. By the time of his death in 1892, forty-two schools had been established in northern Tone county for teaching the Nagai method. He himself made frequent tours of them, giving lectures. Even after his death, his wife, travelling on horseback, continued lecturing throughout Gunma prefecture.

In Hariyama there is a shrine dedicated to Anakannon, the god of silkworms. The shrine was originally dedicated to the hamlet's tutelary god, Kannonsama, a Buddhist diety, and had no specific relationship to the god of silkworms. After the Nagai discovery, however, the hamlet somehow incorporated the worship of the two deities. As the Nagai method spread the shrine became the centre for an ever increasing pilgrimage by sericulturalists north of Numata. Sometimes people came from as far away as Takasaki. Old people in the village told me that until after the Second World War, on 17 of May each year, hundreds of pilgrims used to line up outside the shrine in Hariyama, the queue extending nearly a mile all the way to Kajiya.

Locally, it is believed that the god of silkworms uses foxes to run errands. The people of Hariyama therefore began selling the pilgrims paper charms of the god and pairs of earth-baked fox figures. Pilgrims would buy the fox figures and place them in front of their house god shelves, and then the following year bring the pair back to the shrine to be smashed. When I went to Anakannon shrine for the ceremony in 1982, in front of the main building I found a building of about nine square metres (three metres by three) that was entirely filled with smashed pieces of earthern fox figures. Excluding the residents of Hariyama and myself, however, there were only about a score of pilgrims. The fox figures were no longer sold although paper charms made locally were still popular. Most sericulturists still have a pair of fox figures in front of their god shelves, but they no longer take them to the shrine every year to be smashed and exchanged for new ones. Most of the villagers no longer observe a day for the real silkworm god Oshirasama either, although until some twenty years ago an elaborate ritual was held every year on the first 'horse' day of February.[5]

The decline of religious concern in relation to silkworm raising was not paralleled by a decline in the industry itself. In fact the scale of sericulture in the region increased. Before the war, poor people, families that were short of labour, and tenant farmers were largely unable to raise silkworms. The silkworms used to be supplied in the form of a loan by individual merchants from Nagano prefecture. These merchants would later come back to the village to collect payment. Since there was no other substantial source of cash income, in years when the harvest was not very good it was very difficult for poorer farmers to repay the loan in cash and this discouraged them from raising silkworms. After the war, however, the establishment of the agricultural co-operative, whose main functions included the provision of cheap loans to promote agricultural enterprise, enabled many more farmers to engage in sericulture. In 1946, for instance, only 531 households in Katshina *mura* were reported to have raised silkworms, but in 1956 the number had increased to 706 and the total number of cocoons produced was more than doubled.[6]

Another factor which discouraged poor farmers from silkworm raising was that a considerable amount of cash was needed to pay wages. In the past, it was believed that all the mulberry leaves should be plucked off the branches before they were given to the worms. For about a week to ten days before the worms started spinning, the task of feeding them leaves became so demanding that every household in the village had to hire extra labour. This labour was provided by migrants from Niigata prefecture to the north and from the area near Numata to the south. According to the villagers, the ecological conditions in Niigata were even less favourable than in Katashina, so there were many poor farmers who had to supplement their income. On the other hand, many also came from the Numata area because the weather there was warmer than in Katashina *mura* and the sericultural season was over earlier. Some of the labour was also supplied by families within the village who were unable to raise silkworms themselves.

63

The extra household labourers were commonly known as *yatoi* or *hiyatoi*, but some families employed *hōkōnin*. *Hōkōnin* differed from *yatoi* in that they were not employed on a daily basis. They were more like temporary live-in servants. The system of *hōkō* ('service') seems to have been most frequently utilised by the people in this area as a means of settling debts. Households that were in debt but unable to pay back in cash used to send one of their children to the creditor house for an agreed period. When there was no child available, sometimes the household head went. Those who were sent as *hōkōnin* were often very badly treated and exploited to the maximum. Unlike the *yatoi* labourers who were treated with respect and equality by their employers, the *hōkōnin* were usually served inferior food in the barn by themselves, and it was not uncommon for them to work until late at night. As resident servants, the *hōkōnin* helped with all agricultural work, not only with the silkworms. On the whole, however, there are only a handful of families in the village which have ever hired *hōkōnin*. In Hanasaku, the landlord and money-lender family in Hariyama most often kept two or three *hōkōnin*. A much bigger landlord in Surubuchi is said to have had an average of ten *hōkōnin* throughout the year until just before the war.

The employing of outside *yatoi* labourers or the use of *hōkōnin* for sericulture greatly declined when it was learned the worms can be fed without first removing the mulberry leaves from the branches. This new knowledge greatly reduced the labour required.[7] After the war, many additional new devices were introduced to further reduce the labour force and to bring about better results. As people began to rely more heavily on post-war scientific methods made available to them through the agricultural and sericultural co-operatives, the religious concern in relation to the enterprise seems to have declined proportionately.

The co-operatives have also achieved the relative stabilisation of the price and marketing of the cocoons. Before the war the villagers used to sell their cocoons to visiting merchants, and the price a household got often differed greatly from that of other households even in the same hamlet. Villagers with less bargaining ability often got considerably lower prices, and the old villagers told me what an anxiety this used to be. After the war, the agricultural co-operative offered the same price for all the cocoons produced in the village as long as they met a set standard and, unlike the merchants, it guaranteed an unconditional purchase every year. In addition, with the establishment of the Agricultural Mutual Aid Association in the *mura* in 1948, compensation funds were made available to farmers against loss due to natural conditions.[8]

All these factors – the new knowledge, the new benefits and the new Land Reform by which most farmers gained access to the mulberry trees – contributed to the increase in silkworm raising that continued for some time after the Second World War. A decline began, however, during the early 1970s due to the gradual expansion of commercial vegetable cropping in the area. Extensive vegetable cropping, is incompatible with silkworm raising. Once insecticide is spread at least three or four days must lapse before the leaves from mulberry trees in adjacent fields can be safely given to the silkworms, and the fact that most mulberry trees in this area are planted between fields rather than in a field of their own makes them even more vulnerable to the poisonous effect of the insecticide. As a result, many people have had to reduce the scale of their sericultures. Villages like Tsuiji, Shimotaira and Suganuma where it had been carried out on the largest scale were the first to give it up.[9]

The decrease in the total agricultural population and the increase in general agricultural wages also had some effect on the level of sericulture. Despite the introduction of many new devices, many one-person farming households in the village have found it increasingly difficult to maintain past levels of sericulture. Except in families with elderly people who can at least help with the care of the worms in the house, many have had to reduce their sericulture activities greatly or give them up completely. Villagers also say that agricultural wages are now so high that it is not worthwhile to raise silkworms if one has to hire extra household labourers for the job, and even if one wishes to hire them, there are no longer as many migratory labourers coming into the village as in the past.

Nevertheless, Hanasaku has a relatively large proportion of farmers still engaged in sericulture compared to other villages in the *mura*. In 1980, seventy-five households (35% of the households in the village) still raised silkworms. Compared to the 131 households (63.9%) that did so in 1965, the proportion has certainly declined. The decrease has been even greater in hamlets like Noboto and Tochikubo where *minshuku* have developed, but some hamlets like Yamazaki still had more than half of the families raising silkworms in 1980. An explanation may be found in the strategy of allocating available resources to the widest possible range of products including silkworms.

Work in the mountains
Although there is now only one man in Hanasaku for whom charcoal-burning is a full-time occupation, the subject is worth a brief discussion for its past importance in the village economy. Charcoal-making enjoyed

65

particular importance here because of the village's relatively good communications with the outside world. Despite the fact that all the villages in Katashina *mura* had the same easy access to the resources, charcoal-making did not become a profitable winter occupation in other villages until the early 1920s, when the major prefectural roads began to be constructed. Before then, it is said that the cost of transportation often exceeded the price that could be got for the charcoal produced.[10] On the other hand, Hanasaku had two major roads connecting it to Numata before the prefectural roads were constructed, and many were engaged in the occupation even before the Meiji period.

The occupation was pursued by most villagers until the late 1950s, when it began to decline; it had almost completely disappeared by the late 1960s.[11] When almost everyone pursued charcoal-burning as a winter occupation, the trees were obtained jointly by the members of the village from the regional forestry office, which was in charge of the state-owned forests in the area. Some time in August every year, the representatives of the hamlets held a meeting to decide which part of the mountains would provide them with sufficient trees for charcoal-burning that winter. The village officials then sent a written application to the regional forestry office requesting that the government sell the trees on the designated mountain to the residents of the village at a suggested price, which was often only nominal. The trees the villagers asked for were usually in a natural forest and the government then encouraged the locals to utilise such natural forests, so it is said that the permission was not difficult to get as long as the application was submitted in the name of the village.[12]

The part of the state-owned forests disposed of in this way was known as *tokubaiyama* (specially purchased mountain forests), although only a certain type of tree grown there was actually bought. Once the *tokubaiyama* was obtained, the representatives of the six hamlets in Hanasaku divided it into portions and cast lots to decide each hamlet's share. The residents of each hamlet then held another lottery known as *chūsen* to divide the trees in their sector between the households in that hamlet. Each household's share of the *tokubaiyama* obtained in this way provided trees for charcoal-burning and firewood over the coming winter.

Like most other economic activities, charcoal-burning was also pursued as a household enterprise. Every member of the household co-operated in it. In early December when the harvesting, threshing and shipping of the crops were over, family members began to build a kiln for that year's charcoal-making. The construction of a charcoal kiln used to be an arduous job often requiring the total labour force available in the household. Before the first snow, stones of a suitable shape were gathered into a dome approximately two metres high. Then a special type of earth known as *neba* (the dialect form of the word *nendo*) was collected from the mountain and carried home.[13] The earth was later spread onto the surface of the stone frame and carefully pounded all around. If the pounding was not thoroughly done, villagers say, the kiln often broke into pieces at the first firing and the family had to repeat the whole job from the beginning. Therefore, the treading and the pounding usually required the co-operation of the whole family. Once the kiln was constructed, however, only the adult men participated in the making of charcoal, for which the women made sacks.

The sacks were made of *kaya* (*Miscanthus Sinensis* or *Eujalia Japonica*: a type of reed used for thatching) which had been collected in November from communally owned miscanthus mountains (*kayayama*). Before the war, the *kayayama* were leased from the state as were the *tokubaiyama*. The difference between the two was that access to *tokubaiyama* had to be obtained every year, but the *kayayama* contract remained relatively permanent. The division among the hamlets was made according to the size and location of the *kayayama* and the number of households in each hamlet at the time of the lease. After the war, as a part of the Land Reform, all the *kayayama* were sold to the villages or hamlets to which they had been leased. There are three small mountains which were bought by Hanasaku, one belonging to the residents of Tochikubo and Noboto, one to those of Kajiya, Yamazaki and Hairyama, and the smallest to those of Kuryu.

The miscanthus provided not only sacks for the charcoal but also thatch for the houses. Even though all the households needed the miscanthus, the amount available was limited, so the hamlet exercised strict control over its utilisation. For instance, no one was allowed to enter the miscanthus mountains except during the two days in November set at the hamlet meetings. On these two days of 'miscanthus cutting' (*kayakari kamaaki no hi*), two persons from every household in the hamlets which had *kayayama* rights used to enter the mountain simultaneously at a whistle. Whatever a household could gather on those two days comprised its yearly share of miscanthus for charcoal sacks, and the remaining plants were left to grow until the next year.

In the past, almost all the houses in the village had a roof which needed to be rethatched every thirty to forty years. Each house in the village had to take its turn because *kayayama* materials were only sufficient for rethatching one or two houses each year, so material for the roofs was collected by a different method. Even on the miscanthus cutting days, villagers were not allowed to enter a certain part of the mountain which was reserved for the 'miscanthus for house repair' (*fushinkaya*). At the beginning of each year, the village council examined the houses for which an application for rethatching had been submitted, to decide which one was in most urgent need. Once a house had been chosen, all the households in the village were asked to contribute a certain amount of miscanthus from their *kayayama*. When each villager went into the *kayayama* individually to collect his contribution of rethatching miscanthus, however, he could not enter the part of the mountain reserved for the miscanthus for charcoal sacks, nor could he collect more miscanthus than his contribution to the rethatching. If he was caught taking more than this amount, he was reported to the hamlet council and ostracised by various means.[14]

In addition to the *kayayama* and the *tokubaiyama*, there was another type of communally owned mountain in the village, known as *kusayama* (mountain for grass). These mountains provided pastures for horses and cattle. Like the miscanthus mountains, they had also been leased out from the state for a long term, until they were divided and bought by the villagers at the time of the post-war Land Reform. While the miscanthus mountains were bought communally, the grass mountains were divided according to the number of households in each hamlet and bought individually. Since only a few households in the village raise cattle nowadays, a large part of the mountains is no longer utilised, and the Noboto people sold theirs in 1978 to the immigrants from the Tokyo area mentioned earlier. On the other hand, the communally owned miscanthus mountains are leased out to the ski ground and thus yield some income.[15]

The annual lease of the *tokubaiyama* has also long ceased. The decline of charcoal-burning in the area can be attributed to a number of factors, the most important of which is the gradual decline in the national demand for charcoal as a fuel since the 1950s. Another contributory factor was the government policy of afforestation, which is closely related to the history of timbering. According to available records, the first timbering enterprise in Katashina was in the early 1900s, when a few people who were able to acquire private ownership of forest land started a small-scale timbering business in what is now Tokura village. Later, in 1915, a much larger timbering enterprise was launched under prefectural sponsorship and it is said that this project, which lasted several years, employed nearly a thousand people from all over the *mura*. Until then, the felled trees all had to be carried to the river and floated. Because of the difficulties involved, timbering could only be done in areas located near the Katashina River, which flows into the Tone River and near the urban area in the south. Villages like Hanasaku thus could not actively participate in the enterprise. Only after the 1920s when the prefectural roads began to be constructed did the timbering industry begin to develop to any significant scale. The production of timber in 1946 was more than double that of 1921.

As the timbering industry grew after the Second World War, the government initiated a nationwide policy of afforestation.[16] The policy was mainly geared toward the planting of acicular trees, unsuitable for charcoal-burning. Therefore, it became very difficult for the villagers to obtain materials for charcoal. Also, technological innovation in the Japanese paper industry in the mid-1950s greatly raised the price of the broad-leaved trees used for charcoal and this factor further discouraged charcoal-making.[17] Timbering itself began to decline after the mid-1950s. The country started importing timber from America and the Soviet Union with the result that both the price and the demand for home-produced timber fell. Not only in Hanasaku but also in other mountain villages, therefore, neither the recently developed timbering industry nor the rapidly declining charcoal industry was able to provide people with sufficient agricultural off-season occupations. Sugano argues that the two related factors, the deteriorating conditions for charcoal-making and the subsequent decline of the timbering industry, eventually led to widespread rural depopulation in many mountain villages in the north-east and the west.[18]

In Hanasaku, only one man from Kajiya *buraku* now carries on charcoal-making from trees individually obtained through the *airinkumiai*, another post-war organisation set up through liaison between the *mura* residents and the regional forestry office.[19] Five people operate small-scale independent timbering businesses, employing about twenty villagers altogether. In addition fourteen villagers are employed by the regional forestry office and another ten or so work for timbermen in other villages in the *mura* during the agricultural off-season. Thus the number of people engaged in timbering and charcoal-burning now comprises less than ten per cent of the total working population of the village, while the ski grounds and construction field provide the major sources of supplementary cash income during the agricultural off-season.

Animal husbandry

In the summer of 1981, only four households (ten per cent) in Yamazaki kept any animals in the house. The number of animals totalled seven, and they were all breeding-cattle and calves.[20] Each animal is kept for only a short period, and the number of animals varies with the time of year. As commercial stock, animals are traded as frequently as possible. Most calves, for instance, are kept for less than one year after birth and are then sold at the bidding market held five times a year in Niiharu *mura*.[21] Although there are other bidding markets in the southern part of the prefecture, all the animals from Tone county must by law be traded at the one in Niiharu *mura*, and most village stockmen now use the transportation services privided by the agricultural co-operative. The co-operative also privides a licenced bidder. Although people can sell their animals to individual cattle agents (*bakurō*) as in the past, with the decline of animal husbandry such agents rarely come to the village unless specifically asked for, and there is no such agent operating within the village.

Although it is difficult to assess the exact effect of the decline in animal husbandry on the village economy as a whole one can tell that the scale and significance of animal husbandry have undergone considerable change over the past twenty years or so. For instance, the agricultural census for 1965 showed twenty-three cows, nine horses and six pigs in Yamazaki alone. In the village as a whole, there were 172 cows, twenty-three horses and twenty-eight pigs. In addition, some households also kept sheep (seventeen) and goats (twenty-four), and there were 546 chickens that year. Although I was unable to collect a complete census of animal stock in the village, especially because of seasonal variations, I found that including the seven in Yamazaki there were only twenty cows and calves in the whole village in the summer of 1981, and there were no horses or pigs. Chickens were found only very rarely, and two households in the village kept one she-goat each.

Animal husbandry has undergone drastic changes in terms of scale and significance. In the past most cattle were kept for agricultural purposes. For instance, 127 out of the 172 cows kept in the village in 1965 were work cows aged over two years old. Nowadays, the primary purpose of cattle husbandry is trade, although its scale has been greatly reduced. Horses were also kept as farm animals, but their more important function was transportation. Before the war, horses and horse-drawn carts provided an indispensible means of transport for most villagers in their mountain work and long-distance transportation of agricultural products for marketing. As road conditions improved and other means of transport and labour such as small lorries and agricultural cultivators were introduced into the village after the war, horses lost their most important functions. People then found it more practical to keep cows instead of horses especially since cattle were more useful in making barnyard manure. Still later, however, the cattle were also displaced by farm machinery.

The relationship of people with their animals has also changed considerably. In the past, because animals were kept for a longer period than nowadays and used extensively in the fields, farmers were greatly attached to their cattle. In the old house, because of the cold weather, animal sheds were usually built inside the house, often right next to the open bathtub, and the villagers jokingly told me that whenever they got into the bathtub, animals looked over the separating bar and sometimes licked their shoulders.[22] Also children used to play with the cattle quite a lot while grazing them after school. Sharing living quarters, and working and playing together all contributed to a greater emotional attachment between the farmers and their animals. Animals were considered as much a part of the family as the humans, and one villager told me how horses used to find their own way home when their masters were drunk and had fallen asleep on the cart behind.

In 1981, only one family in Yamazaki still kept their animals inside the house. When the villagers began to build new houses with tiled roofs instead of thatched ones they incorporated the idea of separating the animals from the household, and I was told that many families got rid of the animals altogether when they rebuilt their houses, in the hope of keeping the new houses clean. Until three or four years ago, there were still quite a number of households with animals in the village. The economic functions of cattle and horses had begun to change long before, but many families continued to keep them because of their emotional attachment rather than out of economic interest.[23] It was not easy to think of animals purely in economic terms or to sell them, because they were 'part of the family'.

However, even the families still living in old-style houses now have separate cattle sheds built outside the house. Animals are now considered a source of filth from which many villagers wish to be spared. Also, since, for hygienic reasons, the villagers are prohibited by law from building tourist lodging facilities within a certain distance of animal sheds, many people gave up their animals when they started *minshuku*.

One additional factor contributing to the decline of animal husbandry is again the lack of sufficient labour in most farm households. Cattle feeding especially requires considerable time because, as commercial stock, they have to be fed very well and carefully. Families without spare hands are unable to keep animals and with the changes in the distribution of farm household labour described previously, few families in the village now have such spare hands. To encourage cattle husbandry, the agriculture co-operative provides special grants for old people who wish to be engaged

71

in the occupation, so anyone who wishes to raise cattle can do so with less cost and greater profit. Nevertheless, as there are many ways of earning cash which the villagers consider less troublesome than cattle raising, the incentives provided by the authorities seem to have had little effect in promoting and reviving animal husbandry in the village.

New economic opportunities

The opening of a ski resort in Hanasaku in the early 1960s was an event of significant consequence in the village economy. I will discuss the event and subsequent development of the tourism industry in Hanasaku in the following chapter and limit myself here to the changes that have taken place in the general employment pattern of the village population, especially among those not directly involved with the tourism industry.

As indicated in the previous chapter, most farm households in Hanasaku now only contain one or two full-time farmers, and most of these are women. Most household heads, the inheriting children and their spouses, and a few of the non-inheriting children who still remain in the household after finishing school are employed in one of the non-agricultural occupations available in the village. Excluding those who work for the ski ground and *minshuku*, construction labourers are the most numerous. They mainly work on road construction. Since the Second World War, numerous roads, paddy fields, irrigation ditches, and school and office buildings have been constructed in the area. These works are usually financed by the *mura* and prefectural governments,[24] and carried out by a number of subcontractors for the construction department of the *mura* government. There are two such subcontractors operating in Hanasaku, employing eight and twelve villagers respectively. Another forty or so people from the village work for subcontractors outside the village. Altogether, therefore, about twelve per cent of the total village working population is engaged in full-time construction labour, and in addition there are a number of farmers who work in the construction field during the winter.

Although most construction labourers are employed on a daily basis, a certain feature of the construction work-gangs guarantees them relatively permanent employment. This feature is known as the *oyabun-kobun kankei*, literally meaning 'parent-child relationship'. While the term itself is rarely mentioned by the villagers, it signifies a kind of personal tie which one can find in the relationship between the subcontractor as the work boss (*oyakata*) and his individual employees. The relationship is based on

72

a set of mutual obligations commonly referred to as *giri* by the villagers. When a villager starts working for a particular subcontractor, for instance, it is his *giri* in his newly established personal relationship with the latter that he show honesty and loyalty in carrying out the subcontractor's work.

Such *giri* sometimes cuts across one's own interests, since a labourer quite often sacrifices his own convenience for the interest of the efficiencey of his work gang and of his boss. For instance he would not let his boss down by absenting himself from his work without full notice or by taking a job in another construction field where the wages are slightly better. His boss, in return, is expected to acknowledge such *giri* on the part of his employees and to treat them appropriately. It is the *giri* of the employer that he does not dismiss employees who show loyalty to him for economic reasons alone. In short, *giri* provides a mechanism by which a relationship of mutual dependence and trust is established between the employer and his employees and by which the employer/employee relationship in construction work gangs is personalised. The personal element stabilises labour relations and works ultimately in the interest of both parties. By acting on the basis of *giri* and by expecting his employer to act on the same principle, a worker can achieve a goal of more or less permanent employment and the employer can rely on constant loyalty from his employees. For this reason, most construction workers in the village do not change their work places often despite the fluctuation in availability of work and despite the slight variations in the wages offered by different subcontractors. In fact, most full-time construction labourers in the village have worked for the same company for the past fifteen to twenty years or longer. Even the part-timers who work only during the agricultural off-season usually go to the same company year after year.

As mentioned previously, about ten per cent of the village working population works in forestry, including fourteen villagers employed by the regional forestry office in Hanasaku and five who own private businesses as timber subcontractors. The labour relations in these fields are similar to the *oyabun-kobun* relationship described above,[25] although the availability of work in this field fluctuates more and people tend to change their work places more often than in construction.

About seventy people in Hanasaku or about fifteen per cent of the total working population can be classified as *tsutomenin*, i.e. as salary-earning commuters. They include those who work for the *mura* government office and the agricultural co-operative, those who are employed in factories within and outside the village, and those who work for the shops, super-markets, petrol stations and so forth. Among them, about ten people commute to the shops and factories in Numata, which is about three quarters to one hour commuting distance from Hanasaku by car but most of the work places are nearer to the village than this. Most commuters belong to the age group between twenty and thirty-five. Some of these occupations, however, are often less stable than construction wage-labour. Factories in this area often open and close within five years and there is little trace of the 'traditional element' in the employer/employee relationship between factory operators and their workers, particularly because most factory operators are not locals.

I have already discussed the case of the most successful businessman in Hanasaku, who owns a timber sub-contracting company, a supermarket, a *minshuku* and a petrol station. There are a few such entrepreneurs in the village, though others operate on a much smaller scale. The five men operating small timbering businesses belong to this category. Two other men in the village have been very successful in running a carpentry business and have accumulated considerable wealth with the recent boom in house construction and inn building. The increase of construction work in the area has also led some of the younger villagers to become drivers of heavy vehicles such as dump trucks or concrete mixers, working for a number of different construction subcontractors. One family operates a vegetable-pickling company in the village, two, run button factories, and another two, fish farms.

Apart from their perhaps more enterprising personal character, however, it is difficult to characterise these village entrepreneurs as a group. One of the most successful businessmen in Kajiya, for instance, had already inherited a certain amount of wealth, with which he and his wife expanded the business. Others have acquired special skills in demand at the time such as carpentry or heavy vehicle driving. One person in Sukagawa village in northern Katashina *mura*, for instance, started as the free-lance driver of a concrete-mixing truck some fifteen years ago and has now grown into one of the largest construction subcontractors in the whole *mura*, employing more than a hundred people. The two fish farm owners in the village apparently had considerable knowledge about bureaucratic procedures and were able to manipulate some of the *mura* officials to obtain government funds for their own needs.[26]

Individual ability and knowledge, good timing and a certain amount of luck thus seem to be major ingredients in producing successful entrepreneurs in the village. Apart from the timber subcontractor in Kajiya who also owns a petrol station, and the bosses of two carpenters' corporations, however, the other businessmen in Hanasaku have not been conspicuously successful. Many young men followed the example of the two successful

74

carpenters, and there are now about twenty people in Hanasaku working individually as carpenters or as members of the two groups. Similarly, there are seven free-lance heavy vehicle drivers in the village, mostly people in their late twenties and early thirties. However, since competition is much fiercer nowadays in both fields, the future of these young adventurers is uncertain. In general, although economic opportunities have grown considerably for the past twenty years or so, many people in Hanasaku are acutely aware of the instability of most of the new occupations compared to agriculture. This awareness is partly reflected in the great value still attached to land as an ultimate source of security.

Notes

1 *Katashina Sonshi* 1963: 331.
2 Although it is difficult to assess the relative value of Tokugawa currency units (*ryō*) in terms of the present, the following data provide some idea of the proportionate increase in cocoon prices. In 1826, for instance, one *kan* (approx. 3.75 kg) of cocoons cost one *ryō*. By 1866, however, the price had risen to 6.2 *ryō*. *Katashina Sonshi* 1963: 331–332.
3 Most old-style thatched houses in the village are two-storeyed. The upper floor of the house is usually a farm workplace where the silkworms were placed in their early stages and the ground floor provides living quarters for humans and animals. By the time the worms had started making cocoons, however, they occupied almost every corner of the house, leaving only a small area for the family members to lie down at night.
4 Cf. *Katashina Sonshi* 1963: 276–7, 333, 507–8; *Katashina no Minzoku* 1960: 60; and stories still told in the village.
5 Each day of the Japanese calendar is associated with one of the twelve birds and animals of the Chinese zodiac. For a brief account of the implications of the Japanese calendar for everyday ventures, see Hendry 1981: appendix B.
6 *Katashina Sonshi* 1963: 332.
7 Unlike in warmer areas where mulberry trees can be kept short, those in this area are mostly fully grown. The task of picking leaves from these trees thus used to be difficult. Also, since the trees are usually not planted in a field of their own but on the boundaries of other fields, many tenant farmers of pre-war years were unable to use them for their own purposes. It is said that even when the fields were rented out the mulberry tree leaves on the boundaries were taken by the landlords.
8 The Agricultural Mutual Aid Association has now become affiliated with the local government office in the *mura*. Any farmer who is willing to pay in 1,500 yen (approx. £3.50) at the beginning of the year is eligible for the compensation funds. In 1981 when the mulberry buds were almost completely killed by a late frost in May, some farmers received as much as 200,000 yen (approx. £480) from the funds.
9 For Katashina *mura* as a whole, the changes in the scale of sericulture between 1965–80 are as follows:

	1965	1970	1975	1980
No. of households	608	643	448	224
Silkworm eggs bought (g.)	3153.5	3818.8	2379	1092

*Source: Agricultural Census Data, 1965–80.

10 *Katashina Sonshi* 1963: 342–3; The impact of the construction of the new prefectural roads on the production of charcoal in the area was dramatic. In 1921, the total production of charcoal in the *mura* is reported to have been about 100,000 *kan*. By 1946, it had increased to 850,000 *kan*.

11 Some villagers continued to produce charcoal but mostly on a very small scale to meet household needs. Nowadays some old people in *minshuku* households make charcoal for tourism purposes.

12 The disposal of the state owned forest was much harder to get when individually applied for and the disposal price was also much higher.

13 The charcoal kiln used to be built near the house while clay earth could be found only in certain areas in the mountains. When there was no other means of transportation except human shoulders, carrying a considerable amount of heavy clay home was not an easy job.

14 A number of ways by which a hamlet can insure the co-operation of its members has been reported. See Takeuchi 1938; Beardsley, Hall & Ward 1959: 257–8; T. Smith 1959: 62; Smith 1961: 522–33.

15 The Tochikubo and Noboto miscanthus mountain has been leased to the Olympia ski ground since it opened in 1964, and the Kajiya-Yamazaki-Hariyama one has been leased to a private ski club in Tokyo since 1978. That of Kuryu, the smallest of the three, has been left idle. Households which have branched out or moved into the village since the war have no rights in these communal mountains.

16 Sugano 1976: 23.

17 Until then, it is said, paper was mostly produced from acicular trees. But by the early 1960s techniques for producing paper from broad-leaved trees had nearly replaced the older methods. Sugano 1976: 22.

18 *Op. cit.*

19 In carrying out the afforestation policy after the war, the government intended to mobilise the local labour force in return for the disposal of natural forest grown on state-owned mountains (*tokubaiyama*). The *airinkumiai*, literally an association to promote concern for forests, was initially set up as an organisation taking charge of the negotiation between the government and the local people concerning the terms for this labour mobilisation.

20 Two households in the hamlet kept some chickens for eggs and for household consumption. Chickens however are not traded, and there was no household in the village which raised horses or pigs.

21 One calf from Yamazaki born in July 1981 was sold at the bidding market in March 1982 for 290,000 yen (a little over £700). Altogether five calves from Katashina *mura* were sold at the same bidding at prices ranging from 290,000 yen to 340,000 yen.

22 In new houses as well as in old ones with new fitted-in interiors, bathrooms are usually separated by a sliding door. In the past, however, they were separated only by half walls and the other part of the wall adjoining the animal sheds was often left open. Even nowadays, catching people naked inside the house is not unusual, especially in the evenings when all the family take a bath in turn. Compared to other east Asian countries like Korea and China, nakedness in Japanese culture does not seem to constitute a source of extreme shame.

23 With regard to the changeover from horse to cattle husbandry, Sugano finds that the increase in the number of cattle was not always matched by a proportionate decrease in the number of horses: Sugano 1976: 19. In many mountain villages in eastern Japan, the rate of decline in the number of horses had been much slower, and I believe this phenomenon confirms my interpretation.

24 If the road to be constructed passes through a village, those whose houses are situated near the road also contribute a certain portion of the expenses, under the assumption that they are the direct beneficiaries of the new road. Due to the expenses involved, however, villagers often object to the construction of new roads, thus blocking many new projects. In 1981, two road projects were under blockage in Hanasaku as a result of such objections.

25 Relationships of a similar nature based on culturally defined mutual obligations have been observed in various other contexts of Japanese life, and have been referred to by many social scientists as *oyabun-kobun* relationships. See in particular, Ishino 1953; Bennett and Ishino 1963.

26 The money had been made available as part of the local government's effort to promote tourism. Although it is difficult to understand why people should come hundreds of miles to fish for artificially stocked trout in three foot square concrete pools, the government seemed to believe that such a fish farm would attract more tourists to the village.

4

The development of the
tourism industry

Katashina *mura* has a relatively long history of tourism. In the eastern and northern part of the *mura*, there are three huge lakes surrounded by deep green marshes and forests which had become famous nationally as early as the 1920s. In the local government office there are documents recording visits by well-known people to one of these lakes.[1] Some of the local hot springs were visited by outsiders even during the Tokugawa period. The first ski ground was opened in Oze, in the north, in the early 1950s, and it is said the Crown Prince came there to ski in 1952. Therefore, the opening of a ski ground in Hanasaku during the early 1960s was not a novel event for the local people.

As conditions for charcoal-making deteriorated toward the end of the 1950s, and as some villagers became migratory labourers during the agricultural off-season, numerous discussions had already taken place among them about the possibility of developing a tourism industry in the village. Prior to the present ski ground, which is known as 'Olympia' because it was opened in 1964, the year of the Tokyo Olympics, another attempt had already been made: a ski resort known as 'Oshina' was opened in 1958 by a person of the same name. It closed down only a year or so later, however. The chief reason for its premature closure seems to have been its operator's failure to gain sufficient support from the people of the village. The owner of the ski field, it is said, had attempted from the beginning to bring in all of his employees from outside in the belief that he could make a better profit. In consequence he not only caused general apathy among the local residents but also encountered great financial difficulty. A ski ground can operate only during the winter, and one not locally based and without local co-operation will find it difficult to continue.

In the meantime, several offers had been made by other outside capitalists, mostly from Tokyo, to open another ski ground in the village. While some villagers favoured the idea, others were more reserved, fearing the complications and disturbances that a ski ground in the village might bring to community life. The decisive factor was the deaths of two fellow migrant labourers from the village. In 1960, one villager from Kajiya *buraku*, while working as a labourer on the construction of a power station, fell into the river and died in Okuanimi in Fukushima prefecture. Two years later a man from Noboto *buraku* was trapped under a tree and died in Oze in northern Katashina *mura*, where he worked as a timberman. Shocked by the accidents, the villagers held numerous meetings focusing on the creation of more jobs within the village in order to prevent further mishaps. In 1963, it was decided to accept one of the ski ground offers already made, and in the autumn of 1964, a delegation of three village representatives including the headman was dispatched to Tokyo to make further enquiries.

The chief responsibility of the delegation was to reach the most acceptable terms of agreement. After several talks, it was finally decided to accept the offer made by a company named Tokyo Tower Kankō. The basic agreement was that while the company would provide the capital and dispatch a few 'supervisors', the construction and the actual running of the ski ground would be done mostly by the residents of the village. The ownership of the ski ground has remained with the same group of joint-stock companies to which the Tokyo Tower Kankō belonged although its chief stock holder has since changed to another company based in Osaka. The terms of agreement reached between the company and the villagers with regard to the running of the ski ground has been maintained however. In 1981–2, there was one man from the main company who visited the ski ground during the peak season, but there was no permanent resident 'supervisor'. The actual running of the ski ground has been carried out entirely by the locals, including around a score of 'regulars' employed directly by the company and about a hundred 'part-timers' employed seasonally by the local manager.

The ski ground

The significance of the ski ground in the village economy can be indicated by showing its relative position in the employment market. Those employed by the ski ground can be divided into three different categories: the 'regulars' (*nenkan*), the 'seasonal regulars' (*shiizunchū*) and the 'part-timers' (*baito* or *arubaito*). The nineteen 'regulars' are employed throughout the year and received a monthly salary from the company. The 'seasonal regulars' are employed regularly every winter, and in 1978 this group formed a labour union whose relationship with the local management body of the ski ground will be discussed presently. The number of 'seasonal regulars' varies slightly from year to year, but there were forty-eight of them in 1981. In addition, there are fifty to eighty people who are employed only at weekends and holidays or during the busiest season in December and January. Altogether, therefore, the Olympia ski ground provides full-time and part-time jobs for about one hundred and fifty people or nearly thirty per cent of the village's total working population aged between eighteen and sixty-five.

Apart from the Olympia there are two other ski grounds in the village, one operated by the local government office and the other by a private company based in Maebashi. Both of them are less than five years old. Although the two ski grounds are located within the official administrative division of the village and can only be reached by passing through the village, the land on which they are situated actually belongs to the state and the villagers have no rights in regard to their operation.[2] About sixty people from Hanasaku however, work for one of these two ski grounds during the agricultural off-season. Including these, nearly half of the village working population or more than two thirds of the families living in Hanasaku are dependent on ski grounds for their supplementary income.

While these statistics indicate the relative significance of the ski ground in the village employment market, the opening of a ski ground has other consequences affecting community life. The recent formation of a labour union by the 'seasonal regulars' employed by the Olympia is one example. One reason for its formation was apparently the opening of the other two ski grounds in the village a few years ago. When the Olympia was the only ski ground in the village, many people were simply 'grateful' for being offered a job there. With the opening of two other ski grounds, however, the villagers were provided with a choice and so were in a better position to bargain with the management body of the Olympia over working conditions and wages. To consolidate their improved position and to exercise their newly gained power more effectively, the workers decided to form a union of their own. The management body which represents the owning company, on the other hand, has no choice but to sit at the negotiating table with the union leaders, since it realises that it would be very difficult to secure sufficient labour during the busiest season without the union's consent.

As mentioned above, there are about twenty full-time employees in the ski ground. Although skiing is possible only from December to March, the Olympia hotel which was built as an adjunct to the ski ground is open throughout the year, and the full-time employees work mainly on the maintenance of the hotel and the facilities attached to it such as sports grounds, tennis courts, ski lifts etc.[3] These employees do not belong to the union, but stand on the management side, which is represented by the present manager, the previous manager and one or two senior full-timers who are closely related to the manager. The main items negotiated every year between the union and the management include the period of work, the wages and the nature of the food the workers are allowed to eat at the hotel during work hours. The work period is the most important of these. Being temporary employees, the villagers used to be employed on a daily basis whenever there were guests in the hotel or at the ski ground,[4] and their number used to vary greatly even during the peak ski season depending on the amount of snow that fell. With the establishment of the union, however, management was asked to employ a certain number of people every year for a set period of time, e.g. from mid-November to mid-April the following year, regardless of the number of tourists. In return, the union side is responsible for securing a sufficient work-force including 'part-timers' throughout the season.

The present manager is a man in his mid-thirties from Yamazaki *bura-ku*. He is the eldest son of the person who, as the village headman at the time, went to Tokyo in the early sixties to negotiate opening the ski ground in the village. Among the many villagers who work for the Olympia, this manager is the only one officially recognised by the company as a member; all other employees including the full-timers are theoretically his employees. As a company man on the one hand and as a member of the village community on the other, this man has told me on various occasions of the difficulties involved in his position, especially in dealing with the union. He knows very well that his performance as a successful manager in the eyes of the company depends solely on the amount of profit he can bring in.[5] At the same time, he is also fully aware that the ski ground can never be run successfully without the support and co-operation of his fellow villagers. If he were an outsider, the man often complained, he would gladly sack all the workers who make undue demands in the name of the union and employ people from other villages. He is unable to do that since he is aware that such an act would cast him and his family out of the community completely. It is also very difficult nowadays to find labourers, even from outside.

At present, by detaching himself from his employees as much as possible, he tries to identify himself as a company man in order to gain a better position in his dealings with the union. For example, he rarely mixes with the workers on social occasions and only 'shows his face' (*kaodashi*) briefly. Even on the annual trip the company provides for the Olympia people as a bonus at the end of the ski season, he never travels with his employees, but joins them later on just to show his face. In handling the company finances, he does not discuss them with or seek advice from other senior employees. The manager seems to believe that such careful tactics help to create a 'boss' image which helps him deal with the other villager employees. Some of his senior employees, however, find it difficult to accept him as a boss, and tension exists between the two sides.

As in the case of most other social relationships in the village, any overt expression of tension is carefully avoided. The following incident, however, clearly revealed to me the nature of the resentment felt by some of the villagers against the manager. I will relate it at some length, since it also illuminates certain ways in which conflicts within the village are handled.

I asked the manager if I could participate in one of the company's annual trips. The manager, who had become a good friend of mine, rather boisterously accepted the request, saying that 'there should be no problem'. Unaware then of the tensions existing between the manager and some of his employees, I told my neighbours and the relatives of the household to which I officially belonged in the village that I was going to observe the trip. As days passed, however, I realised that some talk had been going on among my neighbours, indirectly indicating to me that it might not be possible for me to join the trip. About a week later, I was told by the head of 'my household', who had been informed by his relatives working in the ski ground, that it might be a good idea for me to ask the new union leader[6] about my joining the trip. Following his advice, I made an official call on the house of the leader and politely enquired about the possibility. With equal politeness, however, I was told that it was very likely that some union members might object to my participation, although he did not explain why they might. I was asked to call on him again during the next few days to find out definitely. Before I had a chance to call on him again, however, he visited my house very early the next morning. The ostensible reason for his visit was a sympathy call (byōkimi-mai) to an old lady in my house who had been in bed for the past few months. Before concluding his brief visit, however, he told me that he had no time to hold a union meeting before the trip, and without putting my case before the membership, he was unable to accept my request. He regretted the fact very much indeed, he said; if he were at the end of his term as union leader, it might not have mattered much for him to disregard the general opinion slightly, but because he was just starting a new term it would be rather unwise of him to act on his own discretion even in a minor matter. Then he told me several times 'not to feel offended' (*ki o waruku shi naide kudasai*), because he had 'absolutely no choice' but to reject my request for the sake of general opinion. Personally, however, he said that he felt extremely sorry.

I later learned that the union leader had called at the manager's house on his way back from my own. That afternoon the manager's father, a former headman of the village, came up to my room and repeated on the manager's behalf the exact content of the apologies and reasoning made by the union leader earlier in the day. He also emphasised that I should understand the difficulties of the union leader and not feel personally offended. At the end of the trip which I was unable to join, I received a small gift from the union leader. The subject, however, was never brought up again by the manager himself, who stopped visiting my house for some time after the incident.

From this incident and from the way it was subsequently handled, we may discern certain rules which people in the village seem to apply when dealing with conflicts. First of all, as I mentioned before, it is best to avoid any overt expression of conflict or tension. In this particular incident, however, it had already become difficult to avoid the issue since I had been careless enough to let it be known before any background negotiation could take place that I would join the trip on account of the manager's invitation. The union leader and possibly some other senior members were apparently not very pleased that the manager had not consulted them before inviting me. To prevent the manager from arbitrarily disregarding the opinions of his employees, therefore, a break was necessary.

Such a break would, however, inevitably involve a degree of confrontation. The second rule is to avoid as much as possible any 'direct' confrontation. In his attempt to stop my joining the trip, therefore, the union leader took every opportunity to let it appear that his decision was not for his own sake but for the sake of the general opinion of the union members. Because the ostensible reason for his callling at my house was a sympathy call and because it was made very early in the morning, the household head and most of the family members as well as several neighbours were present, and the union leader repeated in front of them all a number of times, as though despairingly, that the local people tend to complain a lot (*Koko no hito wa urusai dakara*). To minimize complaints from members of the union, he had to act on the safest ground possible, i.e. not to invite any outsider to join the trip when there might be members of the group who had worked the whole winter but might be unable to join the trip due to the insufficiency of the funds provided by the company or other reasons.

It was, however, not very difficult to find out from other villagers who worked for the ski resort that this was a mere excuse. The fact that I made my formal application to him very late provided him with an even better excuse. Because it was only a few days before the trip, his claim that he was unable to hold a general meeting and thus unable to accept my application would sound even more plausible.

The third and final important element is the act of reconciliation. The gift presented to me after the trip was one example. Although the union leader and possibly some other members had apparently decided to use me as a scapegoat, formal apologies were made and a gift was presented to heal the damaged relationship. An exchange of gifts, sharing of a feast or a call of sympathy (*mimai*) are the most commonly adopted mechanisms on such occasions.[7] The call by the union leader on the father of the manager may also be interpreted as a gesture of some significance. Although many excuses had been put forward by the union leader to explain his 'inevitable' rejection of what the manager had already decided, the fact that the relationship between them had been damaged by the incident was recognised, and an attempt had been made by the union leader to reduce the damage as much as possible by seeking the understanding and sympathy of the manager's father. One should, however, note that no formal apologies were made directly by the union leader to the manager himself. Such an act would mean an open acknowledgement of the existence of conflict and confrontation, and hence was avoided.

The consequence of the incident was that, while the conflict had been expressed and the message of dissatisfaction on the part of the union leader and his colleagues had been fully conveyed to the manager, no one was 'overtly' offended, or at least no one was supposed to be. The only effect was that the manager had lost face slightly in his relationship with me and in the eyes of people in the village in general. In private conversation, many villagers agreed that the union leader had been very 'clever' (*atama ga ii*) in dealing with the matter, but even my closest friends in the village did not wish to pursue the matter further and discuss it with me. It was generally agreed that the matter had been properly handled.

By quoting this example in detail, I have attempted to indicate the nature of tensions newly developing within the community as a result of the opening of the ski ground. Such tensions, however, do not only seem to exist between the management and workers. Among many of the manager's close relatives and among many other villagers who are not involved with the ski ground, the general feeling is that forming a labour union has not been a very good idea. Many of them believe that the existence of a union within the village is harmful to community harmony, which is an always emphasised and, ostensibly at least, ultimately sought after goal in everyday life. They consider it improper for the temporary workers of the ski ground to form a union. Since the latter are part-time workers employed only during the agricultural off-season, those who are not satisfied with working conditions there should make way for other villagers. This is the majority opinion in Hanasaku and can act as a powerful deterrent against any extreme action being taken by the union members. The union can in principle withhold all the work-force from the ski ground if negotiations fail and their demands are not appropriately met. However, just as the manager fearing community opinion finds himself unable to dismiss all the workers, it is very doubtful whether the union members would ever withhold their labour during the peak season. The traditional value placed upon good community relations and co-operation has still such a great force in directing people's behaviour in Hanasaku that it is more likely that both management and union would strive hard for an agreement even by curbing their own interests, rather than to go to an extreme.

The *minshuku*

Another important consequence of opening the ski ground in the village has been the development of many hotels and inns (*minshuku*) in the countryside for the lodging and entertainment of tourists.[8] The word *minshuku* has apparently come into wide use since the early 1960s with the growth of *rejabumu*, the Japanese translation of 'leisure boom'. The literal meaning of *minshuku*, 'staying with the people', seems to have attracted many city-dwellers, especially young people, because of its romantic suggestion of learning about country life and mixing with rustic people. As the volume of tourism increased with the general improvement in economic conditions in the early 1960s, many *minshuku* villages have appeared in the Japanese countryside. At first, *minshuku* villages usually appeared where there were natural tourist attractions such as well-known mountains, lakes or hot springs. More recently, however, people have started *minshuku* first to earn suplementary cash income and then have developed tourist attractions there. The bulletin of the national association of country-inn operators includes such newly invented attractions as hot milk baths, perfume baths and herbal saunas. Others concentrate more on local specialities such as special mushroom cooking, mountain vegetable

85

dishes or genuine seafood dishes to attract tourists from the cities. Another way of attracting city people is to build sports facilities such as baseball or football grounds, tennis courts or gymnasia. Spiritual as well as physical discipline is strongly emphasised in Japan, and sports seem to provide an effective means toward both ends. During the summer, for instance, many young people are encouraged to undergo training together in one kind of sport or another. Such an activity is commonly known as *gasshuku*, 'staying together', and the large number of *gasshuku* teams of young people have been one of the major features of *minshuku* villages. In most *minshuku* villages including Hanasaku, therefore, one can find numerous sports facilities, which are sometimes used in the summer by professional teams for conducting their intensive short-term training away from the heat of the cities.

Minshuku in Hanasaku began to appear immediately after the opening of the Olympia ski ground in 1964. As the tourists began to overwhelm the lodging capacity of the Olympia Hotel, the parent company and the local branch of the Association for Commerce and Industry (ACI) began encouraging local people to open *minshuku*. As the business developed further, however, the *minshuku* operators began building sports facilities to attract tourists all year, especially during the summers, which remain relatively cool in this area. There are now in the village two gymnasia (one owned by the Olympia Hotel and the other by the village), several sports grounds equipped with electric lights for night games, and numerous tennis courts. There are also sports grounds for baseball, a very popular game in Japan, and for football. Many *minshuku* in the village have their own tennis courts for their guests. Some of the facilities were built with substantial subsidies from the local government. Since they were built under the aegis of the village, their maintenance is also supposedly the joint responsibility of the whole village. This fact aroused strong resentment among residents of agricultural hamlets who do not directly participate in their use. As the nature of this conflict will be discussed later, this section will concentrate only on what kind of people start *minshuku* and how they operate them. I will describe three actual cases which are fairly representative.

Case A

The Tomaru family was one of the six original *minshuku* founders in 1964, the year the ski ground opened. The family owns one of the larger holdings in the village, about 0.5 hectare of paddy and 1.6 hectares of dry fields. Prior to the advent of tourism, therefore, the family were relatively large-scale full-time farmers who also raised silkworms extensively. When talk of the ski ground began in the village, Mr Tomaru was the hamlet representative for Noboto and was thus deeply involved in negotiations. Also, two of Mr Tomaru's close relatives in the hamlet, including his *shinrui*,[9] happened to own land in the area where the ski ground is now situated. On behalf of these two families, and especially as the *shinrui* of one of them, Mr Tomaru also held numerous discussions with the company. According to Mrs Tomaru, this circumstantial involvement initially led the family to consider establishing a *minshuku*. At the same time, as the traditional off-season work had become increasingly difficult to find, it seemed a good idea to open a *minshuku* as a winter occupation. There was also a good deal of encouragement from the company people themselves. The couple therefore decided to enlarge their house to accomodate about twenty people. Several years later, they tore their silkworm-raising house down and built more guest rooms to accommodate another fifty people or so, and built three tennis courts on their paddy fields. In 1981, the family was building another house to accommodate eighty more people, featuring a huge banqueting-hall equipped with 'empty orchestra' music boxes (*karaoke*) to entertain the guests. Their *minshuku* is now one of the largest in the village and the business appears to be prospering.

The family borrowed most of the construction money from the ACI. According to the usual contract with that association or with the local banks and credit associations from which most *minshuku* operators obtain money, borrowers are not asked to pay either interest or principal for the first few years. The interest builds up during those years, however, and when they start paying it back, they have to pay the accumulated interest as well.[10] Payment is usually made twice a year, in summer and winter (when money comes in to the *minshuku*), and it took the Tomarus nearly ten years to clear their initial debt. They had to borrow another sum, however, for the new house being built in 1981. Mr and Mrs Tomaru were not willing to give the exact amount of their current debt, but they claimed that borrowing one billion yen (approx. £25,000) would require one guarantor and they needed two guarantors.[11] If we assume they borrowed two billion yen at an annual interest rate of eight per cent, this means that the family have to pay 1.6 million yen every year in interest. Most *minshuku* in Hanasaku charge their guests about 4,000–6,000 yen per person per day for accommodation and two meals. Even if we disregard the expenses required to run the *minshuku*, therefore, the Tomarus need at least 400 guests per year just to pay the interest. To make any profit and to pay back the principal, the family may need double or treble that number of guests every year. Even by a rough calculation, therefore, it is understandable that the *minsuku* people are so keen on comparing the numbers of guests each of them is able to secure. Most *minshuku* in the village have debts of at least one billion yen and some as much as five billion. Therefore, ill feelings sometimes arise among neighbours when some *minshuku* get more guests than others, or when an overflow of guests is sent elsewhere.

The Tomaru *minshuku* has so far had few difficulties in securing a sufficient number of guests each season. Initially, their guests were introduced by the ACI and by some company people who stayed with the Tomarus during the negotiation period. The number of guests gradually increased through recommendations by the first guests. Having once stayed in this house, guests usually come back and bring some of their friends. This pattern is true of other *minshuku* as well. If they have an overflow of guests, the Tomarus usually send them to another *minshuku* in the same hamlet, whose head acted as the go-between for their marriage, and to the latter's branch household which also opened a *minshuku* a few years ago.

When they started the *minshuku*, the parents continued farming. Now their eldest daughter, who recently obtained a professional chef's licence in Takasaki, is helping them. Since the Tomarus only have three daughters the chef took in an adopted husband a few years ago, and she and her husband will inherit the business. When business is very good during the holiday season, they employ a few of their youngest daughter's friends. This daughter is seventeen and in the second year of high school. The advantages of employing children, in Mrs Tomaru's opinion, are that not only are their wages lower than those of adults, but also they tend to gossip among themselves less than do the village women they might employ.

The couple still farm some of their land, about 0.4 hectare of paddy and about 0.2 hectare of dry fields. They have, however, long given up silkworm raising and animal husbandry, both of which they found incompatible with *minshuku* work. By continuing farming, they are able to be self-sufficient in the rice and vegetables they serve their guests throughout the year. On the rest of their land they have planted trees for timber, mostly larches, which they believe will bring them some income in about twenty to thirty years. Mr Tomaru also works as the manager of a local hotel, recently built by a Tokyo businessman. The *minshuku* work is mainly carried out by Mrs Tomaru and their eldest daughter. The eldest daughter's husband and their second daughter, both of whom commute to work in a shop in Numata, also help in the evenings and on Sundays, as does Mr Tomaru's mother. There are therefore always sufficient hands except during the peak holiday season.

Case B

The Iizukas also belong to the first six *minshuku* families. Their background, however, is completely different from that of the Tomarus. Mrs Iizuka was born in Hanasaku but married into Shibukawa where she and her husband once operated a small bar. The business failed, however, and the couple moved to Hanasaku in 1950. Since they did not own any land, Mr Iizuka worked in timbering and charcoal-burning throughout the year, while Mrs Iizuka farmed about 0.5 hectare of dry fields they rented from her natal household, headed by her elder brother. Since these together did not provide a sufficient livelihood, the couple and their two children had a very hard time when they first moved into the village.

When the Olympia ski ground and hotel were built, one of Mr Iizuka's friends happened to be working on the construction of the water pipe for the building. On his recommendation, five or six people who worked on the same job came and stayed in the Iizuka house, even though it was extremely small. While these people were staying with them, it occurred to the Iizukas that it might be a good idea to start a *minshuku*. They felt slightly more confident than other villagers, perhaps because they had operated a public house in a city. With Mrs Iizuka's brother as guarantor, therefore, the couple borrowed some money from the ACI and enlarged their house. Since then the house has been completely rebuilt and can accommodate forty to fifty tourists.

During the summer Mr Iizuka now works in Oze, another tourist resort in northern Katashina *mura*, and during the winter he works at the state-run ski ground in Hanasaku. The management of the *minshuku* is almost completely Mrs Iizuka's job, with the help of a sister who has married into the same hamlet. The Iizukas have two sons. Their eldest son is employed by the regional forestry office and is stationed in Numata. If he comes back to Hanasaku next year,[12] his wife will also work for the *minshuku*. Their second son has finished high school in Katashina and is now employed in Maebashi. Since they do not own any land, Mrs Iizuka usually stays at home even when there are no guests, although sometimes she travels to Tokyo with other *minshuku* operators to visit tourist agencies there.[13]

89

Case C

The Hoshinos started a *minshuku* only three years ago. Before then they were dedicated farmers, cultivating about 0.4 hectare of paddy and 1.3 hectares of dry fields. They were not particularly interested in starting a *minshuku* even though their main household and two of Mr Hoshino's cousins in the village did already. When they decided to rebuild their house three years ago, however, many relatives and neighbours suggested they build the house slightly larger than the family's needs and start a *minshuku*. Not only would they end up with a bigger house but they could also secure a winter occupation. The couple was persuaded.

They borrowed about one billion yen from the agricultural co-operative to build the house. Both Mr and Mrs Hoshino, however, were rather afraid of getting deeply into debt. When they needed more money later to add facilities such as a central heating system and flush toilets, they sold part of their 'grass mountain'. They now have a house which can accommodate up to fifty people although it rarely becomes full even during the peak ski season.

Compared to other *minshuku* operators in the village, the family is not in much debt. Mrs Hoshino is worried, however, since their prospects do not seem sufficiently promising to even pay the interest on their loan. Being a shy person, she finds it very difficult to spend time with guests. She and her husband much prefer farming to entertaining tourists. Business skill, according to the couple, is something that is given, and they do not consider themselves to have been born with that particular talent. The couple does not make any specific attempt to attract more tourists. At times, Mrs Hoshino wishes that tourists would not come at all, although she feels dismayed when she thinks about the debt they face.

The couple still farms most of its holding and has no intention of reducing it. They even continue to raise some silkworms. Unlike in other *minshuku* in the village, there are rarely any guests here during the summer. Since it is seldom full during the winter either, Mrs Hoshino and her daughter-in-law can manage the work between them. Mr Hoshino works as a full-time farmer in summer and at the Olympia ski ground in winter as one of the 'seasonal regulars'.

The three cases described above show the different backgrounds of *minshuku* operators in the village. As one may note, there is no direct relationship between size of land holding and *minshuku*. Of the forty-three *minshuku* opened by original residents of the village,[14] only one third (fourteen households) belong in the category of extremely small holdings (owning less than 0.5 hectare). Most of these fourteen households are either branch households or those of returned children as in case B described above. For them, the lack of sufficient farmland is one of the chief reasons for starting a *minshuku*. Another fourteen *minshuku* households own more than 1.5 hectares of farmland, belonging in the category of relatively large holdings. Eight households own more than two hectares, as in case A, and most of these are main households.

Geographical proximity to the ski ground and circumstantial involvement in its negotiations have initially led some people in Noboto to open a *minshuku*, mainly through the encouragement of the ski company and of the ACI which seeks to promote tourism in the area. Some followed later upon building a new house as in case C, or in the hope of securing a winter occupation. Agriculture being only a half-yearly occupation and becoming increasingly a one-person job, many felt a serious need for full-time non-farming jobs. Some of the new jobs such as construction labour are hard for women and older men to perform. Operating a *minshuku* thus seems to be a good solution, since it not only eliminates the physical exertion involved in outdoor work but also provides stable supplementary occupations for the older generation within the household and for the younger one, for whom only a few stable jobs are available locally.

On the other hand, some people in the village are afraid of going into debt, and fear the loss of their houses and land if they fail in business. Since people tend to expand their business in the mere hope that better facilities may bring more guests and thus help them to clear debt rather than according to a more realistic economic calculation, it indeed seems that starting a *minshuku*, debt and further expansion make a vicious circle complete, which once in is difficult to get out. Some do not like the idea of entertaining tourists, especially during holiday seasons such as New Year and *Bon* (the midsummer festival for the dead), which are nowadays almost the only occasions for the reunion of families and the gatherting of relatives. Some also prefer outdoor work to *mishuku* work, which is usually conducted indoors by village women. Other factors such as a relatively disadvantageous location or a great distance from the ski ground seem to affect opinion. In general, those who are employed in one of the more stable jobs in the village tend to be less interested in *minshuku*, and they often say that, by starting a *minshuku*, people in the village have become more competitive than in the past and that it is therefore harmful to good community relations. It may also lead to the taking over of village property by outsiders. The recent appearance of the 'Tokyo *mura*' is often quoted as an example of such a case.[15]

Here again one may note the ever-recurring concern for the community. People start *minshuku* for various individual reasons. If the number of *minshuku* continues to increase, it will lead to more competition among community members and to a greater dependence on external forces such as the general economic condition in cities, which affects the number of tourists. When people make decisions, however, they act largely in their own 'self interest' which the people of Hanasaku perceive in terms of the well-being of the household, and are usually unconscious of how their decision affects social relations within the community in general or village economy. This explains why more *minshuku* are opening and why existing ones are constantly expanded. The pursuit of self-interest is generally tolerated and sometimes considered positively in that it may eventually bring prosperity to the entire community if everyone works hard for their own household's interests.

If the pursuit of self-interest is carried too far, to the extent that it threatens the interests of other community members, however, it invariably meets with strong disapproval by the community. The family which built a four-storied building with a lodging capacity of more than two hundred people is a good case in point. By improving and expanding their own facilities to an extent that threatens the prospects of other *minshuku* businesses, the household has almost been ostracised by the rest of the community. In comparison, it is interesting to note that another entrepreneur family in Kajiya which owns supermarket and a petrol station as well as a *minshuku* still enjoys considerable popularity. Some people may envy this family, but the general opinion is that they are simply more able and clever. The way they expanded their business has not directly interfered with other people's interests. Although it is true that such community opinion may not stop people from acting purely in terms of individual interest, it certainly discourages extreme 'selfishness' and promotes caution, especially when the pursuit of private interest is likely to clash with that of others'.

Notes

1 The national rail line of the Jōetsusen was extended to Numata in 1924. The journey from Numata to Katashina *mura*, however, was mostly carried out by horse until the late 1930s when regular bus services between Numata and Kamada were first introduced.
2 There are in Katashina *mura* seven ski grounds altogether, including the three in Hanasaku. Of these, three are owned and run by the local government.

3 The hotel has a capacity of over four hundred people. The hotel rooms, mostly Japanese-style with straw-matted floors, can accommodate as many as ten people per room. It also has a few 'western-style' rooms equipped with straw matted beds.

4 Many of the tourists from the southern cities of the prefecture come skiing for only a day. There are four lifts altogether in the Olympia ski ground, and the largest number of part-timers during the winter work in lift-ticketing. Others work as patrol men or at the various car parks belonging to the hotel. The patrol men are responsible for dealing with accidents. Some of the younger villagers also work as ski instructors.

5 The previous manager, a man aged fifty-six from Kajiya, was persuaded by the company to resign from his post after consecutive years of deficit running.

6 The union leader is a man in his fifties from Yamazaki. In the autumn of 1981, he was elected the third leader of the Olympia labour union for the following two years.

7 *Mimai* is the word used for all kinds of general expressions of sympathy for family misfortunes, such as fire (*kasai-mimai*) or sickness (*byōkimimai*), hot weather, cold weather, individual hardship and so forth. It is expressed by exchanging cards or letters, or by a call accompanied by the presentation of gifts.

8 Some of the *minshuku* in Hanasaku have a lodging capacity of nearly two hundred people and their facilities are often as good as small urban hotels, but others are just slightly enlarged farm houses and can accommodate about twenty people.

9 The word, *shinrui*, means a patron household in this area. For further details, see Chapter 6.

10 The interest rates of the ACI and the various credit associations are between seven and eight per cent per year. For those able to borrow money from the agricultural co-operative, however, the interest rate is sometimes as low as two per cent per year.

11 It is not difficult to see that the local financial associations encourage people to borrow money. They only require one gruarantor while the agricultural co-operative requires two and even the spouse of the borrower is eligible to serve as guarantor. The money is also often given out on the basis of assessments of business conditions rather than on the security of any material property.

12 One of the three regional forestry offices in Tone county is located in Hanasaku. Those with clerical jobs are circulated every two or three years among these three local offices, and Mr and Mrs Iizuka hope that their son's next post will be in Hanasaku.

13 All the *minshuku* operators in Hanasaku formed an association (*minshuku-kumiai*) several years ago. The association produces a pamphlet every year advertising the *minshuku* in the village, showing their locations, facilities, and so on. It also dispatches a regular delegation to Tokyo to circulate these pamphlets among tourist agencies. In addition, the members of the association hold numerous parties at the beginning and end of the year, and organise group-tours, pop song contests and so forth.

14 There are sixty-one *minshuku* in Hanasaku. Of these, three are run by outsiders, i.e. non-residents of the village. Another fifteen are run by recent immigrants from Tokyo area as discussed before. Only forty-three are run by original community members.

15 Some villagers cynically refer to the separate residential quarter of recent immigrants in Noboto as 'Tokyo mura'. Although people are generally reluctant to sell land, the pressure of debt might inevitably lead some to do so.

5

The household

I have outlined the traditional economic relations in Hanasaku and how they have changed as a result of external forces. The mechanisation of cultivation and the need to increase cash income have moved a large population from agriculture to wage-earning jobs. The decline of traditional supplementary occupations such as charcoal-making, timbering and animal husbandary has coincided with the development of a tourism industry. The following discussion will focus on how social relations have affected, and have been affected by changes in the economic sphere.

Structure and composition

I have used the term 'household' as a rough translation of the Japanese *ie* in the belief that it is a closer rendering than 'family'. As many writings on Japan have already shown, however, neither 'household' nor 'family' fully conveys the connotatons of *ie*.[1]

The *ie* is the basic social and political unit in Japan. Households and not individuals are the constituent members of the hamlet assembly where each household has one vote regardless of size. Individuals are not socially recognised in the village other than as members of a household, and people are often referred to by their status within the household, e.g. 'the father of the house' (*uchi no oyaji*), 'the mother or wife of the house' (*uchi no kaka*), 'the young man' (*wakashi*) of such and such house, and so forth. It is for this reason that one is invariably given the number of houses rather than individuals when enquiring about the size of a hamlet or village. Although official statistics exist, no one in Hanasaku, not even the village headman or any relevant officials in the local government office, had any clear idea about the village's actual population, while most people in the village could immediately provide me with more or less accurate information on the number of houses in each of the six hamlets.

The chief characteristic of the *ie* is continuity. The *ie* exists 'independent of the individuals who pass through, and the primary duties of the living members are to honour the ancestors who went before them and ensure that descendants will follow after them'.[2] In this regard, the word 'household' only applies to a synchronic representation of the *ie*.

In the past, membership of the *ie* was not confined to kin; non-kin such as servants (*hōkōnin*) were also included. Although no household in Hanasaku nowadays has servants, people still use such symbolic expressions as 'under the same roof' (*hitotsu no yane no shita*) or 'a relation with whom one has shared rice from the same pot' (*onaji kama no mesi o tabeta naka*) to incorporate any long-term resident into the group.[3] When such phrases are applied, the recipient is expected to behave as a member of the group. For example, an anthropologist incorporated into a village household is expected, by the members of the household and others alike, to be represented in the community by its head and not in his or her own right. The head of the family with whom I stayed considered it his responsibility both to gain consent from other members of the community before I could participate in any hamlet or village meetings, and to present gifts on my behalf whenever appropriate.

As a residential group, each household in Hanasaku is more or less permanently linked with a particular house in the village. People in the village almost never move from one house to another, nor change the location of their house. That people so rarely move is significant. As will be discussed later, a considerable amount of institutionalised social interaction takes place between members of households situated close to each other. Each house in the village, therefore, provides its residents not only with shelter but also with an already established framework of social relationships. In other words, to change the location of one's house often involves a change in the whole set of social and ritual ties developed over generations between nearby households.

In the past three generations or so, only three families out of forty in Yamazaki have changed the location of their houses. In one case, a family had their house rebuilt at a cost greatly above their means and was unable in the end to pay the carpenter, who claimed his right to the house and sold it to the money-lender in Hariyama. The money-lender gave the house, which is zinc-roofed and the largest in the hamlet, to his second son, who subsequently passed it on to his own son, the present household head. The original owner of the house now lives in a small thatched house built for his family by the money-lender.

In another case, the family was forced to move out of its house on the grounds that it had lost its right to the building. The family had one

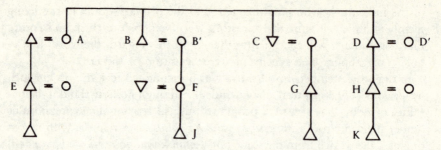

Fig. 6: The case of house exchange

daughter and three sons. The house was originally inherited by the first son. The second son was sent as an adopted husband to another household in the same hamlet, while the third son branched out. The daughter, the eldest child, had also married and lived in the same hamlet (see Fig. 6).

The first son (B in the diagram), however, died without offspring or adopted children. His wife (B′) then adopted one of her sister's daughters (F) and continued to occupy the main house. The third son (D) also died young, but he had a son (H) before he died. After her husband's death, D′ left the village and married elsewhere, leaving the child (H) with her husband's sister (A). The child was brought up by A so the house built for the child's father (D) was left empty for one generation. When H reached the age to marry, however, his two cousins, E and G, who were both living in the same hamlet and were considerably older than H and F, thought that H had more right to the main house than either B′ or F, and thus persuaded the two women to move to the branch house, a small thatched one originally built for D but which had been left empty. H and his wife were made to move into the main house.

The present head of the branch house, J, still begrudges the incident but refers to K's household as his 'main household'. The general opinion in the village is that B′ should have either adopted H as her son in the first place rather than adopting F later, or should have married F to H. Since she was 'foolish' enough to do neither, the change of houses was inevitable.

The final case of a change of house occurred much more recently than the other two. The family moved to another location within the hamlet when they rebuilt their house a few years ago. The family, a branch household, lived in a small thatched house behind their main household in the lower part of the hamlet where houses are more concentrated. They could not enlarge or build a bigger house on that site because of a mountain range behind, and since their fields were in any case in the upper part of the hamlet, they decided to build on some of their land there.[4] This is, however, the only time in living memory that a change of house location under such circumstances has occurred.

What are interesting, however, are the changes in the relative social and ritual status of the households which followed the changes of house location. In the second example mentioned above, for instance, F and H, by exchanging house buildings, also exchanged the status of 'main' and 'branch' households. Although it became necessary under Meiji law to register property as belonging to the head of the household,[5] in practice the property is still conceived of as belonging to the household. This case therefore implies also an exchange of all property rights related to the main and branch households.

The other two cases of house moving accompanied a change in religious status. Both the family which had gone bankrupt and the one which rebuilt their house in the upper part of the hamlet used to belong to the same neighbourhood group at the far end of the lower part of the hamlet. Before the two families moved out, this group consisted of six households all belonging to one 'extended household group'.[6] At the annual village festival held on the second monkey day of the lunar month of September, members of these households used to take turns in performing as the monkey, the prime role in the ritual, on a four year rotational basis (see chapter 8 for details). The family which went bankrupt lost this right after it moved out and joined another neighbourhood group. Similarly, when in 1981 the monkey role came round to the family which had moved to the upper part of the hamlet, it was performed by the second son of a family who had recently returned to the village and was now living in the family's old house with his wife and infant daughter.

Extended household groups, composed of main and branch households, commonly known as *dōzoku* or *ikke*, tend to coincide with neighbourhood groups, as branch houses are often built in the vicinity of their main houses. It appears that the six families mentioned originally acquired the right to perform as the monkey by virtue of their status as members of an extended household group and not as members of a particular neighbourhood group. The example shows, however, that when a redefinition of status is required, group membership based on the location of houses takes precedence over other qualifications. This may be a recent phenomenon. As a result of recent affluence, there is now little difference in the economic standing of households in the village, and people perhaps tend to resent more strongly than before political or religious privileges enjoyed by any

Table 7: Household composition in Yamazaki and Noboto: no. (%)

	Yamazaki	Noboto
(i) One couple only	4 (10.0)	2 (4.3)
(ii) A couple and their unmarried children	14 (35.0)	20 (43.5)
(iii) Two couples only	4 (10.0)	2 (4.3)
(iv) Three generations	16 (40.0)	19 (41.3)
(v) Four generations	2 (5.0)	3 (6.5)

one family or extended household group. Some people, for example, have even proposed that the role of the monkey be rotated among all the households in the village.

Despite the changes that have occurred in the village economy during the post-war years, there has been little change in the historically developed spatial framework of the village community. Not only have few families moved house, but the number of households within the community has remained almost the same for the past twenty-five years despite the constant emigration of individual members. The fact that few households have disappeared from the village reflects the ideology of continuity. The most common form of household composition in Hanasaku is the 'stem family', i.e. a household with two or more married couples from successive generations, but never two married couples from the same generation. In Yamazaki, for instance, twenty-two households out of forty (55%) are of this composition, while the remaining eighteen (45%) are 'nuclear families', containing one married couple or one surviving spouse of the couple and their unmarried children (see Table 7). The proportion is similar in Noboto which has developed as a *minshuku mura*, where twenty-four households out of forty-six (52.2%) are of stem family composition and the remaining twenty-two (47.8%) are nucelar families.

Except for a few households where only the married couples remain, however, most households which are at present of a 'nuclear' composition represent only one stage of the developmental cycle of the *ie*. In other words, in most of the households classified in category (ii) in the table, children are still of school age. When the children leave school and marry, these household may well develop into three-generation households. On the other hand, households classified in categories (i) and (iii) are mostly cases where the children have left the village and their continuity is therefore under threat. There are eight such households in Yamazaki and four in Noboto. Of the four in Noboto, however, one case is a 'retired household' (*inkyoya*) consisting of only one old lady. Another is a case where a barren couple lives with the husband's mother, and there is a possibility of adoption into this household in the near future. Therefore, only in the remaining two households are all the children employed and living elsewhere. In one of these two, however, it is quite possible that the eldest son, now serving in the regional forestry office in Numata, will some day come back to the village and take over the household.

Of the eight households in Yamazaki, similarly, one is a case where the successor to the house has only recently married and does not yet have children. Another is a household consisting of an old lady who used to be a concubine of the previous head of a family in Kajiya (the owner of the supermarket) who 'retired'[7] to Yamazaki after her husband's death. This woman adopted in her name the second daughter of her main household in Kajiya a few years ago, and it is possible that the adopted girl, who now works for her natal parents' supermarket and lives with them, will succeed to this woman's household in Yamazaki when she marries. Another two households are cases in which the children are attending school outside the village and thus are away temporarily. Only the remaining four are households all of whose children, including the successor, are at present employed outside the village. In two of them, however, the would-be successors, one working as a primary school teacher and the other for the regional forestry office elsewhere in the prefecture, have expressed a clear intention of returning to the village, although their jobs may take them away now and again. In the third case, the inheriting son is at present working as a cook in Takasaki and has expressed his intention of returning to the village if his parents start a *minshuku*. It is therefore only one family whose continuity is in any way under real threat. This family is a first generation immigrant household and does not own any land in the village, so their social status within the community is relatively low.

As far as Yamazaki and Noboto are concerned, therefore, one can say that recent economic changes have so far brought little change to their household structure or to the ideology of continuity. It is true that, owing to the scarcity of stable non-farming occupations in the area, many farm households find it difficult to keep their youngsters at home. In more isolated agricultural hamlets like Kuryu and Hariyama, therefore, there are more households which are likely to break up in the near future. In Yamazaki, however, only one household has so far reached that stage. The rest, including the farm households, have been able to secure a successor, although whether the trend will continue is not certain. Under the circumstances, the *minshuku* seem to be one of the most powerful attractions for young people and will thus probably remain one of the most important variables affecting household structure in Hanasaku.

Continuity of the household

How, then, is the household perpetuated? To ensure the continuity of a household, as Bachnik writes, two successor 'positions' must be filled in each generation and the two 'positions' refer to a married couple. Typically one of the two is recruited from among the children of the family and this one can be either a male or a female child. When the family has more than one child, however, there is a general preference for male rather than female, and older rather than younger.[8] In Hanasaku, about half the present heads of households were the eldest sons of the previous heads.

When the eldest son does not want to remain in the household, the second or third son may take his position. Equally, if none of the sons want to remain or if there is no son in the household, a daughter may take a husband who will assume his wife's family name and succeed to the office of the household headship. Such a husband is called a *mukōyoshi*.

Even when there is a son in the household, if he is too young to succeed when his parents have reached retirement, the eldest daughter may take in a husband and assume the responsibility of running the household until her brother reaches marriageable age and can take up the headship. Although there is no set age for parents to retire, in Hanasaku they generally do so when they can no longer be actively productive. The adopted husband and the daughter who have temporarily assumed the responsibility of running the household are usually given land to enable them to establish a separate household. In one case, the adopted husband and the daughter remained in the main household as the son who was to succeed has left the village. This example is considered as an 'exception' by the villagers and talked about as a case where the adopted husband has 'taken over' (*toraretta*) the household.

When there are no children in the household, a male or female child may be adopted. In this case, however, male preference does not necessarily apply. In Hanasaku, in fact, girls are adopted more often than boys. Moreover, although the adopted child is often one of the wife's sisters' daughters, even a completely unrelated child is equally acceptable. In one case the youngest brother of the household head was adopted as the latter's 'son', and in case of an uxorilocal marriage, the wife's youngest sister was adopted as her 'daughter'. Adoption of siblings in this way is called *junyōshi* as against *yōshi* for an ordinary adoption. In a later a stage of the household developmental cycle, adoption of a married couple may take place if no adoption has beeen made before. This is known as *fūfuyōshi*, 'adoption of husband and wife'.

All the practices mentioned above are found in Hanasaku and are considered equally acceptable. In other words, there is no prescribed rule with regard to the selection of the successor, and any of these strategies can be followed, depending on the situation. In the process of deciding, however, the emphasis is always on the continuity of the household as a corporate group rather than any particular individual within the group.[9] This makes it difficult to label succession practices in Hanasaku by conventional anthropological terms such as 'patrilineal', 'matrilineal' or 'bilateral', all of which refer to individual, rather than corporate continuity.

The reversal of the generally preferred strategy, i.e. that based on male/female and older/younger hierarchies, for the greater benefit of the household is by no means uncommon. For example, if the eldest son is physically or mentally incompetent or incompatible with the group for any reason, a younger son may be chosen as successor even when the eldest son wishes to remain in the household. In the case of one household in Yamazaki, the eldest son, who was in bad health, had to establish a branch household while his younger brother succeeded to the main household. This case caused some scandal in the village, however, since it was believed that the branching out of the eldest son was actually was not so much because of his bad health as his wife's bad relationship with his parents. Due to this scandal, the parents later 'retired' to another hamlet and lived there until just before their deaths in 1981.

Several reports indicate that in certain parts of Japan other types of succession, such as by the youngest child or by the first-born regardless of gender, were prevalent at least until the early Meiji period.[10] In Hanasaku, however, except in the cases of temporary succession described earlier or when none of the sons wish to remain in the household, daughters rarely succeed. If the parents wish to live with one of their daughters, the usual solution is to establish a branch household with the daughter and her adopted husband. There were several cases in the village in which the parents branched out with one of the daughters or younger sons. This is known as *inkyo-shintaku*, and will be further discussed in the next chapter.

Once chosen, it is the duty of the successor and his or her spouse to manage the household property, take care of the dead and living members of the household, and ensure that the household will continue by providing subsequent successors.[11] Most of the property including the land and the house, though legally separated from succession to the 'household headship' (*katoku*) following the Second World War, is still transmitted as part of the office in Hanasaku. The non-succeeding children, although they are now entitled to an equal share of the household property usually sign away their rights for the good of the household. In return, the younger sons and daughters receive financial support for education and later marriage.[12]

The recent economic changes seem to have had certain effects on succession practices in Hanasaku. First, the increase in economic opportunities other than agriculture has reduced the number of potential successors. When land was the major means of production, succession to the household also meant access to a livelihood. One may assume, therefore, that parents were in a better position to choose their successor than nowadys when few children are attracted to farming as an occupation.[13] It is true that the eldest sons, and eldest daughters where there is no son, generally consider it their duty to remain in the household and succeed to it. As will be shown later, however, they do not remain for economic reasons as much as out of a sense of responsibility to their parents and to ensure that the household continues. Unlike in the past, therefore, it is difficult for parents to choose their successor either for their own interests or for the interests of the household as a whole.

Even when a child is secured as the successor, a second problem is recruiting his or her spouse. As already mentioned, many farm households in Yamazaki are having difficulties finding daughters-in-law for their successors. One consequence of this is that successors tend to marry late. To find an adopted husband for a succeeding daughter seems to be even more difficult. As a married-in member, the status of the adopted husband within the household is relatively low. Even in the past, it was not considered a desirable position for a man as a saying goes, 'If you have three measures of rice bran, don't go as an adopted husband' (*kome nuka sangō areba, yōshi ni wa ikunazo*). When other economic opportunities were limited, however, many second or third sons had to marry into another household to make a living. This is no longer the case. Younger sons may still agree to marry into another household and continue its enterprise, but nowadays most are unwilling to change their family name. In Hanasaku, even one of the richest families, that of the owner of the petrol station, was unable to persuade its eldest daughter's fiancé, the second son of a *minshuku* household in Noboto, to change his family name upon marriage. The agreement reached between the two families was that the couple should marry and later have one of their children continue the mother's name and inherit the household property.

In Yamazaki alone, two households out of forty had precedents of siblings succeeding father's and mother's natal names respectively. Both happened during the later Tokugawa to early Meiji period. In one case, the great-grandfather of the present household head married into another household in Surubuchi. He was the only child in the household, but left the village after his parents died and worked in Surubuchi as a carpenter. His household in Hanasaku was thus left empty for one generation until his second son, named after his father, returned to the village and revived it. His eldest son, who was named after his mother, remained in the main household in Surubuchi and succeeded to it.

In the second case, a woman from a wealthy household in Koshimoto married into a household in Yamazaki. Although the actual cirucmstances are not clear, it was agreed before her marriage that she would keep her family name and have one of her children continue it. As agreed, one of her sons was named after her while all the other children were named after her husband. Later, this son had to establish a separate household in Yamazaki with land and a house provided by his mother's natal household in Koshimoto. This practice of 'bringing in one's family name' is said to have been much more frequent in the past, and people attributed the diversity of household names in the village to custom.[14]

By providing their successors not only with land and a house but also with an occupation more attractive than farming, *minshuku* households are in a better position to secure a successor than farm households. Conversely, it also appears that the ideology of household continuity has played a significant role in determining the patttern of the changing village economy, especially the development of many *minshuku* as household enterprises, as the following section shows.

The household as an economic unit

According to Befu, one cannot conceive of the *ie* except in the context of its economic activities.[15] This aspect of the *ie* has been reinforced in Hanasaku by the development of the tourism industry.

In the past, members of a household were usually all engaged in the same economic activity, namely agriculture. Although they also pursued a number of supplementary occupations, these were pursued by households as a group and not as individual occupations. For example, when the people in Hanasaku divided the trees of the *tokubaiyama* for charcoal-burning, they divided them not by the number of individuals, but always by the number of households in each hamlet, even though some households may have had no male members to do the job while others had two or three. In such cases, informants said that the former usually sold their share of trees to the latter at a price about three times higher than the original. This method illustrates how the household is indivisible not only as a social, but also as an economic unit.

As shown previously, most farm households in Hanasaku no longer form a corporate productive unit. Members of one household often pursue different occupations and their incomes are not always added to the common family purse. Many old people in the village still consider farming a family occupation and provide labour as long as they can. Similarly, in the households where only the wives now work as full-time farmers, their husbands, in addition to working in one of the wage-earning occupations, usually help, and their incomes are always pooled. Unlike in the past, however, younger members of the household no longer work in the fields, and when they work in non-farming occupations they usually keep their incomes for themselves, as savings or for recreational activities.[16] Older informants said that, since young people these days need so much money for their own expenses, parents had better be satisfied just as long as their children do not ask for more.

Due to the nature of their business, on the other hand, *minshuku* households have largely maintained the character of the traditional household as an economic unit. I have already mentioned that most *minshuku* households in Hanasaku carry on farming to a varying degree as a supplementary occupation. There is therefore a certain division of labour in carrying out the two household occupations. In a three generation household, for example, the older couple tends to concentrate on farming while the younger couple is mainly in charge of the *minshuku* business. The division of labour, however, is not always clear-cut, since there are always tasks to which any member of the household can contribute when required. In the case A *minshuku* family described in the previous chapter, Mr and Mrs Tomaru, both in their late forties, are in charge of the *minshuku* and farming at the same time. While Mr Tomaru's retired mother mainly helps with farming, she also cleans guest rooms and prepares food. The eldest daughter works as the receptionist as well as helping in the kitchen, where the food is prepared mainly by Mrs Tomaru herself. The eldest daughter's adopted husband, who commutes to Numata during the day, also provides help with the *minshuku* in the evenings through maintenance of the central heating system or fetching guests in his car.

The *minshuku* business therefore provides far more occasions for co-operation between household members than farming. Although husbands sometimes lend a hand in transplanting or harvesting rice, most other farm work is now carried out by wives alone with the help of labour provided from outside the household through *ē* or *yatoi*. By contrast, in *minshuku* households, even children of school age, who almost never participate in farm work, usually contribute labour, by washing up in the kitchen or setting the table etc. Unlike kin employed from outside the household, members of the household are not paid separate wages. On the other hand, a married-out daughter or a sister from one's natal household is always paid a fixed wage like other non-kin employees. People in the village explained that household members are carrying out 'the work of the house' (*uchi no shigoto*) which is for the household as a whole and not for any individual member.

A certain change in the status structure of the traditional household is noticeable, however. In the past, when all members of the household were engaged in the same economic activities, whether farming, silkworm rais-ing or charcoal-burning, skills and knowledge largely obtained through experience had always been transmitted from parents to children, from the previous head of the household to the successor. Nowadays, most of the young people have had some experience of the city and hence accumulated a different kind of knowledge from their parents who have never left the village. Some of the inheriting children of *minshuku* households have had training as professional chefs while others have had brief experiencies working in a hotel in the city. Even without such specific qualifications, the simple facts of youth and urban experience make the young better suited to the tourist industry.

Since Hanasaku has a fairly strong dialect with a vocabulary differing substantially from standard Japanese, people from the village find it dif-ficult to deal with tourists from Tokyo and surrounding urban areas.[17] Most young people, however, have a high school education and usually speak standard Japanese. Moreover, most tourists are young, and the young hotel workers understand them better.

Within the household, therefore, there has been a diffusion of authority. In many of the *minshuku* in Hanasaku, the actual head of the household is not always the boss or the *oyakata* of the *minshuku* work. Even when the parents are still in charge of major financial transactions, actual dealings with the guests are often delegated to the younger members of the household. In general, the opinions of the young are much more respected than before.

The changes in status structure are even more striking in farming households in the village. Since most men are not fully engaged in farming, they are no longer the chief decision makers within the household either. In many farm households, it is the wives, the actual farmers, who decide which crop to cultivate, what area is to be given to each crop and so forth. It is also these wives who frequently represent the households in hamlet meetings concerning agricultural matters. Moreover, it is mostly the women who order and purchase fertiliser, seed, silkworm eggs as well as household goods through the agricultural co-operative. During the harvest, all the farm households in each hamlet take turns in recording each day's crop, another task mostly carried out by women.

Most of all, however, it is knowledge of new agricultural machinery that enhances women's status within the household. To drive the powered cultivator, for instance, one needs a licence which can only be obtained by taking a written and practical examination in Numata and which has to be renewed every two years. In 1981, nineteen women in Yamazaki held a licence. In addition, most women under sixty could manipulate a powered huller, thresher or rice mill. Such knowledge is something unknown to the previous generation. In the traditional Japanese household, the male head is often referred to as the 'principal pillar' (*daikoku bashira*) of the house. Commenting on the increased responsibilities of women and their importance within the household, one old lady from a farm household remarked that the *yome* (the daughter-in-law of the house) nowadays is as much a *daikoku bashira* as the household head.

The diversification of the farm household economy has also affected the traditional authority of the household head over his successor. In the past, the household head was the manager of the household property, the supervisor of the household work group and the keeper of the family purse. In the traditional Japanese household, the head would usually bathe first and receive preferential treatment at meal times.[18] Even nowadays, in most houses in Hanasaku, a special seat known as *yokoza* is reserved around the fire place (*irori* or *kotatsu*) in the living room for the household head, and its is still considered rude for a casual visitor to occupy this seat. A saying goes, 'Only fools, cats and priests sit on the *yokoza*'.

When land was the only meaningful source of livelihood, the authority of the household head was often economically reinforced. As more people have become involved in wage or salary earning occupations, however, the economic basis of this authority has also inevitably been undermined. A dispute which arose over the inheriting son's marriage in one household in Hanasaku is indicative of the declining authority of the household head in this regard.

The would-be successor fell in love with a girl who was the only child of a family in a neighbouring village. Her parents wanted to adopt him, so that he would succeed to their own household. Realising this, the boy's parents tried for some time to discourage the relationship. When their efforts proved fruitless, the boy's father threatened to disinherit him. To the parents' dismay, however, the boy, who works full time at the ski ground and had no interest in farming, expressed little concern over the threat. The son thought his father mean, but said he did not care if his father named his younger brother as successor. He was sure that his younger brother, who worked in the city, would not be very keen to return. Nevertheless, he said, should he ever decide to stay at home against the wishes of the girl's parents, it would be because of his personal affection (ninjō) for his parents and feeling of obligation (giri) towards them, and certainly not for fear of losing the property.

It is in the light of these changes that starting an inn becomes a significant advantage for parents who want to consolidate the household unit. Unlike in farm households where successors now merely inherit (apart from land and the house) the household headship, duties for parents and ancestors and community obligations, in minshuku households they also inherit the business. Although the latter may involve a certain debt as well, it nevertheless seems to be more appealing to the young, both male and female.

Household gods and ancestors

The fact that the ie remains an important institution despite recent economic changes is reflected in the numerous rituals centring on the houses and household members. Each house in the village, for instance, has its own tutelary deity known as inarisama or yashiki inari. Inarisama is a small wooden or stone statue contained in a miniature house, usually found in a corner of the back garden, and is believed to protect the contents and inmates of the house. Despite the decline of certain religious practices in recent years, the guardian deity of the house is still faithfully attended to, and in the many newly-reconstructed village houses one often finds that the abode of their inarisama has also been smartly redecorated.[19] Its surroundings are usually kept tidy and rice is offered at least once a day.

In addition to the *yashiki inari* of the main building , there are a number of minor deities for each of the smaller buildings usually found in a farm house compound. These include the god of the barn (*monooki*) where agricultural tools are placed, that of the godown (*dōzo*) where household valuables such as clothing, bedding, table-ware and grain are stored,[20] and that of the farm house (*shiikujō*) where rice seedlings and silkworms are kept in their earlier stages. Most of the farm households in Hanasaku also have their own gods somewhere in the mountains to protect their fields and water sources. Although no specific rites are performed for each of these gods, they are all recognised each New Year by an offering of a pine branch called *hinoki*.

Sometime toward the end of the year, for instance, the head of each household in the village chooses a 'safe day',[21] and goes to the mountain to collect suitable branches of *hinoki* for the New Year decorations.[22] These branches are then decorated with auspicious objects such as dried cuttlefish (*surume*), sardine (*iwashi*), mandarin orange (*mikan*) and sometimes a kind of dried seaweed called *konbu*, all in odd numbers of three, five or seven. They are then placed at all the 'important' places in the house where gods are believed to reside. These 'important' places vary from house to house, but commonly include the entrance of the house, the *tokonoma* (an alcove in the most formal room in a Japanese house where special objects are displayed), the *kamidana* (house god-shelf), the bathroom, the kitchen and the lavatory in addition to the *yashiki-inari* and minor buildings mentioned. The purpose of this ritual decoration is to purify those places for the new year and it is often preceded by a general cleaning up of the house.

Apart from the purifying decorations of pine branches, the month of January, the least busy agricultural month, used to be the month devoted to numerous ritual activities centering around the household group. Many rituals have now disappeared,[23] and religious practices differ slightly from house to house as well as from hamlet to hamlet even within the village. The rite of the 'first fetching of water' from the stream, which used to be performed by the head of every household first thing on New Year's day, for example, has disappeared since water pipes were introduced some twenty years ago. Similarly, the New Year's visit around the hamlet by household heads, which is said to have been customary in the past, is no longer practised. In fact, even on New Year's day, many of the household members including heads and their wives were away at the ski ground, and members of *minshuku* households were mostly busy entertaining guests.

The rite of *yakudoshi* for those who that year reach ages regarded as especially vulnerable or inauspicious, however, is still performed in all six hamlets in Hanasaku.[24] In Hanasaku, these *yakudoshi* are the nineteenth and thirty-third year for a woman and the twenty-fifth and forty-second for a man. Some informants said that these years were 'dangerous' because they are the years when people 'change'. Such an idea has been mentioned by an earlier writer on Japan[25] and is found in other societies as well. To prevent possible attack by an evil spirit, therefore, a purification rite should be performed, which in Hanasaku consists of a joint burning of the New Year decorations by all hamlet residents. It is believed that like any other offerings *hinoki* branches which have been offered to the household gods, should never be thrown away but always burnt. Hence, around 13 January, people in the area take down the decorations, remove the items of food and leave the branches on their door step. The branches are then collected by those who have reached an unlucky age that year. On the 14th, a bonfire is built with these branches by family members of the *yakudoshi*. During the bonfire, to which all hamlet members are invited, the mandarin oranges and dried cuttlefish grilled on the fire are distributed by family members of the 'unlucky' people. According to the villagers, while burning the pine branches 'purifies', sharing the food shares the 'spiritual danger' (*yaku*) which has fallen on one of their household members.

The hamlet-wide ceremony with bonfire, or *dondoyaki* as it is called here, is no longer carried out in Noboto where the hamlet assembly decided a few years ago to drop it because many of the *minshuku* people were too busy at that time of the year and were thus unable to participate. Even in Noboto the household *yakudoshi* feasts are still held, however. In the evening, the families of *yakudoshi* hold big feasts at their houses for relatives and neighbours. The idea of 'sharing the spiritual danger' is still prevalent. The occasion also provides an opportunity to recognise the respective social standing of each household within the community, especially when the *yakudoshi* are men, household heads or would-be successors. When it is a daughter for a daughter-in-law who reaches an unlucky age, those invited to the household feast usually include only members of the immediate neighbourhood group (*tonari-kumi*)[26] and relatives living within the same hamlet. For succeeding sons and household heads, though, they include the members of all the associations to which the *yakudoshi* belongs, those of his work place and age group as well as neighbours and relatives. Relatives living in other hamlets are also supposed to visit, and not only the immediate neighbourhood group but also a few adjacent ones are invited, as well as the family's own extended household group (*ikke*).

The larger the number of visitors, the better since all visitors are believed to share the 'spiritual danger' (*yaku*) of the person concerned. Since there are usually a number of *yakudoshi* every year, people usually make a round of visits during the course of the night, or different members of the household are sent to different houses according to the sex and age of the *yakudoshi* concerned.

All the rites observed during the month of January for the benefit of the household are concluded on the twentieth when the god of wealth, locally known as Ibesu-sama,[27] is supposed to leave home for work. During the previous night, all the New Year decorations are removed, and early the next morning a special table is set up for Ibesu-sama. The table usually contains rice, some freshly-made noodles, soup, a pair of sardines and other side dishes (*okazu*). In some cases, money is also placed on the table as pocket-money for the god, though the amount should be moderate or the god will waste time spending the money instead of working hard to ensure a good harvest. In November, a welcoming rite for this god is also observed by many Hanasaku households. In the past people used to make cakes from the newly harvested grain and gave them to the children who went from house to house singing. Though they no longer make cakes for the occasion, they still give money to the children.

Most household rites are closely related to the traditional agricultural cycle. Around 20 January when Ibesu-sama is said to leave home, for example, people used to start 'planting earth' on barley fields.[28] Similarly, the return of Ibesu-sama in late November coincides with the end of the harvest. Even though the work cycle of the people in Hanasaku has changed and some of the traditional household rites have been abandoned, especially in *minshuku* hamlets, in general the attitude of relating good fortune, prosperity and safety of the household to supernatural forces (*kami-sama*) still prevails in Hanasaku. Therefore, although many people in the village describe any attempt to relate particular events in everyday life to supernatural forces as 'superstition' (*meishin*), they still buy amulets and talismans and place them in front of the god-shelves (*kamidana*) found in every house in Hanasaku.

In nearly every house in Hanasaku, one can find, alongside the god-shelf, an altar where wooden tablets (*ihai*) of dead household members are placed. This altar is called the *butsudan* or simply *hotokesama*,[29] and is attended to with care in most houses. Offerings of water and rice are usually made daily and flowers are changed frequently. Gifts received by members of the household are usually placed in front of it before they are opened.[30] At the New Year and *O-bon*, the midsummer festival for the dead, as well as during the weeks of the spring and autumn equinoxes (*higan*), relatives visit each other's houses to pay repects to their ancestors.

While new households in the village may have only a few tablets on the alter, old ones often have more than fifty, some dating as far back as the early seventeenth century. There exists, however, a conceptual distinction in people's attitude toward these tablets. If asked to whom offerings are made, people normally say to the *hotokesama*, i.e. the dead. Further questioning reveals, however, that they conceive recipients of their action to be recently deceased individuals and not the dead of the household as a whole. In dealing with the tablets of those recently dead, people treat them as if they were still alive. The rest of the tablets, on the other hand, are dealt with more out of obligation and general respect. Indeed, people often do not know who the tablets represent.[31] On some of the tablets, personal names are inscribed on the back. Most of the tablets found in the village, however, have only posthumous Buddhist names (*kaimyō*) together with the date of death.

As years pass by, tablets of individual kinsmen eventually join the more general category of 'the dead of the household' sometimes referred to as *senzo* (ancestors). The application of the term 'ancestors' in this context is relevant only in the sense of 'the forerunners of the house', and not as 'ancestors of an individual', an Oxford English Dictionary definition of an ancestor being 'one from whom a person is descended, either by the father or mother'. The term *senzo* may have been borrowed from China, a society with highly developed unilineal lineage groups. In a patrilineal society like China or Korea, an individual can join the rank of 'ancestors' after death only if he or she had married, and given birth to or adopted a son in that marriage. In the Japanese context, however, the term *senzo* seems to have become closely merged with the indigenous concept of the household as a residential unit, and the ideology of lineage based on kinship is almost completely eliminated. Among the tablets collectively referred to as *senzo* or ancestors, therefore, one may find tablets of children who died as infants, as often happened in the past. In one household in Yamazaki, the tablets also included that of a woman who had once married out but later returned home after contracting an incurable disease. As indicated previously, due to the rules governing the succession of the household, an individual occupying the house now may have no kinship ties at all with one who occupied the house three generations ago. Even in such a case, the tablets of the latter are referred to by the former as belonging to his *senzo*. As long as one remains a member of the household until one's death, one is included in the category of *senzo*, regardless of age, sex or marital status.[32]

At the *O-bon* festival, however, a special rite is held for all the dead of the household including the *senzo* and the recently deceased. *O-bon* is a three-day period in August when the spirits of the dead are said to return to the house. On 12 August (always the same day since people adjusted it to the solar calendar), therefore, all the tablets are taken down and dusted before being placed on a specially decorated altar in the main room of the house. At dusk, people light a small fire at the entrance of their houses to welcome the spirits and to 'show them the way to the house'. If there has been a death during the previous year, the household concerned holds a special 'first *bon* ceremony' (*arabon*) in which the household head, after feasting with relatives and neighbours, goes to the grave site and carries the spirit home on his back. The welcoming fire for the spirit, called *mukaebi*, is lit every evening for three days (until the 15th). During this period relatives visit each other's houses to pay respect to the special altars, and gifts are often presented to the *hotokesama*, the ancestral spirits of the household. The occasion also priovides an opportunity for a reunion of the living members of the household since children who are temporarily away generally return to the village. On the 16th, the spirits are supposed to leave the house and go back to the grave site. Early on the morning of the 16th, therefore, a 'sending-away' ceremony (*okuribon*) is held at the family grave site, and incense, water and specially made rice cakes called *tango* are offered at the grave. Rites of a similar nature are also held during the weeks of the spring and autumn equinoxes, but on a much smaller scale than *O-bon*, and they are usually limited to the hamlet level.

Notes

1 Several other English words have been used to translate *ie*, including 'house', Beardsley, Hall and Ward 1959: 217; Fukutake, 1967: 40; Dore 1958: 99; 'stem family', Befu 1971: 38; 'genealogy', Takeda 1968: 124; and 'religious society', Hearn 1924: 67. For a useful discussion on *ie* in historical context, see Hendry 1981: chapter one.

2 Hendry 1981: 15.

3 Cf. Nakane 1980: 9.

4 Each parcel of land is registered according to use, e.g. farmland, house plot, etc. As a means of protecting agriculture, a change of use from farmland is subjected to strict regulations, and permission from the Agricultural Committee is needed before one can build a house on farmland.

5 Isono 1964: 40–1; Dore 1958: 101.

6 In the past, the six families had a shrine dedicated to the deity of their 'extended household group' called *fukusenji*. For this reason, this neighbourhood group is still referred to as *fukusenji-kumi*. See Chapter 7 for details.

7 In this area, the older couple of a household who are not on good terms with the

successor couple sometimes set up a separate household and 'retire' to it. Such a household exists only during the lives of the old couple and is referred to as an *inkyoya*.

8 Bachnik 1983: 164.
9 Cf. Befu 1962; Bachnik 1983.
10 Cf. Takeda 1951; Izumi and Nagashima 1963; Naito 1970; Suenari 1972; Maeda 1976.
11 In the Tokugawa period when peasants were not allowed family names, personal names of household heads were often transmitted to the successors as family names. Succession thus also involved giving up one's 'youth name' and taking on the household head's personal name; Dore 1978: 138.
12 Cf. Watanabe 1963: 386; Bernstein 1976: 49.
13 According to Nakane 1980: 16, the authority of the household head was greater in wealthier families. Reeports also indicate that choice other than the eldest son was much more frequent for big merchant and warrior households during the Tokugawa period. See Nakano 1964; Takeuchi 1954; Moore 1970.
14 Thirty-five different household names exist in Hanasaku. Of these, twenty-four are represented by one or two households only. Fourteen of these twenty-four are first or second generation immigrant households.
15 Befu 1971: 39.
16 This is especially so when the children are not yet married. In some farm household with young married couples, part of their income is sometimes given to their parents for household expenditure. In contrast, villagers who have worked as forestry labourers since the pre-war period said that they used to give their whole wage to their fathers who, as heads of the household, were in control of the family purse.
17 Many people in Hanasaku consider that it is in the areas of food and language where the greatest changes have occurred since the introduction of the tourism industry. People often speak of their own local dialect as a 'bad language' (*warui kotoba*) and regard the general sophistication of language positively. More English words have been introduced as well since such new food items as coffee, black tea, mayonnaise, asparagus and lettuce are all referred to by using the Japanese transcription of the English words: *kohi, tei, mayonezu, asupara* and *retasu*.
18 Cf. Embree 1939: 80; Nakane 1967: 19; Fukutake 1967: 47.
19 The *inarisama* of more recently built houses are not in this style, but only paper charms.
20 When the household head and his wife retired from the headship, the most important items to be handed over to the succeeding couple used to be the key to this godown and the family purse.
21 Usually a *daian* day, the most auspicious day in the Buddhist six-day cycle incorporated in the Japanese calendar. Cf. Hendry 1981: 241.
22 When collecting these branches, it is important to remember to collect them on the way to the mountain, since this is believed to affect the fortunes of the household in the coming year. According to some, however, it is more important to collect from east to west than upwards.
23 Cf. *Katashina no Minzoku* 1960: 71–7.
24 Cf. Norbeck 1955: 107; Lewis 1986.
25 Jōya 1955: 75.
26 For a discussion of institutionalised neighbourhood groups, see Chapter 7.
27 More commonly, this god is referred to as Ebisu and is supposed always to travel with his brother Daikoku. Cf. Cornell and Smith 1956: 171; Embree 1939: 240–1; Norbeck 1954: 123; Sakurai 1968: 17.
28 If snow was left to lie on the fields until it melted, the pressure of snow and lack of air used to ruin the young barley plants. Towards the end of January and throughout

February, when it snows most heavily in this area, people used to come out very early in the morning to make holes around the fields. Earth was then dug up from these holes and spread over the snow to quicken its melting. This task was called *tsuchimaki*, 'planting of earth'.

29 In ordinary speech, no distinction is made between the spirits of the dead and the Buddhas and Bodhisattvas of the Buddhist faith. Since the two are differently conceptualised, however, Dore 1958: 313 has suggested distinguishing the two as *hotoke* and *Hotoke* respectively. The suffix '-sama' is honorific.

30 Cf. Smith 1974: 136.

31 In some places, the individual *ihai* is destroyed after a certain period of time (usually fifty years or so), and the name added to a common tablet (Plath 1964: 302–3), or simply subsumed under one genral *ihai* for the household (Dore 1958: 313).

32 In some households, tablets of the parents of the married-in members of the household are also included. These tablets are specifically referred to as *gaiseki*, literally 'out-relations', signifying that they have not been actual members of the household. Similarly, when a branch household is established for a younger son, the latter may take a duplicate of his father's tablet from the main household and worship it at his own altar. The latter practice is said to have been widespread in the past (Yanagita 1970: 26–7).

6

Kinship and affinity

Households in Hanasaku are categorised in two ways, one based on ties between the main household and its branches and the other on the territorial divisions of the community. In most literature on rural Japan, these groups are referred to as *dōzoku* and *kumi* respectively, although different names are in fact used in different localities.[1]

The co-operative system based on territorial divisions will be discussed in the next chapter, while this chapter concentrates on the *dōzoku*, the extended household groups.

Division of the household

A *dōzoku* group, locally referred to as *ikke*, consists of households related by a series of branch relationships. A branch household may be established for sons or daughters who are not eligible to inherit their own household. Many non-inheriting sons in Hanasaku move away to work elsewhere and establish households in cities or enter other households as adopted husbands. Similarly, daughters usally marry into another household as a *yome*. Sometimes, however, they may be set up in the village with land and a house provided by their natal household. Such a household is known as a 'branch house' (*bunke*) or a 'new house' (*shintaku*). Households thus related maintain special relations for generations even when consanguineous connections can no longer be traced.

In Hanasaku what characterises the main/branch relationship seems to be land transactions rather than kinship. Hence, a household established in a city by a second or third son is not considered a branch of the original *ie*. Similarly, if a separate household is established without help from the original *ie*, the latter is not necessarily referred to or related with as the 'main household'. There are two such cases in Noboto. The present heads of the two households, younger sons of a Noboto *ie*, returned to the village during the war and have remained there ever since. When they first came back they rented some land from their original *ie* and cultivated it while also working at other jobs. When their father died, however, their brother who succeeded him took away the land which they had been cultivating and which they had been promised by their father. The brothers remained in the village, but often had to work outside as migrant labourers to support their families. The two households are now securely settled in the village, although neither owns any land. The head of one household works as a full-time employee in the regional forestry office while the other works for a fuel company in Tone *mura*. When I interviewed them about the main/branch relationships, both men maintained that although the household of their elder brother, now headed by his widow, is 'the household into which they were born' (*umareta uchi*), it is not their 'main household' in the proper sense since they received nothing from it. In this connection, it is noteworthy that the main household is sometimes referred to in Hanasaku as *chiwakasare*, '(a household) from which one has received a division of land'.

The second type of branch household is the *inkyo-shintaku* mentioned previously. When a branch household is established, parents usually remain in the main house. If parents do not like the eldest son who is normally the successor, they may establish a branch household for the eldest son and bequeath the main household to another son. If the eldest son is married and has worked for the household for long enough before any other son or daughter reaches marriageable age and if he refuses to leave the main house, however, such an arrangement is difficult to make. In such a case the parents sometimes move out with one or all the other sons or daughters. Similarly, if the household head remarries, he often retires with his second wife and her children into another house, leaving the main house to the eldest son by his first wife. A household established in this way is known in Hanasaku as *inkyo-shintaku*, combining the word for the 'retirement of the parents' (*inkyo*) with 'branching of a household' (*shintaku*), and it is considered a branch of the household where the eldest son remains.

When a branch household is established in a normal way, for a younger son or daughter, the portion of land given to it rarely exceeds a third of the total holdings of the main household, and frequently much less. When parents move to the branch house, however, they may take a larger portion of land with them, and this sometimes leads to conflict. Before the Second World War it seems that land was divided by mutual consent between the main and branch households, while the legal issues were left unclarified. After the parents died and the members of the two households changed, therefore, disputes sometimes arose as the head of the main household claimed land which had hitherto been 'thought' to belong to the branch household. Such disputes have rarely developed into court cases in Hanasaku, but usually ended up with the branch household returning the land concerned to the main household. There were two such cases in Yamazaki, one involving most of the branch household's land and another only a piece of forest land. The former household, an *inkyo-shintaku*, finally returned most of its land to the main household, but had also severed all ties with the latter until very recently.

Parents, or one parent, sometimes retire on their own without accompanying other children. A temporary household called *inkyoya* is set up with a small portion of land known as *inkyoda*. The *inkyoda* is cultivated by the retired parents during their life time and returned to the main household after their death. An *inkyoya* comprises a member without full rights and duties in the *dōzoku* which will be discussed later. Unlike other kinds of branch households, however, it is not considered a full member of the village community. For example, an *inkyoya* is not liable for hamlet dues, does not have a vote in the hamlet assembly, and it is not obliged to provide labour for the community pool.

In some parts of Japan, it seems that most parents move to an *inkyoya* when they stop being household heads.[2] In Hanasaku, parents who have retired from the household headship are referred to as *inkyo* even when they remain in the household. However, they do not normally establish a separate household unless there is some conflict, such as between in-laws. The establishment of an *inkyoya*, therefore, usually causes a slight scandal in the community and the parents are seen as having been 'driven out'.

Formerly, a branch household was sometimes established for a resident servant (*hōkōnin*). One household in Hariyama was set up before the Second World War by the money-lender and landlord family for one of their servants, who married one of the family's daughters and was later given some land and branched out. For some reason he did not change his name to his wife's as was normal under such circumstances. Nevertheless the household is considered a member of the landlord family's *ikke*.

A main/branch relationship of a similar nature may also be established between a newcomer's household and the household which helped him settle in the community. Before the war many of the immigrant households settled in Hanasaku were started by tenant farmers. In relation to the household which initially provided lodging and rented farmland, an immigrant is called *waraji-nugi* ('to take off'). The *waraji-nugi* households maintain with their original helper households a relationship similar to the main/branch one, although they refer to the latter as their *ōya* rather than *honke*. While the *ōya* may have helped *waraji-nugi* to settle in the community by lending farmland or house plots, few *waraji-nugi* households have actually received any free land from their *ōya*, and hence the latter is not referred to as *honke*.

Extended household groups: *ikke*

Households related by main/branch ties form a group, locally referred to as *ikke*. Some researchers have described *ikke* or *dōzoku* as descent groups. Brown,[3] for instance, maintained that *dōzoku* are cognatic groups since they allow a male or female link as the basis for membership. Befu,[4] on the other hand, argues that they are patrilineal groups because preference is given to a male descendant when establishing branches. In Hanasaku, however, branches are often established for a daughter, even when there are younger sons. Similarly, branches can in theory be established for any non-kin members of the household. Hence since what initially links the main and branch households is common membership of the main household, I translate *ikke* as 'extended household group'.

As shown previously, common membership of the main household is not sufficient for a persisting main/branch tie between households. It is the provision of land or some other economic support provided by the main household that creates a relatively permanent relationship. In this regard, the main/branch relationship is similar to the relationship between parent and child in that the latter owes its very existence to the former, a debt of gratitude (*on*) which has to be recognised and repaid.

The term *ikke* is used in Hanasaku to talk about groups at two different levels. First, it designates a group of households which holds a yearly rite in honour of a group guardian deity (*ujigami-sama*). There are two or three such groups in each hamlet, the number of households involved ranging from eight to fifteen. The only households excluded are a few recent immigrant households. In many cases, the ritual group is divided into two or three subgroups of households whose interrelationships are clearly recognised, and among whom more social interaction takes place. Some villager's apply the same term *ikke* to designate this subgroup. To avoid confusion, one may distinguish the two by referring to the larger group as 'religious *ikke*' and the sub-group as 'social *ikke*'.

One religious *ikke* in Yamazaki, for instance, consists of nine households which are divided into two subgroups. Fig. 7 shows how the nine

(Sub-group I)

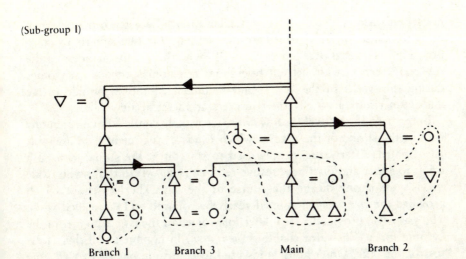

Branch 1   Branch 3   Main   Branch 2

(Sub-group II)

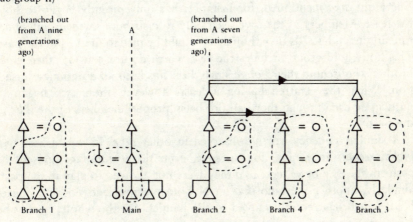

Fig. 7: An example of *ikke*

119

households are related. In this particular case, however, no main/branch tie is recognised at an inter-subgroup level, and the two subgroups comprise separate social *ikke* independent of each other. Only members of the subgroup *ikke* provide help at household ceremonies or visit each other during the weeks of the vernal and autumnal equinoxes or during the midsummer festival to pay their respects at ancestral altars.

In the past, the festival for *ujigami-sama* usually consisted of a ceremony held at the shrine of the *ikke* in which heads of the member households participated. Afterwards, people used to stay on at the shrine to have a drink together and distribute festive red rice (*sekihan*) to those who came to visit the shrine during the course of the day. The household which provided the rice was determined yearly by rotation and was called *yado*. The *yado* also provided a meal later for women of the *ikke* who met in the evening for a joint sutra chanting (*nenbutsu*) in honour of all the ancestors of the *ikke*. Other households used to contritute one or two *gō* (one *gō* is approximately 0.4 pint) of rice to the *yado* household toward the cost of preparing the food and *sekihan*.

Only two extended household groups in Hanasaku now hold this shrine festival. In the case of a third group, the Hujii *ikke* in Noboto, women of the eight member-households gather at the *yado* during the day to prepare a feast which the heads of the households participate in later in the evening. For other extended household groups, the occasion now only consists either of distributing *sekihan* to the member households by the *yado* or women chanting surtra in the evening; sometimes the rice contributions are not collected either.

The *ujigami* festival in Hanasaku, however, is not necessarily declining. The Hujii *ikke* mentioned, for instance, has only recently begun to hold the feast. Members of the *ikke* used only to distribute *sekihan*, but sometime in the mid-1970s they thought it would be nice to meet as in the past. This household group includes the two which do not consider their elder brother's household their *honke* since there has been no economic transaction. When they started having a feast, however, these two began to participate even though they had not been 'proper' members of the *ikke* in the past.

A similar tendency can be observed in other *ikke*. In the case of two Hoshino *ikke* in Kajiya, for instance, even the *waraji-nugi* households perform the role of *yado*, a role they were not allowed to play in the past. Similarly, another Hoshino *ikke* in Noboto includes one Yoshino household, which has recently moved to the hamlet. On the whole, it may be said that the *ujigami* festivals in Hanasaku are more of a social than a religious occasion nowadays. Perhaps for this reason, people seem less concerned that originally it was necessary to be a member of an extended household group to participate.

It has been reported that, in some parts of northern Japan, especially during the pre-modern period, extended household groups comprised an effective economic corporate group.[5] In such villages almost all household group under one powerful main household which was also the major landlord. Branch households were tied to this main household by tenancy and were economically, socially and ritually dependent on it. Even in the past the *ikke* groups in Hanasaku do not seem to have possessed such a character perhaps because there have never been large landlords in the village.

Branches in general, however, used to be more dependent on their main households. Main households were, on the whole, economically superior to their branches due to the practice of land division. In times of need such as sickness in the family or bad harvest, therefore, branches often relied on their main households for help. Similarly, when people had to borrow money, farm implements or farm animals, it was usually to their main household that they turned. Moreover, since a branch household was not immediately given full community membership upon its establishment, it also had to rely on its main household for a share of communal rights until it acquired full membership. The most important of these rights included the use of a water-powered mill of which there were one or two in each hamlet, and the lottery right (*chūsenken*) in the division of trees from Tokubaiyama for charcoal-burning.

The economic dependency of branches seems to have led to their social subordination as well. Therefore, villagers reported that, in the past, members of branches did not dare to contract economic transactions or to marry off one of their members without consent from their main household. Similarly, at *ikke* meetings, the head of the main household used to be treated with much more respect than nowadays.[6] He was usually given the best seat in the room, served the best food and so forth. Branches also had to provide free labour for the cultivation of the main household's estate when required. Status distinctions can rarely be observed at *ikke* meetings nowadays, nor is consent always sought from the main household whenever a branch contracts a marriage or disposes of its property. Branches are much less dependent on their main households, economically or otherwise. It is on a more or less equal footing, therefore, that social and ritual ties are maintained between the main and branch households, especially in the form of *shinrui-sama*.

The *shinrui-sama*

In Kenkyusha's Japanese/English dictionary, the term *shinrui* is defined as 'a relation, a relative or kinsfolk in general'. Apparently, this is the sense in which the word is normally used in standard Japanese.[7] Once or twice I heard people in Hanasaku use the word as a blanket term for all the people to whom one is 'related' by kinship, affinal ties and membership of the same extended household group, as opposed to the 'non-related' (*tanin* or *tanin-sama*) such as neighbours (*kinjo no hito*), people of the same village (*mura no hito*) and outsiders (*yoso no mono*).[8] More frequently, however, the term *shinrui* in this area refers to a particular household which performs certain ritual and social functions in relation to another. It is therefore a dyadic inter-household relationship. Such a role is hereditary in the household, and the word *shinrui-sama* with its honorific suffix '-sama' refers to the head of the *shinrui* household.

Shinrui relationships are closly linked with main/branch relationships. For a branch household, therefore, it is often its immediate main household which plays the *shinrui* role. In the case of a main household on the other hand, it is usually performed by its first branch.[9] In the past the main household of an extended household ggroup used to exchange the role with the main household of another extended household group in the village. Through this means alliances were formed between certain *ikke* groups, though such cases are no longer found in Hanasaku. The *shinrui* role is always exchanged between households of one extended household group, and frequently within the subgroup *ikke*.

The main household of an extended household group also used to play the *shinrui* role for all remaining members of the group including the incorporated immigrant *waraji-nugi* households. Households which perform the *shinrui* for *waraji-nugi* households are specifically referred to as *tanomare shinrui*, 'requested *shinrui*'.[10] Nowadays, however, the main household does not always assume the role of *shinrui-sama* for all of its members even in a subgroup *ikke*. When a branch establishes a branch of its own, it sometimes changes its *shinrui-sama* from its original main household to its newly established branch. Thus, the *shinrui* role is generally exchanged between households related by the most recent main/ branch tie. Similarly, there are a few cases where a main household with two or more branches recently changed its *shinrui* from its first branch to another with which it has a better relationship. In 1982 when a *waraji-nugi* household in Hariyama married off its succeeding daughter, it asked a branch of its original *ōya* to perform the *shinrui* role. The new *shinrui* household, which owns a fish farm, now enjoys a relatively high social and economic standing in the village, while the original *shinrui*, the *ōya*, has somewhat declined in status in recent years after the premature death of its previous head.

This tendency to switch *shinrui-sama* is said to be new in Hanasaku. Although only a minority of households in Hanasaku have changed their *shinrui*, this new phenomenon, together with the division of a religious *ikke* into a number of smaller social *ikke*, is suggestive of ways in which extended household groups might adapt themselves to changing economic situations. Branch households are no longer economically dependent on their main households, yet still retain social and ritual ties with the *shinrui* system.

In some ways the *shinrui* system in Hanasaku closely resembles the *oyakata-kokata* system originally reported by Kitano.[11] In the mountain districts of Yamanashi prefecture, some influential households become *oya*, literally 'parents', of other households through a formal ceremony known as *oyakonari*, 'taking an *oya*' or 'becoming parent and child'. The *oya* household then provides the *ko* household, 'the child household' with patron-like protection in all aspects of life while the latter performs certain services in return. An *oya/ko* tie is, however, often initially established between individuals and sometimes does not prevail beyond their deaths. Moreover an *oya* is not always a member of one's own extended household group, while a *shinrui* relationship in Hanasaku is an inter-household relationship from the beginning, and is almost always established on the basis of main/branch connection even when people change their *shinrui-sama*. Moreover a *shinrui* relationship in Hanasaku is not necessarily hierarchical, although it might have been so in the past, as stories of main housholds of different *ikke* groups exchanging the *shinrui* role seem to suggest. Nowadays, the role is often exchanged between a main household and one of its branches on an equal basis.

The *shinrui-sama* plays a vital role in many aspects of the social and religious life of people in Hanasaku. In the past when most marriage ceremonies were held at the groom's house, *shinrui-sama* used to accompany the bride along with her personal kindred to the groom's house. During the course of ceremony he sat next to the bride's father in front of the *tokobashira*, facing the go-betweens at the other end of the *zashiki*.[12]

123

Nowadays when most marriage ceremonies are held at a special wedding hall in a nearby town, it is usually the *shinrui-sama* who makes the first of many formal speeches given at the reception.

When a death occurs in the household, the first person to be informed is the *shinrui-sama* who then organises the ceremony on behalf of the bereaved family, making the list of people to be invited, deciding how many neighbourhood groups are to be asked for help, allocating roles among people who come to help and so forth. One of the most important functions of the *shinrui-sama* is to draw a bow into the sky in a northerly direction to prevent evil spirits from attacking the corpse. This is done twice during the course of a funeral ceremony, the first time just before the corpse leaves the house and the second when it arrives at the grave.

After a funeral, the children of the deceased meet in the formal room to express gratitude to the Buddhist priest who carried out the ceremony and to discuss the expenses involved. This meeting is called *o-shō-sama-zashiki* in Hanasaku and is participated in by the priest, three hamlet representatives who handle the expenses of the ceremony, and one person representing each of the children's households accompanied by their *shinruisama*. Children who have married into another village are accompanied by the *shinrui-sama* of the household in their new village. The main obligation of the *shinrui-sama* on this particular occasion is to negotiate, on behalf of the household they represent, the latter's share in the funeral expenses. People explained that it is 'difficult' for those directly involved to discuss such matters without it leading to friction among siblings. Hence *shinrui-sama* are present to settle matters smoothly.

It is also the *shinrui-sama* who at a house construction ceremony, sits at a table receiving and recording gifts and donations. When there was a fire in a neighbouring village, many Hanasaku men went to help, including the fire brigade. Afterwards, the family which met with the misfortune sent round a card expressing gratitude to all the households from which it had received help, signed by both the head of the household concerned and its *shinrui-sama*. When there is a dispute between households in the village, it is the *shinrui-sama* of either household involved who usually acts as mediator. Similarly, if a household causes communal trouble, people representing the community often contact its *shinrui-sama* first in order to convey the general feelings to the household concerned.

Shinrui-sama[13] is often a household within one's own hamlet. When a household branches out into another hamlet, however, its main household in the original hamlet may continue to play the role. When a household branches out from another village, on the other hand, within one or two generations it usually changes its *shinrui* to one in its new hamlet. Though rare, an affine's household may assume the role for a household which does not have a main or a branch household within the same hamlet. For the two siblings' households in Yamazaki which broke up their main/ branch tie after a quarrel over land, the household into which one of their father's sisters had married assumed the *shinrui* role for some fifteen years until the two households were finally reconciled. Now the two households play the *shinrui* for each other.

The general principle is that, although the *shinrui* relationship is ideally between a main and a branch household, when a household does not have a household in the same hamlet related in this way, it has to find for the role of *shinrui-sama* a household 'related' in another way. Nevertheless, the idea that one has to have a *shinrui* household is so strong that except for the residents of the 'Tokyo *mura*', most recent immigrant households have established the relationship with one of the native households. In Yamazaki, for example, only one household out of forty does not have *shinrui-sama*. This is the household of a Shinto priest who settled in the community during the years immediately following the Second World War. It used to have an *ōya* in Noboto where it originally settled. When a child of the priest and his adopted daughter was born, however, it became too scandalous for the family to stay in Noboto, and thus it moved to Yamazaki. Since then, it has neither kept a special relationship with its original *ōya* in Noboto, nor yet established a *shinrui* relationship with a household in Yamazaki.

Personal kindred and affines

The discussion so far has concentrated on inter-household relationships. On occasion, however, people interact with an individual and not the household unit, a category of kin which one might term 'personal kindred' following Freeman.[14] In contrast to the vast amount of literature, especially in Japanese, on the nature of the 'extended household group' (*dōzoku*) and the household organisation (*ie*), surprisingly little work has been done on this aspect of the Japanese kindship system, and even in the few studies available, there is some confusion with regard to the concept and how it operates within an ethnograhpic context.

Some have applied the term *shinrui* to the category of personal kindred in Japan.[15] I will avoid this for two reasons: the term *shinrui* refers to an institution of a completely different nature in Hanasaku, and even when the term is used as a blanket term for all 'relatives', it often covers not only one's personal kin but also those who belong to one's *ikke* group whose membership is determined by inter-household relationships. A term more often used by the people in Hanasaku to designate the category of personal kindred is *miuchi*. For example, apart from the *shinrui-sama* and the go-between (*nakōdo*), only people of one's own *miuchi* participate in the ritual part of the marriage ceremony (*san-san-ku-do*).[16] Similarly, at a funeral ceremony, the *miuchi* of the dead person are distinguished from other guests by a piece of white paper participate in the 'send-off' (*miokuri*) of the dead person's spirit. The task of washing the corpse also falls to the *miuchi no hito*, people who belong to one's own personal kindred.

The etymology of *miuchi* is suggestive of its conceptual category. The two Chinese characters used to write the word literally mean 'inside the body'(*mi-*: body; *uchi*: inside). Therefore, *miuchi-no-hito* may be seen as those related to one through an element inside the body. This is interesting if one considers that *miuchi* is a strictly bilateral category and that there is no distinction in terms of address between kin on paternal and maternal sides. If one asks who the *miuchi* are, the commonest answer is 'up to the first cousin' (*itoko made*). *Itoko* is indeed the term applied to all categories of first cousin, parallel and cross on both paternal and maternal sides. Although people sometimes use the term *hatoko* to designate kin beyond the boundary of first cousin, recognition of the concept is ambiguous and blurred. For example, anyone more distant to one than first cousin is often described as 'something like *hatoko*' (*hatoko mitai*) or 'relatives of yore' (*mukashi no shinseki*). The necessity for recognising kin beyond the first cousin boundary is not so important since people usually cease to interact on kinship terms beyond first cousins even when they live within the same village.

The term *miuchi* as used in Hanasaku therefore refers to the maximum category of cognates with whom one interacts. Those who fall into the category of one's *miuchi*, however, do not always form an autonomous action group. For example, only a part of one's *miuchi* participate in one's marriage ceremony in this area, including normally one's siblings and parents' siblings (see Fig. 8). On the other hand, for a more general household ritual like the celebration for a house reconstruction (*shinchiku iwai*), everyone belonging to the *miuchi* of the eldest generation living within the household are invited. Since *miuchi* is a category conceived of with an individual at its centre, the *miuchi* group differs from generation to generation. First cousins of parents, for example, are no longer invited after both parents have died.

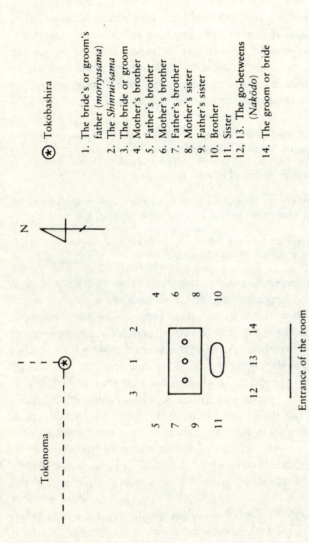

Tokobashira

1. The bride's or groom's
   father (moriyasama)
2. The Shinrui-sama
3. The bride or groom
4. Mother's brother
5. Father's brother
6. Mother's brother
7. Father's brother
8. Mother's sister
9. Father's sister
10. Brother
11. Sister
12, 13. The go-betweens
   (Nakōdo)
14. The groom or bride

Fig. 8: An example of traditional marriage seating

127

Confusion may arise, however, since those who are supposed to be present at a certain ceremony are often represented by other members of their households. At a marriage ceremony, a father's brother may be represented by his son if the former is already dead or not available. Similarly, a mother's sister or a father's sister is often represented by her husband. The same applies to other ritual occasions. When a person dies, all cognates up to his first cousin are supposed to 'send-off' his spirit. However a cousin of the dead person may be represented by his or her daughter-in-law from the same household. This phenomenon has led to the following statements by Nakane, who applied the term *shinrui* to designate the group of commonly interacting cognates.

> For the understanding of this Japanese concept of *shinrui*, the unit of a household is of prime importance. Though a *shinrui* is recognized in terms of kinship relations and with reference to a single person, the function of *shinrui* is carried out on the basis of household units. A *shinrui* is recognized as a set of households.[17]

> The *shinrui* of the members of a household tends to be framed along the lines of the *shinrui* of the household head, rather than of each individual member. The recognition of kinship itself with reference to each individual does not always establish *shinrui* relationship, unless it is supported by some activity. It is the kin of the household, not of individual, that are most significant socially.[18]

Such statements are misleading in that they fail to distinguish the level of action from that of conceptualisation. The *miuchi* is not a discrete set of households 'framed along the lines of' close cognates of the household head, nor can one talk about the 'kin of the household' at the conceptual level of the household members. As shown above, the boundary of cognates to be invited varies depending on the occasion. Thus, for a marriage rite, it is 'only siblings' (*kyōdai dake*). Since a marriage is perhaps as important an occasion for parents as for those who actually get married, this category includes the siblings of the parents as well as the siblings of the marrying couple. On the other hand, those invited to celebrate a new house, include 'up to the first cousins of the grandmother' (*obā no itoko made*). This indicates that the category of cognates to be invited is clearly conceived with an individual at its centre and that people adjust the category taking into consideration the *miuchi* of each individual member living within the household. Therefore, when people say *uchi no miuchi*, '*miuchi* of the house' as they sometimes do in this area, they use the word to describe those who fall into the category of *miuchi* for any member of the household, and not to designate any particular household which is in a *miuchi* or '*shinrui*' relationship with one's own. Similarly, though at the level of action a cognatic kinsman may be represented by another member of his household, the latter is representing not the household but the individual.

Some confusion may also arise regarding affines. Nakane has suggested that:

> The category of *shinrui* is somewhat analogous to that of *kindred*. However, if kindred is defined 'to refer only to cognates and never extended to embrace affines' as suggested by Freeman in his recent work (Freeman 1961, p. 202), a *shinrui* is not a kindred because it embraces affines as well, though it is based on the kindred category. In fact *shinrui* involves marriage relationships no less importantly than cognatic relationships.[19]

It is interesting to examine the content of this remark in relation to a particular ethnographic context. In Hanasaku, those who have been present at one's marriage ceremony are referred to as 'honourable guests' (*o-kyaku-sama*), and people say that, since the 'honourable guests' are the *miuchi* of the married-in member of the household, one should interact with them as though they were one's own *miuchi*. Indeed, after marriage or even after betrothal, one begins to apply exactly the same kin terms for the close *miuchi* of one's spouse, such as the spouse's siblings or his or her parents' siblings as for one's own *miuchi*. The *o-kyaku* or the 'honourable guests' are then invited to most household ceremonies, and at one's funeral, the siblings of one's spouse also participate in the 'send-off' of one's spirit together with one's own *miuchi*. They are, however, invited as affines or as the *miuchi* of a married-in-member with whom 'one should interact as though they were one's own *miuchi*'. It is therefore mistaken to classify them in the same category as those with whom one interacts as cognates. Confusion seems to arise when one attempts to consider all those present at a household ceremony as a homogeneous group, especially as 'a set of households', when in reality they include a number of differently conceptualised groups, e.g. cognates of each member, those of the extended household group, affines, go-betweens, *shinrui-sama*, neighbours, friends and so forth.[20]

The relevance of understanding the importance of the household unit, the nature of inter-household relationships and the kinship system in this study arises from the fact that, along with the territorial bonds discussed in the next chapter, these relationships still comprise the major focus of social interaction for people in Hanasaku. Interestingly, some household rituals have increased considerably in number in recent years. In theory, memorial services for ancestors are supposed to be held on the first, third, seventh, thirteenth, seventeenth, twenty-third, twenty-seventh, thirty-third and finally the fiftieth calendar year after the death of a person. In former times, however, these services could only be held by the most well-to-do families in the village, and even then only for a certain number of years. They are much more widespread nowadays. According to people in the village, the *yakudoshi* feast is another example of a household ritual which has increased in popularity. With the general improvement in living standards, these household rituals have provided many with a means by which they can translate their newly-gained economic prosperity into social influence and thus enhance their relative status within the community. Household feasts are also often used for political ends. Anyone interested in a local political office, such as a place in the *mura* assembly, often holds many household feasts and invites neighbours and relatives. While giving out money to the voters is illegal, feasting is considered acceptable.

Similarly, new prosperity is expressed in new houses and new gravestones. In the past, people apparently erected a small gravestone for each dead member of the household. Nowadays, they often erect a huge gravestone in the name of the household as a whole. At grave sites, therefore, one often finds large gravestones engraved as the 'House of such-and-such' with a smaller flat stone beside it bearing the names of recently deceased household members. To erect such a house gravestone costs about £2,500–£3,000,[21] and most people in the village can immediately tell approximately how much it cost by its size and shape. Like house buildings, therefore, these stones clearly express the relative prosperity of each household. Another example is the posthumous Buddhist names presented to dead members of the household. The rank of posthumous names differs with the kind of Chinese characters used (e.g. *tokuingō, ingō, kengō*, etc.) as well as depending on the number of characters. The rank of one's posthumous name is supposedly determined by one's deeds and achievements during one's lifetime. In reality, however, it more often reflects the worldly success or failure of one's descendants, and for this reason, they have provided another opportunity for people to express their relative status.

The standard price charged by the priest in Hanasaku varies from about £200 to £500 depending on the rank of posthumous name. The price is determined by the priest himself with the consent of leading members of the village temple association. In the past, the better names such as *tokuingō* or *ingō* were very rare. Nowadays, even a child is given a posthumous name of at least six Chinese characters.

Notes

1 The two systems are not equally developed throughout Japan. The most strongly developed *dōzoku*, for instance, are found in north-eastern Japan, while in some areas of southern Japan households related by a series of main/branch ties do not form a separate corporate group. Cf. Izumi and Gamo 1952; Ishino and Bennett 1953; T. Smith 1959.

2 Nakane 1967: 11–14.

3 Brown 1966.

4 Befu 1963.

5 See in particular Ariga 1943; T. Smith 1959; Nakane 1967.

6 In some parts of Japan where the *dōzoku* was well established, kin terms for one's elders were used by members of branch households addressing members of main households regardless of the relative age of the speakers. See, Befu and Norbeck 1958; Norbeck 1961. Such incidences however are rarely found these days even in the same areas.

7 Cf. Nakane 1967: 26.

8 'Yoso no mono' is a relative term which people sometimes use in opposition to 'uchi no mono', people of one's own household or 'tochi no mono' which may be translated as 'people of our land', a category which varies depending on the context.

9 A branch of a branch household is sometimes referred to as a *mago-shintaku*, a grandchild branch, and the main household called *ōhonke* by the grandchild branch.

10 Norbeck reports a similar custom in north-eastern Japan; Norbeck 1961: 308. According to him, however, the custom is disappearing in all but one of the five communities he studied.

11 Kitano 1939.

12 The *zashiki* is the most formal room in a Japanese house, where important guests are received and all ceremonies held. The *tokobashira* is the main pillar in this room.

13 *Shinrui-sama* can refer to the head of the *shinrui* household or to the whole *shinrui* household as a group.

14 Freeman 1961.

15 Cf. Iwamoto 1978; Kanabe 1967; Nakane 1967: 26–40.

16 See Hendry 1981: 174–77.

17 Nakane 1967: 27

18 *Ibid.*: 31.

19 *Ibid.*: 27.

20 The role of go-betweens is generally played by a couple from a respected household in the community. In this area, the go-betweens are referred to as *nakōdo oya*, 'the go-between parents'.

21 Equivalent to nearly half an average farm household's yearly income.

7

Politics and co-operation

This chapter examines the socio-political functions of groups organised on the basis of territorial divisions as well as age, sex and other individual factors. Its purpose is to discern the basic principles of group organisation and show how they have been affected by changes in the village economy. The first section deals with the historical background and present form of village government; the second with the structure and function of various associations found in Hanasaku; and the third with the community's co-operative system based on its territorial divisions.

Village government[1]

The village council
The present-day village council in Hanasaku, the third *ku* of Katashina *mura*, consists of eight members, the district chief (*kuchō*), the deputy chief (*kuchō-dairi*) and six hamlet representatives (*kumichō*). If there are important items on the agenda, the six deputy hamlet representatives, the three *mura* assemblymen and the three members of the *mura* agricultural committee are also present, making a complete council of twenty.

The selection of the present village and hamlet officials is based strictly on principles of rotation. The six hamlets take turns in choosing the district chief and deputy chief every six years, although the same hamlet does not simultaneously provide both. In each hamlet, on the other hand, there exist a different number of territorial divisions and these divisions take turns among themselves to provide the hamlet representative and his deputy. Since in all six hamlets this year's deputy *kumichō* serves as next year's *kumichō*, only the deputy *kumichō* needs to be elected. While the office of district chief, who represents the village to the outside world, is still largely limited to a few particularly respected individuals from households of a certain standing, no such concern is shown in the selection of hamlet representatives. Not only are most people in the village now literate through the spread of education, but also the growth of a cash economy in recent years has greatly reduced the gap between wealthier and poorer families. Moreover, official posts no longer require as much individual expenditure as in the past and thus this is no longer a limiting factor. Indeed to fill a post at least once or twice is now virtually an obligation since so many villagers are reluctant to spare the time required.

There are no fixed dates for district council meetings in the village except for the two ceremonial occasions at the beginning and end of each fiscal year in early April. Following individual hamlet election meetings, there is a village council meeting known as the 'transfer' (*hikiwatashi*), in which the village officials of the previous year ceremonially hand over their duties to their successors.

Probably the most important village councill meeting, however, is one held for the ceremonial hearing of villagers' requests. Sometime at the end of January, the head of the local government, accompanied by all his department heads, goes round the eight districts in the *mura* to hear requests from residents. Individuals or individual households are not allowed to make requests in these hearings. Prior to the hearing, therefore, each hamlet holds a general meeting to hear individual wishes and to decide priorities. Then the district council (which in Hanasaku is the same as the village) meets and examines each request made in the name of individual hamlets, and some of these are made into district requests. At the grand hearing itself, each of the six hamlet representatives reads out their requests before the district chief lists items requested in the name of the whole district. In return, the heads of the relevant local government departments explain the difficulties involved in accepting the requests, and the meeting ends with a speech from the head of the local government concerning its general policy and another from the head of the *mura* assembly on its budget.

These hearings appear to be the remnants of a form of 'citizen participation', that was first introduced into local politics after the Second World War by the Occupation.[2] Whatever their origin, the meetings now clearly function to bring local government and the residents of its sub-units into closer contact. All requests submitted in the name of each hamlet and district in the *mura* are taken to the next *mura* assembly meeting where local government expenditure is allocated for the coming year. The hearing is therefore taken seriously by local residents since items which have not been put forward there will not be considered at the *mura* assembly's budget meeting. Not all the requests made are met, however, and priorities are always given to those made in the name of the larger unit.

Once a demand has been made in the name of the village its consequences are the responsibility of all concerned and this sometimes causes conflict. In 1980, for example, *minshuku* operators in Hanasaku wanted a set of electric lights for the village sports ground to enable night games to take place, and they managed to persuade members of the village council to put forward the item as a district demand at the hearing. The request was accepted and electric lights were installed with a local government subsidy. The facility was built on such a scale, however, that maintenance plus the minimum connection charge cost almost £2,500 per annum, even when the lights were not used at all. Originally, it was agreed between the district council and *minshuku* owners' association that the latter would take charge of the facility and maintain it by renting it to individual inn operators. Inn operators who borrowed the facility from the association were required to pay about twelve pounds per day, which it was hoped would cover the electricity bill and maintenance costs. Contrary to initial expectations, however, the facility is used less than ten days a year, leaving the association with a large unpaid bill. For the initial year, the association borrowed money from the village council. When it tried to borrow for a second time, however, many village council members objected, and at the 'transfer' meeting in April 1982, an unusual row took place. The newly elected officials including many representatives from the agricultural hamlets, argued that from the beginning the bill should have been equally divided among the *minshuku* households and paid by them alone. On the other hand, the representatives of the association and many inn operators who were not themselves interested in using the facility felt that the electric lighting was a district facility, and hence its maintenance was the responsibility of the whole village. Since the only solution seems to be to have the electricity cut and to stop using the facility altogether, many fear the village will appear 'irresponsible' in the eyes of the local government and this will weaken its position when applying for funds in the future.

District income is provided by three major sources: *kuhi, hana* and *shūnyūjigyō. Kuhi* is the district contribution paid by all households in the village, the exact amount being determined by the amount of national tax for which each household is liable. *Hana* refers to donations received from local shops and companies as well as from individuals in the village at various village festivals, of which the midsummer dance festival (*bonodori*) is usually the most lucrative. Under the *shūnyūjigyō* scheme, one person from each household in Hanasaku is required to work for the timber subcontractor in Kajiya, the owner of the petrol station already mentioned, for one day a year. Their wages (6,500 yen per head) are then paid directly into the district account. Though people are allowed to work at any time of the year convenient, if a woman provides the service, the household concerned has to pay the male/female wage difference in cash to the district council.

Other village council activities include an annual party for the elders, preparations for the *mura* athletic meetings, the baseball and volleyball tournament matches held twice a year between the hamlets, and various village festivals. Every spring a huge banquet is held under the auspices of the district council for all residents over seventy years of age, of whom there are more than eighty in Hanasaku.[3] It is an occasion aimed at promoting respect and concern for the old. Village schoolchildren, members of different associations and each hamlet in the village show their skills in acting, dancing, singing and story-telling. Splendid food specially prepared by members of the village Housewives' Association is served, and gifts are distributed to all those present. Youth Group members are responsible for transporting all the old people from their hamlet to the school gymnasium where the party is usually held. It is said that in the past people used to carry the old people on their backs. Nowadays, however, a few round trips in a car solve the problem. The occasion also provides competition between districts within the *mura*. Local governement officials like the mayor of the *mura* and the head of the *mura* assembly are invited to the party, and they often make speeches comparing similar parties in other districts, thus encouraging a competitive spirit.

Another occasion for competition among districts is the annual *mura* athletic meeting. First instituted in 1955 on the initiative of the local government, it is one of the most widely attended activities of the *mura* as a whole. On the day of the meeting in September 1981, almost every one in Hanasaku went to one of the school grounds in Kamada, where they sat with others from their hamlet. Tents and seating are divided into the eight districts and again into different hamlets within each district, and competitors from one's own area are enthusiastically supported. Events include long and short distance running for all age groups, a 400m relay race for companies and offices in the *mura*, an egg and spoon race for the eight districts, a mock cavalry battle by the school children, and a competition between the eight district Fire Brigades. The climax is a tug-of-war contest held between the districts. Baseball matches for men and volleyball matches for women are held separately, but their results are included in the final assessment of each district's performance. After the prize-giving ceremony at the end of the meeting, each district holds its own party for all its competitors.

The occasion provides an opportunity for reinforcing territorial solidar-

135

ity as well as for a reunion of kin-folk living in different districts. One could see many women going around the different tents to meet their kin, though they never cheered for their own natal village even when their own siblings were running. Territorial attachments are always emphasised, and the same is true when tournament matches are held within one district, where primary loyalty always goes to the adopted rather than the natal hamlet.

The hamlet assembly

Unlike the village or district council, there is no specific form for a hamlet assembly. Hamlet meetings are, on the whole, participated in by one member from each household, and all dicisions made by consensus rather than majority vote. Hence whenever there is a difference of opinion among hamlet members concerning a particular issue, the meetings are often repeated again and again until ostensible unanimity is reached. In one case concerning the widening of the prefectural road passing through Yamazaki, one resident strongly objected since it would mean that he had to move his animal shed into the mountain area on the other side of the road. Moreover, when the road had been widened and paved about fifteen years ago, his family had already had to concede a considerable part of their house site. Although many initially sympathised with his cause, the degree of sympathy diminished as meetings on the same item were repeated. In the meantime, unspoken pressure built up to compel the man to conform to the majority interest. Finally, after several meetings held over an eight-month period, he could no longer object openly at the meeting, and the agendum was 'unanimously' passed.[4]

During all the apparently sterile and endless meetings that went on, however, hamlet members showed a remarkable degree of perseverance. No specific attempts were made to persuade the man concerned at the meetings themselves, although the house was frequently visited in between by hamlet officials and representatives from the subcontracting company. This pattern of behind-the-scenes negotiation and long-term perserverance always accompanies complicated issues in hamlet meetings. 'Selfishness' and 'causing trouble to others' are two of the most discouraged attitudes in community life, and hence no matter how justified one's claim may be, concern for these values usually overwhelms all argument.

Because of the diversification of interests among its members nowadays, hamlet meetings are held almost every other week throughout the year. Not all meetings, however, are general gatherings; some concentrate on a particular crop and are attended only by those who cultivate that crop, while others are held by a particular association and attended only by its members. In addition, there are five regular hamlet meetings known as *jōkai* at which annual hamlet activities are discussed including joint disinfection, repairing the hamlet irrigation system, the annual communal clear-ups and so forth. Most of these activities are carried out under the initiative of the local government through the *mura*. Actual services are provided by hamlet labour pools (*ninsoku*) and each hamlet has its own representatives in charge of each activity. When the statistics department in the local government takes an annual census, for example, the actual collection of data is carried out by the 'statistics representative' in each hamlet with the co-operation of other community members. Similarly, each hamlet has people in charge of individual crops and services, which should in theory be provided by the agricultural co-operative such as the purchase of seeds, shipping of products and so on, are provided by these crop representatives. As unpaid, 'voluntary' workers, services performed by local community members therefore comprise an indispensable part of the functioning of local government as well as of other official organisations such as the agricultural co-operative.

More recently, some of these delegated functions began to be remunerated. The representative of each hamlet (*kumichō*) who collects the national tax for the local government is now allowed to keep a three per cent share of the total collected in his own hamlet for the hamlet's expenses. Similar arrangements have been made for the collection of other taxes, pensions, etc. delegated to different associations in each hamlet. Apart from this share of the tax collection, hamlet expenditures are partly supported by 'hamlet operational expenses' (*buraku uneihi*) contributed to equally by all constituent households, in addition to the national and prefectural taxes and the district allowance mentioned earlier.

Village associations

There are at present sixteen village associations in Hanasaku:
  (1) Shrine Association
  (2) Communal Forest Co-operative
  (3) Environment Preservation Society
  (4) Forest Protection Society
  (5) Welfare Society
  (6) Local Development Association
  (7) Tourism Development Association

137

(8) Sports Society
(9) Patronage Society for the Youth Sports Club
(10) Friendship Society
(11) Fire Brigade
(12) Old People's Association
(13) Housewives' Association
(14) Youth Group
(15) Village Primary School Parent-Teacher Association (P.T.A.)
(16) Village Nursery School P.T.A.

Many of these societies are fairly uniformly found in all the other villages in Katashina *mura* and have certain links with the local government. After the annual village election meeting, for instance, each village or district sends the local government the names of officials elected to represent each society, and meetings concerning broader local issues are often held in the new *mura* government building. Within Hanasaku, the six hamlets in turn elect their own representatives for each of the sixteen associations and the village representatives are rotated from among the hamlet representatives. In addition, each hamlet has a number of other offices to fill each year, including representatives for the agricultural, sericultural and stock-breeding co-operatives, statistical survey, agricultural aid association and those for each crop. There are so many offices that almost everyone serves as one kind of official (*yakunin*) or another each year.[5]

It was only after the Meiji Restoration and the implementation of the present local government system that most of these associations were created in Japanese villages. The uniformity of most local associations reflects their historical background, as Fukutake writes:

> none of them were formed by the voluntary and spontaneous adhesion of the villagers. They were, rather, created first in the village local government units on instructions and models provided by the central government and, utilizing the hamlet's traditional capacity for unified action, branches of these organisations were then created in every *buraku*. But these were not the kind of organizations that villagers had freedom to enter or leave voluntarily as they desired. The nature of these organizations shows both how strong was the social unity of the hamlet and also how deep was the penetration of the political power of the central government into the remotest corners of the country. Administrative guidance has been a preponderant influence in the formation of associations in Japanese villages.[6]

The Housewives' Association

The local Housewives' Association arose out of the Patriotic Women's Society founded in 1902, which had concentrated its major activities on supporting the war effort following the Russo-Japanese war in 1905. In 1936, the name of the society changed to the Women's Society for the

National Defense of the Great Japanese Empire, and its war-supporting activities were reinforced. Old women in Hanasaku described how all the women in the village lined up in white aprons with patriotic banners to cheer off any new conscript. A similar scene is reported by the Russian Ella Lury Wiswell who with her American husband John Embree was one of the first Western ethnographers of Japan.[7]

After the Second World War, the society was banned. Locally, however, it was revived in 1946 under the new name of Katashina *mura* Housewives' Association, its objectives having changed from national defence to the 'construction of a new Japan'.[8] However, despite a new emphasis on the voluntary nature of the association, even since the war it has still functioned mainly as a vehicle for implementing government policy, such as popularising the government-initiated family planning programme in the mid-1950s. It has also organised many adult schools for housewives, through which new ideas from the central government are disseminated.[9]

Although all married women in the village are theoretically members of the Association, less than a third actually participate in its activities nowadays, mostly women in their forties. Many of the younger women in the village find the Association's activities uninteresting, and they recently formed their own separate group called the Young Wives' Association.[10] While the Housewives's Association (*fujinkai*) still collaborates closely in most of its activities with the local government and the district council, and puts great emphasis on educational events, the Young Wives' Association (*wakazumakai*) concentrates more on recreational activities such as sports, village festivals, annual outings and so forth.

The Youth Group

The *seinendan* or Youth Group was also created under the auspies of the central government during the Meiji period. Unlike the Housewives' Association, however, this group had already had its precedent in most Japanese villages.[11] In Katashina *mura*, for instance, before the current Youth Group was created under government instructions in 1904, there was a similar association called *wakashū* or *wakarenchū*[12] which included all men in the village between around fifteen and forty as well as women from around thirteen until their marriage. On the second day of every lunar New Year, all boys and girls reaching the age for entering the Association were required to visit a house in the hamlet called a *yado*, carrying a bottle of Japanese rice wine.[13] The family whose home was designated as that year's *yado* then provided a big feast for all new and old members of the *wakashū*.

139

Functions of the old *wakashū* included the protection of village girls from harrassment by outsiders, premarital inquiries of possible marriage partners from other villages, and preparation for village festivals.[14] The group also carried out functions which now come under the jurisdiction of the police and the Fire Brigade.[15] When it was reorganised into *seinendan*, however, its major activities centred on supporting the war effort by helping war-bereaved families, collecting war supplies from the village and organising send-off ceremonies for new conscripts. Even today, many old people in the village still refer to *seinendan* as *wakashū* or *wakaren*.

Nowadays, the *seinendan* in Hanasaku is not particularly active. Apart from preparing the midsummer dance festival and the *Gion-matsuri*, traditionally a festival for young people (see Chapter 8), the group rarely meets. Following past tradition, however, all young men up to about thirty and girls before marriage are automatically considered members. As an official village association, it also has a representative known as *sōken* in each of the hamlets.

The Sports Society and the Friendship Society

Some of *seinendan*'s past functions have been taken over by more recently organised voluntary associations such as the Sports Society and the Friendship Society. Most young people in the village belong to the Sports Society, the major sponsor and organiser of annual village athletics meetings and the numerous other sporting activities already mentioned. It is also mainly members of this society who run the village ski school, and the three amateur baseball teams.

The recently formed Friendship Society, *shinbokukai*, consists mainly of married men in their mid-thirties and early forties, who organise joint trips, singing contests, and softball matches, etc. An interesting feature of these newly formed associations is that, even as voluntary groups initiated by a few interested individuals, they have all adopted the traditional group organising principle based on administrative and territorial divisions. The *shinbokukai*, for instance, now has branches and representatives in all six hamlets, and the position of chairman rotates among them. By changing from a voluntary, random group into a village association, it has assumed the character of an age-group, whose members' common political interests are represented in the village council. In fact, although the *shinkbokukai* does not have headquarters at a higher administrative level, since it consists mostly of active young household heads, it occupies an important position in the village community perhaps much more so than the historically developed Housewives' Association and Youth Group.

The Tourism Development Association

Another local association developed through a similar process is the *kankō-kaihatsu kyōkai*, the Tourism Development Association, which basically represents the interests of the *minshuku* people, and thus theoretically cannot be represented in the village council since there are hamlets where as yet no inn exists. To incorporate such hamlets and thus become a politically legitmate organisation, therefore, the *minshuku* people have had to adopt a broader title such as an association for the development of tourism, and hence ostensibly represent community interests in general rather than those of any particular segment. In other words, the principle of utilising the hamlet's traditional capacity for unified action has remained the basic organising principle, not only for traditional government-created associations such as the Housewives' Association, the Fire Brigade and the Youth Group, but also for voluntary associations. Unless each constituent hamlet is equally represented, no association is considered politically legitimate. For this reason, although more than eighty per cent of all households in the village are affiliated to the Pure Land sect temple located in Yamazaki, its association is not considered a village organisation.

Other associations

Other associations cover various aspects of village life which either the government or the people in the village regard as communal. The main responsibility of officials of the Communal Forests Co-operative is the management of the communal *kaya* mountain, a jointly-owned mountain from which hamlet members used to collect a type of Japanese reed to make charcoal sacks and to thatch their houses. The plants are not much in demand now and hamlets mostly rent out their mountains for tourist purposes, and hence the co-operative representatives' task is to collect and distribute the rent money to the hamlet households. Officials of the Environment Preservation Society, usually female household heads, concern themselves with the maintenance of public roads, annual communal clean-ups, etc.

Anyone between the ages of sixty and seventy belongs to the Old People's Association, one of the few associations whose membership is not by household.[16] There are few hamlet-level activities for this group. At the village level, its members often meet for 'gate-ball' games, a Japanese version of croquet said to have been specifically invented for the old and disabled. Tournaments are held twice a year between the hamlets, and some go to Kamada to compete with members of Old People's Associations from other districts. In addition, members of the association offer services to the community such as weeding the village shrine ground. Recently, as a part of nation-wide measures to deal with the problem of an aging society, the government introduced a new form of school for old people known as *kotobuki daigaku* in which *kotobuki* means 'long life' and *daigaku* 'a university or college'. Each year, two people elected from the Old People's Association in Hanasaku attend the school in Shibukawa at government expense.

The Fire Brigade is a self-help organisation of young men, responsible for village safety in times of emergency, such as fire and flood disaster. Recently, this group has often been required to fight bears attacking the maize fields. There are two fire engines jointly owned by the village which members of the group maintain. As part of a national organisation, its members receive occasional training from the professional fire fighters in Numata. Each hamlet is required to provide a set number of young men for the brigade, usually between the ages of twenty-five and thirty-five.

The Parent-Teacher' Associations (P.T.A.) for both the village nursery and primary schools are participated in only by families with children in the schools. Unlike urban areas,[17] however, participation is not limited particularly to women, especially in the case of the primary school P.T.A. of which the headship, rotated among the six hamlets, is usually held by a man. One of the major activities for the primary school P.T.A. is to organise an annual trip for the children to visit a sister school in Chiba prefecture. When children from the sister school return the visit in the winter, they also organise a welcoming party. In all these activities, fathers and mothers participate jointly. The nursery school P.T.A. meetings, on the other hand, are mostly attended by women and have the character of a women's age grade.[18]

The Welfare Society is another government-created organisation set up mainly to assist the administration of new pension schemes. The chief responsibility of its officials is to ensure that all hamlet members eligible for agricultural and old people's pension schemes, as well as the war reward scheme, receive their money. More recently, however, members have spent time discussing juvenile problems, after an article, published in a local newspaper, reported a 'shocking' degree of juvenile delinquency in Katashina middle school in Kamada. The article quoted statistics concerning smoking, drinking and carrying knives. Katashina middle school happened to be slightly higher than others in these figures, and the 'statistical data' provided material for a minor local newspaper to relate the development of tourism to social vice in general. From an outsider's viewpoint, there seemed little ground for worry either from the content of the article or real life where no serious incident of juvenile violence has so far been noted locally. Nevertheless, since the school was described as the worst in northern Gunma prefecture, numerous official meetings particularly of the welfare Society followed to 'counteract the problem' (seishōnen mondai no taisaku).

In general, as Norbeck has pointed out in his study of the urbanisation of Takashima,[19] the number of associations in villages seems to be increasing with their functions becoming more specialised in recent years. As mentioned previously, however, the basic group-organising principle of household membership and hamlet sub-units has always been maintained, and it appears that the activities of various new associations have only increased the amount and diversity of interaction among community members.

The hamlet as mutual aid group

For the inhabitants of Hanasaku, the hamlet unit or buraku comprises the primary, face-to-face community in everyday life. Although it is not an official political division, a certain degree of autonomy is recognised, even in matters concerning official administration, where it is now commonly refered to as a koaza or, less frequently, as a buraku.[20] It is this unit whose members jointly own property and exercise control over those who do not conform, control which used to be practised in the form of mura-hachibu, a mechanism by which the community officially ostracised a member household for a designated period.[21] The maintenance of the irrigation system and the prefectural roads passing through it and the recently-constructed water pipe system are the responsibilities of each hamlet. In the past, each hamlet in Hanasaku also possessed its own tutelary deity, although nowadays only Tochikubo, Noboto and Hariyama hold separate hamlet festivals. One of the most important functions of the hamlet, though, is as a mutual aid group.

Mutual aid groups (Tetsudaikō)
The term 'mutual aid group' or tetsudaikō is always used together with the expression 'mutual financing loan association' (mujinkō), designating two different aspects of the same group. Its membership, as in the case of most other village associations, is by household, and each hamlet usually forms

its own *tetsudaikō*. In former days, the chief occasions for a hamlet to act as a 'mutual aid group' were rethatching house roofs and funerals. Once a house was designated for that year's rethatching by the hamlet assembly, each household was required to collect a set amount of *kaya* from the communally-owned *kaya* mountain and take it to the house to be rethatched. The set amount of *kaya* to be contributed by each household used to be six *soku* or bundles, about the maximum a horse could carry at one time. The plant was then left to dry, and sometime in the autumn following the harvest, members of the hamlet worked together to construct the roof. It usually took about fifteen days for the work-force of the whole hamlet plus relatives to complete one roof. During this period, the household concerned provided food and drink for the whole work-force, but were not expected to pay for either the labour or the contribution of *kaya*. The labour and the material were like a kind of saving which people set aside for the time of their own needs, and it is for this reason, people explained, that such services are called *mujin*.

Exchange of labour in this way is only possible when all member households of the group require the same kind of service. As people in Hanasaku started building tile-roofed houses, it became increasingly difficult to continue the system. Although those who had already built tile-roofs continued to provide the service for the *tetsudaikō* of rethatching, those who required the service 'felt bad' because they would be unable to return the labour on the same scale. This is thought to be one important factor which hastened the house reconstruction boom in recent years. A few thatched houses remain in Hanasaku, but it is almost certain that they will be tile-roofed the next time the roofs need to be replaced. To hire wage-labour for rethatching would be as expensive an enterprise as building a new house.

The disappearance of thatched houses in the village, however, does not necessarily imply the breakdown of the hamlet unit as a mutual aid group, since the same principle of labour exchange still applies to building a new house. The only difference is one of scale. *Kaya* is no longer provided, and labour services are provided only for two days for the task of house demolition and later another two days for constructing the basic framework of the new house.[22] The rest is done by carpenters. The principle of reciprocity is also strictly followed: it is conventionally accepted that each member household is entitled to receive this communal labour service only once in a generation or so.

Another occasion for the whole hamlet to act as a mutual aid group used to be at funerals. Unlike marriage, which is a ceremony for families and relatives, funerals are still very much community affairs. Even nowadays, such tasks as making the coffin and other necessary ritual objects,[23] grave digging, informing relatives, commissioning the priest, the preparing and serving of food, are all carried out by the members of the *tetsudaikō*, i.e. the hamlet. All the services are provided free and have the nature of *mujin*, since people provide them under the assumption that they will receive the same service whenever someone dies within their own household. In addition, all households in a hamlet are required to contribute one measure (*shō*) of rice towards the funeral expenses. The rice contributed in this way is specifically referred to as *mujin* and is distinguished from other kinds of gifts, such as *watamashi* presented by relatives.[24] People explained that rice was so rare in the past that many households would have been unable to feed all their guests on such big occasions as funerals and house rethatchings without the *mujin* contribution, the amount of which is determined at the hamlet assembly.

The scale of funerals has been considerably reduced during the post-war period with concomitant changes in the nature of the communal services required. The task of 'informing relatives' (*tsuge*), for instance, used to require five or six pairs of men before automobile transportation was introduced.[25] The funeral ceremony itself is said to have been much more complicated than nowadays. Even the food as in most other household ceremonies, had to be served separately to each guest on a small four-legged table known as *ozen*. Nowadays, however, all guests are served together on large, rectangular banqueting tables set up in the hamlet meeting hall. Most of these changes came about as a result of the government sponsored New Life Campaign (*shin seikatsu undō*) which aimed to 'rationalise' rural life by reforming areas of extravagance. The compaign required a limit on all obituary gifts (*kōden*, literally 'incense money') to 2,000 yen per household except those of closest relatives. Similarly, the 'excessive' return gifts (*hikimono*) which used to include such items as blankets, Japanese quilts and cushions have all disappeared.

The New Life Campaign has also affected the hamlet co-operative system. Funerals are no longer an occasion which require the co-operation of the whole hamlet. At funerals I observed in 1981–2, therefore, only part of the hamlet was present as helpers. The reduction of the scale of co-operation is not random, however, but based on traditional divisions of the community. For example, there are forty households in Yamazaki, divided into six neighbourhood groups (see Map 6). Of these, the upper three comprise an 'upper hamlet group' (*kami-gumi*) and the lower three, a 'lower hamlet group' (*shimo-gumi*). All the other hamlets are divided into

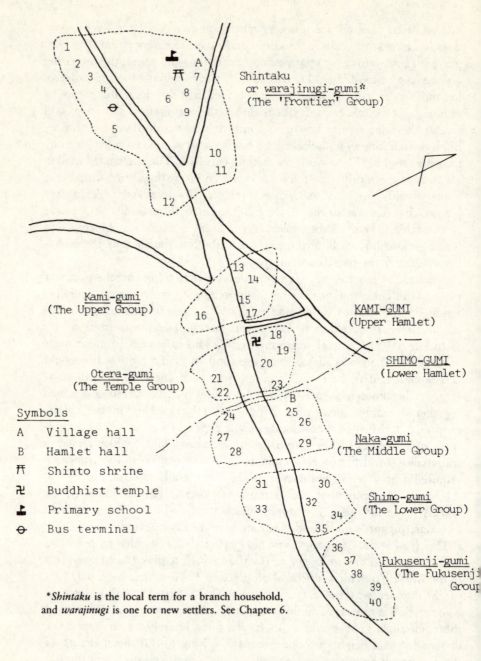

Map 6: Neighbourhood groups: Yamazaki

Within the map:

Shintaku
or warajinugi-gumi*
(The 'Frontier' Group)

Kami-gumi
(The Upper Group)

Otera-gumi
(The Temple Group)

KAMI-GUMI
(Upper Hamlet)

SHIMO-GUMI
(Lower Hamlet)

Naka-gumi
(The Middle Group)

Shimo-gumi
(The Lower Group)

Fukusenji-gumi
(The Fukusenji
Group

Symbols
A   Village hall
B   Hamlet hall
⛩   Shinto shrine
卍   Buddhist temple
⚑   Primary school
⊖   Bus terminal

*Shintaku is the local term for a branch household,
and warajinugi is one for new settlers. See Chapter 6.

146

territorial groups in a similar way. As mentioned previously, these territorial groups alternately elect the hamlet representative. Nowadays, the
tetsudaikō for funerals as well as for other, smaller household ceremonials
also tends to coincide with these territorial divisions. When a death occurs
in one of the households in the middle group, e.g. in the *otera-gumi* or
naka-gumi of Map 6, the services are sometimes requested of the members
of the adjoining three neighbourhood groups, and are thus not necessarily
in line with the larger territorial division. The services are, however,
always asked of a neighbourhood group as a unit, and never just of one or
two households.

In general, about half a hamlet or about three adjoining neighbourhood
groups now form a *tetsudaikō* for funerals.[26] The co-operative group,
therefore, comes to about fifteen or twenty households which usually
provide what is called the 'whole household service' (*uchi chū tetsudai*),
meaning the contribution of the labour of one man and one woman. It is
only the households which offer this 'whole household service' which are
required nowadays to bring one measure of *mujin* rice in addition to the
incense money of 2,000 yen. Other households in the hamlet are only
required to express condolences during the course of the day when the
death occurred. The dead are usually buried on the third day after death
unless it is a day of *tomobiki*.[27] On the day of the burial, a representative
of each hamlet household makes another formal visit to present incense
money. In return, they receive a small 'return gift', usually a white hand-
kerchief and some food contained in a wooden box, nowadays often
ordered from a shop or a *minshuku*. Those households which have offered
the 'whole household service' on the other hand receive, like relatives of
the family, a larger return gift.

After the funeral, women of the households which have provided the
'whole household service' gather again in the evening for sutra chanting,
nenbutsu. These are chanted in chorus to the rhythms of sounds made by
each participant striking a set of bell-shaped metal objects placed in front
of her. Each sutra has different rhythms and each hamlet in Hanasaku has
more than a score of different sets of sutras. To memorise all the different
sets of rhythms for each sutra thus requires considerable skill, and necessitates continuous co-ordination and practice among members. In the past,
each hamlet used to make one sutra chanting group (*nenbutsukō*), participated in by one woman from each constituent household. Sutra chanting,
is performed not only after a funeral,[28] but also at equinoxes, at *arabon*
(the first *bon* after death), at all 'ancestor memorial services' and at the
ujigami festival of extended household groups. It is usually performed in

147

the evenings and provides an exclusive occasion for women to gather. Nowadays, Kajiya and the two smaller hamlets, Kuryu and Hariyama, still form sutra chanting groups at the hamlet level. At midday on the vernal and autumnal equinoxes, for instance, a group comprising one woman from each household in Kajiya gathers together at one house, determined annually by rotation, and chants sutras in the name of all the dead of the hamlet.

All the services people offer as members of the 'mutual aid group' (*tetsudaikō*) or 'sutra chanting group' (*nenbutsukō*) are considered obligations. The force of tradition is such that, once asked to help as a member of the hamlet community, one is obliged to come. It may be assumed that any refusal would soon be reciprocated and the community co-operative system might then break down. In 1982, in fact, one woman in Yamazaki openly declared that she would not return any service in the future to a household which had failed to provide her household with the required service three times during previous years. She recounted these occasions as the funeral of her father-in-law seven years ago, her house reconstruction four years ago and the *yakudoshi* feast of her eldest son the previous year. The wife of the household accused is notorious for laziness, and many neighbours supported the accusing woman's declaration.

This example, however, cannot be regarded as indicating any new trend. As it involves differences in personal character, it is not difficult to imagine that temporary and partial breakdowns of the system under similar circumstances had also happened in the past. Apart from such occasions, the community co-operative system has been largely maintained, despite the tendendy for fission of actual co-operative groups into smaller units. When there was a funeral in Yamazaki in 1981, for example, eleven men absented themselves from their work in a construction business and came to help. People thought that even the employers had no choice but to accept absence under such circumstances. In Noboto, however, community labour is no longer provided for inn buildings nowadays, although they still exchange labour for main house construction, funerals and so forth. Also, since people in general are more time-tabled these days, they try to avoid asking for men's labour during weekdays except on unavoidable occasions like funerals. Even for a woman engaged in farming, people are more conscious of the cash value of daily wages than in the past and consider it bad (*warui*) to ask for help when others are busy. A sign of such awareness is the way many of the ancestor memorial services, which are supposed to be held on the death day of the person concerned, are now often postponed in Hanasaku until sometime in the autumn when people are not particularly busy.

Another community obligation includes providing labour for hamlet labour pools (*ninsoku*). I have already discussed several kinds of agricultural labour pools participated in only by those concerned. There are, however, also a number of general hamlet labour pools. In Hanasaku, for instance, the footpaths on Hotaka mountain are cleared once a year by communal labour. In the past, this used to be done by a village-wide labour pool, but nowadays it is done by a hamlet labour pool, the six hamlets taking turns to provide the service. The preparation of village and hamlet festivals provide other major occasions for hamlet labour pools (see Chapter 8 for details). In former times, public buildings such as meeting halls were also completely built by communal labour. Although each member household is obliged to provide one man's labour for all these occasions, female labour is also accepted for those households headed by women such as widows. For those households which fail to provide any labour at all, however, fines are imposed by the hamlet assembly, as is the case for those who fail to participate in hamlet assembly meetings. Service in these labour pools, as in mutual aid groups, is unpaid and is considered a duty of community members.

Neighbourhood groups (Gochō-gumi)

Due to the fissioning tendency of the co-operative system, many of the previous hamlet-wide co-operative occasions are now participated in only by those of one's own neighbourhood group. When the neighbourhood group system was first institutionalised in Japanese rural communities is not very clear.[29] The system is said to have been reinforced as part of the drive against Christianity and for the purpose of policing during the Tokugawa period, when the members of a neighbourhood group were held jointly responsible for all the crimes committed by the people of its member households.[30] During the last war, the system was revived for 'transmitting the will of those above to those below'[31] and for the 'fostering of ... spiritual solidarity'.[32] Although it was denounced after the war as a system that had been designed for supporting warlike activities, the system has survived in Hanasaku as in most other Japanese villages.[33]

The neighbourhood groups are referred to by different names in different localities, and in Hanasaku, are called *gochō-gumi* or sometimes *tonari-gumi*. The chief functions of the neighbourhood groups nowadays are the distribution of information and tax collection. The five or six households in one *gochō-gumi*, for instance, each year designate one member household to play the 'distributing role' (*fureyaku*). It is then the responsibility of this household to keep its members informed of all official business disseminated from the hamlet assembly, the village council and

149

the *mura* government. All the other village-wide associations also use this means to distribute relevant information. Tax is also collected by members of this household on behalf of the hamlet representative to whom the task is officially delegated. The 'distributing role' rotates annually among the member households and is another compulsory service to the community.

The neighbourhood group also comprises a co-operative unit for various household ceremonies. For ancestor memorial services, for the first *bon* ceremonies or for the *yakudoshi* feasts, and so on, one woman from each member household of the neighbourhood group helps to prepare food along with other relatives. It is also women of this group who are nowadays invited to childbirth celebrations, first birthday celebrations for firstborn children and the 'face-showing ceremonies' of brides, although many of these occasions were for the whole hamlet community in the past. In the village festival, each of the neighbourhood groups provides the two major ritual roles (see the next chapter for details).

In this chapter, I have shown how the traditional political structure, the associations and the co-operative system in Hanasaku have changed during the post-war years, as a result of the growing involvement of its residents in a cash economy. Evidence suggests that, while changes are clearly noticeable at the level of action, basic elements in the structural social relations have remained the same. Instead of the community co-operative system being replaced by a system of a completely different nature, the old system has simply been adjusted to meet reduced needs. Similarly, although the number of local associations has increased in recent years, new groups are always formed following the same principles as old ones. In most anthropological work on social change, there is a distinction between change in which basic elements of the society alter, and change in which social action, while not repetitive, does not alter the basic social forms.[34] The materials so far discussed clearly indicate the latter case. In the following chapter, I discuss the role of community festivals and religion in reinforcing traditional social forms within the village society.

Notes

1 For the history of village government in Japan, see T. Smith 1952; Steiner 1956; for that of Hanasaku village, see *Katashina Sonshi* 1963; Satō 1980; and Moon Kim 1984: 277–84.

2 Cf. Steiner *ibid.*: 196.

3 The banquet is called *keirokai* in which *kei* means 'respect', *ro* means 'old' and *kai* means

'a gathering or party'. The last word *kai*, however, also means 'a society, a club or an association', and in some areas of Japan, the same term *keirokai* seems to mean the association for the old people; Hendry 1981: 247. In Hanasaku, people sometimes use the word in the latter sense when they apply the term to anyone who is over seventy years old.

4 To the same effect, Ward 1951: 1039 writes, 'the technique of decision by concensus often does no more than convey the public impression of unanimity – which the Japanese consider important – while at the same time concealing bitter antagonisms which will continue to be expressed insistently but secretly'. See also Steiner 1956: 190.

5 Even in a relatively large hamlet like Yamazaki, for instance, thirty-six out of forty household heads were elected as officials in 1981. Male heads were generally elected, but some roles are considered household obligations, and any of the household members can in fact perform most services required.

6 Fukutake 1967: 110.

7 Smith and Wiswell 1982: chapter 2.

8 *Katashina Sonshi* 1963: 445.

9 Dore 1959: 486–9.

10 This association is active only in *minshuku* hamlets where there are many young wives. While some young married women from agricultural hamlets participate in its activities through friends, there are no hamlet based sub-branches of the association as in the case of the Housewives' Association.

11 See Norbeck 1953: 376–9; Seki 1962: 143–52; Varner 1977: 464–5; and Yanagita 1957: 217ff.

12 *Katashina no Minzoku* 1960: 46–8; *Katashina Sonshi* 1963: 439.

13 The word *yado* may be translated as 'lodge'. In some other parts of Japan, the practice of groups of each sex spending the night separately in a *wakashūyado* (youth lodge) has been reported; Hendry 1981: 252; Naito and Yoshida 1965: 216–17. In this area, however, there is no record of such a practice nor did anybody remember it from the past. Families in which there had been a marriage during the previous year used to offer their home as a *yado*, and in some hamlets, girls were not required to bring a bottle of rice wine.

14 *Katashina no Minzoku* 1960: 47.

15 *Katashina Sonshi* 1963: 438.

16 Although membership in the Youth Group or the Housewives' Association is in theory on an individual basis, usually only one person from any household at a time participates in them. A daughter-in-law, for example, starts coming to the meetings of the Housewives' Association only after her mother-in-law has retired.

17 Cf. Vogel 1963: 110–11.

18 Cf. Hendry 1981: 71; Norbeck 1965: 53.

19 Norbeck 1977: 59.

20 For postal and census purposes, the *mura* is divided into a number of *ōaza*, of which there are fourteen in Katashina. *Koaza* is a sub-unit of *ōaza*. For detailed description of this unit, see Embree 1939: 23–4; Ward 1951: 1026, 1033.

21 Cf. Smith 1961: 525ff.

22 Most new houses in Hanasaku are wooden framed, and the process of their construction as well as the rituals involved are very similar to those described by others. Cf. Hendry 1981: 216–17; Dore 1978: 214–16.

23 Moon Kim 1984: 315; Sofue et al. 1972: 197.

24 In a book kept by most households in the village for reference when returning gifts, two *shō* of rice presented by the same household which is a member of the hamlet as well as

kin are always separatedly recorded, one *shō* as *mujin* and one *shō* as *watamashi*.

25 In Hanasaku, it is still considered impolite to give the news of a death by telephone or telegram. Even nowadays, therefore, the news is delivered personally within the boundary of Katashina, Tone and Kawaba *mura*.

26 The size of *tetsudaikō* may vary from household to household. As soon as a death occurs, people of the *ikke* and *miuchi* gather at the bereaved house to make arrangements for the funeral. One important item discussed is the number of neighbourhood groups to be asked for service, which varies according to the respective standing of the family.

27 This is a day in the Buddhist six-day cycle, which means 'pulling a friend'. While considered a good day for a marriage, people believe that another death will soon occur if someone is buried during it.

28 People believe that to make metal sounds (*kane no oto*) is very important especially after a funeral since it helps the spirit of the dead safely cross the river separating life and death. For a detailed account of *nembutsu* practice and related beliefs, see Hori 1968: chapter 3.

29 Braibanti 1948: 140 maintains that it was introduced from China during the Taika Reform which began in AD 645. According to him, the decree of the Reform directed that every fifty houses be made a *satō* and that each *satō* be divided into groups of five with an elder as head; see also Asakawa 1903: 275.

30 Sansom 1943: 170; Murdoch 1926: 47.

31 Fukutake 1967: 97.

32 Steiner 1968: 240.

33 According to Fukutake, only about twenty-seven per cent of Japanese rural settlements do not have the neighbourhood group system, and the majority of these are hamlets too small to need division; Fukutake *ibid.*: 98.

34 Firth 1954: 17; cf. Malinowski 1945; Gluckman 1958; Mead 1956.

8

Village festivals

Most Japanese villages have a guardian deity of their own, and village residents are often referred to as 'children' (*ujiko*) of the village god. Similarly, the village sub-units or hamlets (*buraku*) possess separate guardian deities, so that both hamlets and villages in Japan have the character of religious communities. Not only the nature of the village gods but also the ritual forms and processes observed to honour them differ from village to village even within the same locality. Participation in, and co-operation on, the preparing festivals held for the village and hamlet gods have thus clearly helped to foster a sense of belonging among members of a territorial group and strengthened the community character of village society. This chapter describes how recent economic changes, especially the advent of tourism in Hanasaku, have affected the nature of these community festivals.

The temple and the shrine

As in many other Japanese villages, Hanasaku has both a Buddhist temple and a Shinto shrine. While Buddhism and Shintoism represent the two major religious traditions in Japan, in the religious life of people in the village little reference is made to the formal or doctrinal teachings of either. For this reason, some have described religious practices at the village level as 'village Buddhism' and 'village Shinto'.

> The modifier 'village' is used advisedly, since the lay farmer approaches Buddhism quite differently from the priest or scholar, foregoing most of its philosophical subtleties. Buddhism to a layman is a means of venerating his household's ancestors and of understanding and linking himself to the afterworld. Every temple ... is supported by its parishioners mainly for its services on behalf of the ancestors. Whatever else the priests and nuns concern themselves with is of little moment to the ordinary person. Hence, Buddhism has one character in its colleges and monasteries but has a different character in the villages.[1]

The Buddhist temple in Hanasaku is of the Jōdō sect, the second largest Buddhist sect in Japan. The sutras recited by the temple priest when officiating at a village funeral or an ancestral memorial service thus may differ from those recited by a priest from another sect. However, few people in the village claim to understand the sutras, nor does the difference seem to be important to them.

The resident priest of Senfukuji, as the Buddhist temple in Hanasaku is called, indeed seems to be little more than a religious functionary kept by the parishioner households (*danka*) in the village to officiate at funerals and other rituals concerning the household ancestors. He works full time at the regional forestry office, and his priestly work is only a part-time occupation. He is not separately remunerated for maintaining the village temple, but most parishioner households contribute one measure of rice to the temple at New Year, *higan* (vernal and autumnal equinoxes), and *bon* (midsummer All Souls' festival). Some also contribute flowers and gifts on such occasions and, in addition, the priest is paid for each individual ceremony he performs, and receives the money paid at funerals for the posthumous name of the deceased. Other functions of the priest include visiting each parishioner households in the village at New Year, *higan* and *bon*, to recite a few sutras in honour of household ancestors. The priest's eldest son, before joining the *mura* government office in the spring of 1981, had also qualified as a Buddhist priest by receiving two years' education at one of the Jōdō sect schools in Kyoto, just as his father had done some twenty-five years earlier. Nowadays, this son shares the service of going round the village with his father, and will probably inherit the temple work when his father retires.

Senfukuji is considered to be a branch temple of Ryōgenji, a Jōdō sect temple in Numata. However, apart from the fact that Senfukuji's previous resident priest came from the latter, no specific ties seem to be maintained between the two temples, nor does Senfukuji keep any organisational link with other higher institutions within the Jōdō sect.[2] Although the everyday maintenance of the temple building falls to the priest and his household, major repairs or reconstruction are the joint responsibility of all parishioner households in the village. In each of the six hamlets in Hanasaku there is one hereditary patron household of the temple. In addition, each hamlet elects, from among the parishioner households, two representatives who form the temple association and assume responsibility for maintaining the temple over a two year period. It was the decision of the temple association that every parishioner household in the village should deposit 3,000 yen (approximately £8) per month in a local bank for one year toward the expense of changing the temple roof from thatch to zinc, a job which was finally carried out in the spring of 1982. Each parishioner household also provided one person's labour for two days at the beginning of the enterprise. On completion, the priest and his household held a temple-warming party to which one person from each of the parishioner households was invited.

In other aspects of village life, the Buddhist priest does not differ in status from other community members. Just like any other member of the community, for example, he participated in all the communal labour pools organised to prepare village festivals held in honour of Shinto deities. He has, however, never been elected a representative of the shrine association, nor does he take active ritual roles at the shrine ceremony such as *sakaban* or *hitsuban*, which will be described later.

Unlike the Buddhist temple, the Shinto shrine in Hanasaku does not have a resident priest. There is a Shrino priest living in the village, and his son has also recently qualified as a priest. This priest, however, is an immigrant settled in the village after the Second World War and has no connection with the village shrine. Instead, another Shinto priest living in Tone *mura* officiates at annual shrine festivals in Hanasaku. This priest's father and grandfather were also Shinto priests and officiated at Hanasaku festivals. People said it was because of their *giri*, 'sense of obligation', towards his father and grandfather that they invited this particular priest. Local Shinto priests operate much like independent religious specialists working on informal contracts for individual villages or households for which they perform occasional purificatory rites for specific purposes, such as building a new house, starting a business, taking an entrance examination and so forth. The younger Shinto priest living in Hanasaku, for instance, has a number of client households all over Tone county, which call on him for service. On the whole, however, 'pious Shintoists' who require individual services are few in this area, and he claims that it is almost impossible to earn a living simply from being a Shinto priest these days.

Like the term for Buddhism, *bukkyo*, the term Shinto is almost never mentioned by people in Hanasaku. People are more concerned with *hotoke* (the household ancestors) and *kami* (other deities) whose worship is generically referred to by the blanket term Shinto or Shintoism. In fact, the term Shinto (the way of the gods or *kami*), is thought to have been invented after the introduction of Buddhism from Korea around the mid-sixth century to distinguish the traditional forms of belief and practice, namely the 'way of Japanese divinities', from the new alien religion.[3]

155

Shinto is thus scarcely an orderly system of beliefs. Under the state Shinto system created by the Meiji government for nationalistic purposes, however, certain local shrines were made the shrines of larger administrative units such as the shrines of the *mura* (*sonsha*), county (*gunsha*) and prefecture (*kensha*), and these bgan to receive state support. Under this system, the Hotaka-jinja of Hanasaku was made the shrine of Katashina *mura*, and its festivals were attended by the mayor of the *mura* and other government officials. After the Second World War, the state Shinto system was dismantled and all local shrines were again made equal. Accordingly, the compulsory attendance of local government officials at *Hotaka-jinja* ceremonies also came to an end. In 1978, however, the autumn festival of *Hotaka-jinja*, the *Saruoi-matsuri*, was designated a national 'Intangible Cultural Asset' (*mukei bunkazai*) for the richness of its rites. Therefore, people in the village as well as the local government show particular interest in preserving the tradition of the ritual, and though not compulsory, the attendance of government officials has also been revived.

The shrine in Hanasaku is now managed by twelve elected representatives, two from each of the six hamlets. The twelve form an association called *ujiko-sōdai*, which may be translated as the 'representatives of the children of the god-family'.[4] In the past, there was only one annually elected *ujiko-sōdai* in each hamlet. Since the Saruoi-matsuri became an 'Intangible Cultural Asset', however, it became so important 'to observe the right ritual process' that the village council decided to elect a second member from each hamlet. Though those elected as *ujiko-sōdai* now serve for two years, for the initial year they serve only on a provisional basis as observers so that each year, only one *ujiko-sōdai* is elected in each hamlet.

The Saruoi-matsuri

The gurardian deity

The village shrine in Hanasaku houses Hotaka-sama. *Hotaka* means 'high warrior', and Hotaka-sama is a legendary warrior figure accorded divinity, like many other Shinto gods. How this figure came to be related to the village is not clear. One of the mountains north of the village, however, is also called Hotaka, and is considered sacred. In the past, the men who participated in the annual clearing of the footpaths on Hotaka mountain had first to purify themselves by taking a bath and avoiding any defiling activities. Women and those who had suffered misfortune such as a death in the family during the previous year, were not allowed to climb the mountain. People are much less concerned about these prohibitions nowadays, and in any case, little can be done about female tourists who come mountaineering. In the footpath-clearing labour pool in 1981, a widow of fifty-three years of age participated, and no one seemed to object.

There is also a legend which relates the name of the village, Hanasaku, to Hotaka-sama. The literal meaning of Hanasaku is 'flower bloom', and the name is said to originate from an old story which tells of flowers once 'blooming' out of a stone, on which Hotaka-sama had sat down to rest when he came to the village to drive out demons hiding in the mountains to the north. The stone can still be found in the hamlet of Noboto. About two metres in diameter, it has dim scarlet dots all over it. Beside it there is a miniature wooden shrine, looking like a wind-beaten house god (*yashiki-inari*). No specific rite is held at this shrine and, although it was partially destroyed by a typhoon while I was there, no discussions were held regarding its restoration.

Although Hanasaku therefore has a special relationship with Hotaka-sama, he is not the guardian deity of that village alone. In fact, a number of *Hotaka-jinja* or *Hotaka* shrines are found throughout Katashina and Tone *mura* up to Numata on the western side of the Katashina River.[5] Hanasaku is considered to be the origin of Hotaka beliefs, however, and it is said to be for this reason that the Hanasaku *Hotaka-jinja* was designated as the mura shrine (*sonsha*). A common feature of all the areas where Hotaka shrines are found is the avoidance of growing taro plants and sesame trees, an avoidance which is related to another legend. This tells how, when Hotaka-sama was in the area, supposedly Hanasaku, he slipped on a taro leaf and one of his eyes was injured by sesame seeds. Some people in the village told me that Hotaka-sama could see with only one eye, while others claimed that, if one closely examined the drawing of Hotaka-sama in the shrine, which shows an upright warrior carrying a sword, one can see that one of his eyes is a tiny bit smaller than the other.[6]

The ritual process
In former times, three annual festivals were held in honour of the village guardian deity, *Hotaka-sama*, in spring, summer and autumn. The spring festival was dropped some years ago. The summer festival is still held, but is mainly an occasion for village and hamlet officials and members of the Shrine Association who organise the festival, and hence it attracts little attention from others in the village. It is therefore only the autumn and *Gion* festivals which create any festive spirit in the village nowadays. Even in the past, the autumn festival, which follows the harvest, was considered

the main festival of the year. On the festival day, pedlars and itinerant merchants used to flock in from outside to set up their stalls and booths. Every house cooked special food and relatives came to stay from other villages, Girls, especially new village brides, were given a new set of brightly coloured kimonos for the occasion, and had their hair specially set. Everyone went to the shrine to see the celebration.

Saruoi-matsuri, and indeed all the other shrine festivals, are much less of an event these days. The increase in other kinds of recreational activities such as coach trips, sports or shopping in a nearby town, has reduced the importance of shrine festivals in village life. Everybody can now afford good food and clothing, so they do not have to wait for the festival for them. Children are no longer interested in going round different hamlet and village festivals to receive festive red rice (*sekihan*) when they can buy ices and sweets from the local shops whenever they wish. Nevertheless, the designation of the *Saruoi-matsuri* as a national cultural asset has prhaps brought back a little of the old enthusiasm, and people seem to take pride in its 'cultural' value, thanks mainly to the encouragement of the authorities and the media. In 1981, the festival day was made an unofficial half-holiday by the village school and all the children led by their teachers came to observe the occasion. There were also quite a number of villagers present, in addition to a small group of local historians and ethnologists and a reporter from a local newspaper. A number of stalls and booths were set up selling candy floss, rubber balloons and the like, but there were no fortune-tellers or showmen.

Although many events in Hanasaku, including *bon*, are now calculated by the Gregorian solar calendar, the *Saruoi-matsuri* is still held according to tradition on the second monkey day of lunar September. The festival day thus usually falls some time between late October and mid-November by the solar calendar. On the previous day, members of the Old People's Association clean the shrine and its surroundings. Two big banners announcing the festival are then set up on the way up to the shrine by members of the *ujiko-sōdai*. Another banner, hung from two wooden poles and about six or seven metres long, used to be erected at the entrance to the village, for anyone coming in to see. Villagers told me that, in the past, once the banners were raised, strangers were not allowed into the village for fear of possible defilement.

The main rite is held some time in the early afternoon of the festival day. In the morning, the priest goes to Hariyama where a rite is held separately for the hamlet. Being the latest settlement, Hariyama did not constitute in the past a part of the Hanasaku shrine community. Nevertheless, it now has two representatives for the main shrine where they participate in the festival as observers. Early in the afternoon, the priest, village and hamlet officials, and members of the *ujiko-sōdai* arrive at the shrine. The priest then produces amulets or *shide*, folded out of white paper, which officials and *ujiko-sōdai* members place at all the places where gods reside for purification purposes. Apart from the main shrine building inhabited by Hotaka-sama, there are in the shrine compound a number of other smaller shrines which used to be in other parts of the village but which were moved when the local shrines were reorganised under the state Shinto system during the Meiji period. Although the state Shinto system was dismantled after the war, the shrines were left, and their gods, one Fudo-sama, one Tennō-sama and two Suwa-sama, are now worshipped together with the main god of the village, Hotaka-sama. In addition to the *shide* placed inside the shrine buildings, people also sanctify the area by hanging a straw festoon stuck with white cut-paper, called *o-shime* at the entrance of each shrine building including the main entrance (*torii*). While some are engaged in setting up these decorations, others go to the nearby forest to collect *hinoki* branches, with which the priest makes numerous *tamagushi*, the sacred tree offerings used at Shinto rituals.[8]

As the preparations continue, people begin to arrive, most importantly, the *mura* mayor and his officials, and *sakaban* and *hitsuban*, all of whom take part in the main rite. 'Saka-' or *sakaban* comes from *sake*, Japanese rice wine, and '*hitsu-*' is the name for a kind of chest in which people used to carry cooked rice. The word *ban* means 'one's turn', so *sakaban* are the households required to prepare and bring *amazake* (sweet rice wine), and *hitsuban* those which bring *sekihan* (glutinous red rice cooked at festive occasions). Each hamlet except Hariyama is divided into several groups which each provide one *sakaban* and one *hitsuban*. In principle, these groups coincide with neighbourhood groups (*gochō-gumi*). In Yamazaki, however, the Buddhist priest household and the new settlers' group at the upper end do not participate in these roles. Similarly, in Kajiya, only Hoshino households take part, the rest being mostly recent immigrant households. In Noboto, the residents of Tokyo *mura* do not participate. In Kuryu and Tochikubo, all the households participate although their *saka-ban* and *hitsuban* groups are slightly at variance with neighbourhood groups. Those who take part in the ritual, especially the *sakaban* and *hitsuban*, are supposed to come dressed in *montsuki-haori-hakama*, formal garments with a household crest, worn by men on ceremonial occasions. In 1981, however, about one third of those present were dressed in black western-style suits.

159

On arrival, the *sakaban* and *hitsuban* first offer rice and wine to all the house gods lined up at the back of the shrine.[9] After that, everyone enters the shrine and sits down round the two open-pit hearths to drink tea until the preparations are over. In 1981, the tea was served by two women though in general women are not allowed to participate in the main ceremony. Those from Kuryu, Yamazaki and Kajiya sit on the right-hand or eastern side and those from Tochikubo and Noboto on the left-hand or western side. The division is maintained throughout the ritual.

When everything is ready, all walk out of the shrine, most of them wearing black garments except the priest and the mayor. The rite in front of the altar itself is exactly the same as that at the summer festival except that the mayor and his officials are not present at the latter. All squat on the floor in front of the altar, with the priest a step forward in a kneeling position. The priest then calls the spirit by clapping twice and saying a few words in a high-pitched voice. On the spirit's arrival, everyone including the priest bows to the ground. The priest takes out a piece of rolled white paper from his sleeve and reads it out in the same high-pitched, sing-song voice, reporting to the spirit past events in the village, thanking him for his protection and praying for a good harvest, prosperity in business, no illness and no misfortunes in the village for the coming year. The priest again claps and bows to let the spirit know that one stage of the rite is over. After that, each participant comes forward and offers the prepared *tamagushi* (a sprig of sacred tree with white paper stuck on it) to the god and bows to the ground. In 1981, the *tamagushi* were offered, in order, by the mayor, the head of the tourism department in the *mura* government, the head of the education department, the village headman, the three *mura* assemblymen elected from the village in order of seniority, the head of the *ujiko-sōdai* and other members of the *ujiko-sōdai*. The *sakaban* and *hitsuban* do not participate in these offerings. The end of the rite at the altar is again announced by clapping and bowing in which, this time, everyone participates.

All the *hitsuban* then come out of the shrine building and line up in front, people from Yamazaki, Kuryu and Kajiya on the right-hand side, those from Tochikubo and Noboto on the left, and they throw the *sekihan* at each other shouting 'echo', 'mocho', although no one claims to understand what the words mean. This stage of the rite is both confused and messy since it is not easy to throw glutinous rice even when made into small balls! After that, all return to the building and start singing, the two sides taking turns. As they finish the third song, the 'monkey' dressed in white and holding a *gōhei*, a wand with hemp and paper streamers used in

Shinto ceremonies, dashes out from behind the altar where it has been waiting unseen and runs out of the building. All those singing stand up and run after it as it races round the building three times and disappears back into the building where it hands over the *gōhei* to the priest and retreats again behind the altar, quickly changing into ordinary dress and joining the others who have been trying to catch it. The priest then offers the *gōhei* to the god and announces the end of the rite, at which all the participants including the priest and the mayor once more take a seat around the two fire places in the front part of the building and commence a drinking party, as the onlookers gradually disperse.

The drinks and other expenses for the festival as well as those for the general upkeep of the shrine are provided by the *ujiko-sōdai* from the proceeds of the shrine-owned forest land and from selling the shrine's *o-fuda* (amuletic paper bearing the name of the god of the shrine). Before the Second World War, the shrine owned about 0.3 hectare of paddy fields and a little more than two hectares of dry fields, the renting of which sufficiently covered the upkeep of the shrine and the expenses of its festivals. It lost these farm lands during the post-war Land Reform but kept some forest land which is now managed by the *ujiko-sōdai* with the help of the Youth Group or Friendship Society.

Implications

A number of stories are told in the village to explain the origin of the *Saruoi-matsuri*, a word in which *saru* means 'monkey' and *oi* is a derivative noun of the verb *ou*, 'to drive away' or 'to chase'. Though the stories vary and none of them fully explain all the details, a few are worth quoting here since they reflect the ways in which people understand the meaning of the rite. One of the most popular versions runs as follows:

Story A: Once upon a time, a white monkey used to appear in the village every night and damage the crops. Some say that the monkey came from a place called 'monkey rock' (*saru iwa*) on Hotaka mountain. Since the monkey's damage continued for several years, everyone felt very frustrated. Finally, they gathered at the shrine to consult with the village god (*kami-sama*). They decided that they would choose a day and go out as a *ninsoku* to drive away the monkey. (At this point, opinions vary once more, and some say that it was decided to catch the monkey in order to turn it into a god since they believed that, if they worshipped it as a god, it would stop harming their crops.) While they were discussing the matter, the monkey appeared once again. Everyone stopped talking and ran after it. Though they could not catch it, the monkey never appeared again, and since they believed that the *kami-sama* helped them drive it away, they began to hold the rite at the shrine.

Advocates of this story maintain that the throwing of rice symbolises the subsequent abundance of food. When the monkey stopped damaging their crops, people enjoyed such good harvests that they could afford to throw away some of the food in praise of the god. When I asked why the monkey in the rite appears only after the throwing of rice, the only explanation was that the actual process must have changed over times. This seems plausible since most people in the village are now unsure about the 'right' process of the ritual, as was possibly the case in the past as well. At the 1981 festival, for instance, many people started singing just after the rite at the altar. When an old man came up and said that the throwing of rice should come first, however, they all laughed and changed the procedure.

The second version is slightly more elaborate than the first, referring to a number of different aspects of village life. It runs as follows:

Story B: In former times, people used to get extremely drunk at village festivals. One day everybody got so drunk that a big fight broke out. (This story also varies at this point since some say that the fight was not simply between drunken participants in the festival but between those who had lived in the village from the beginning and were farmers (*hyakushō*), and those who came late and claimed to be descendants of a feudal lord (*tonosama*).) When the fight was at its peak, symbolised by the throwing of rice, a white monkey suddenly appeared and began to ruin the crops. At this, everyone ceased fighting and chased after the monkey which ran into the shrine building. When people looked into the shrine, however, they could not find the monkey. People thought therefore that it must not have been a real monkey but the *kami-sama* who appeared in the form of a monkey to admonish them against fighting. Realising the god's will, the two groups made peace and began to hold the rite in his honour.

Even the second story does not explain certain parts of the ritual, such as the singing or the division of the group between Tochikubo and Noboto on the one hand and Kuryu, Yamazaki and Kajiya on the other in the 'fighting'. However, it demonstrates some interesting correlations with other features found in the community.

There are in Hanasaku seven Hoshino *ikke*, 'extended household groups', accounting for a little more than one third of all households in the village. Of these, only members of four groups are entitled to act as the monkey, one in lower Yamazaki, one in front Kajiya and two in rear Kajiya. These four groups take turns in providing the monkey each year — rear Kajiya for two years, front Kajiya for one year and the *fukusenji-gumi* of lower Yamazaki for one year.[10] How the four groups were originally related is not certain. The two groups in rear Kajiya, however, have the same guardian god, O-taishi-sama. Similarly, the one in front Kajiya and one in lower Yamazaki also worship the same guardian deity, O-kuman-sama, although the rites are separately held at two different shrines of the same name. On the basis of this evidence, Satō speculates that the four groups originally belonged to two separate *ikke* groups whose members were probably the first settlers of the village.[11] In this connection it is interesting to note that members of one of the three Hoshino *ikke* which are excluded from the monkey role maintain that the reason they cannot act as the monkey is that their original ancestors were not farmers, but instead they are descendants of a feudal lord.[12] This group has as its guardian deity of Buddhist origin, Kannon-sama, located in the upper part of Yamazaki. The other two groups which are excluded from the monkey role are in Noboto. These groups are said to be offshoots of a Hoshino *ikke* in rear Kajiya, but have a different guardian deity from the latter, Akagi-sama.

While much more historical research is needed to clarify fully the relationship between different extended household groups in Hanasaku, from the available circumstantial evidence, one can at least suggest that the reference in the second version to conflict between the original settlers and late-comers is not totally unfounded. Whichever group arrived later, the limitation of the main ritual role to a certain group seems to signify an internal division within the community or at least a status distinction, and from this, one may well assume that the throwing of rice indeed symbolises conflict between the two groups. On the other hand, in terms of either story A or story B, the message of the ritual is straightforward enough: that the god of the village ensures the prosperity of its residents, and that they should live in harmony, and should co-operate with each other. When harmony is disrupted by persistent conflict within the community, the god sees that it is recovered. As mentioned previously, harmony and co-operation are the two cardinal values emphasised in every aspect of village life; and the *Saruoi-matsuri*, or at least people's understanding of it, clearly expresses these values, although in the face of declining interest in religious affairs in general, how much force this now has in directing people's action is a different matter.

The *Gion-matsuri*

Festivals called *Gion* are found throughout Japan, but the best known is that sponsored by the *Yasaka* shrine in Kyoto, and therefore, many people in Hanasaku believe that their festival originated in Kyoto too.[13] However,

163

the deity honoured in this festival is in fact Gavagriva (Gozu Tennō in Japanese), a god of good health and the guardian deity of the Jetavana monastery (*Gion Shōja* in Japanese) in India. The first *Gion* festival in Kyoto was held in 869 when, to counter an epidemic that had swept the city, sixty-six tall spears (*hoko*) representing the provinces of Japan were erected in the Imperial Park and prayers were offered. *Gozu Tennō* was then enshrined at Yasaka and his festival had become well established by the late tenth century. Later during the Tokugawa or Edo period (1603–1868) when the festival spread throughout the country, the original *hoko* (spears) were replaced by giant, wheeled floats often bearing life-size figures of famous historical or mythical characters.[14]

Unlike the locally developed *Saruoi-matsuri, Gion-matsuri* displays a number of similarities to festivals found in other parts of the country under the same name. The deity honoured is locally referred to as Tennō-sama, and is considered the guardian god against diseases and epidemics. Apart from the village *Tennō-sama* figure found in a corner at the *Hotaka* shrine compound, each hamlet has its own *Tennō-sama* contained in a miniature wooden shrine. On the day before the festival, which now falls on the last Sunday of August by the Gregorian solar calendar, one person per household of each hamlet form a *ninsoku* and decorate the hamlet's *Tennō-sama* on the wayside near their meeting hall. The officials then remain in the hall for the rest of the day drinking the rice wine offered to the god, while individual household members occasionally appear at the decorated altar to offer rice, noodles, newly harvested vegetables, fruit and so forth. While these offerings are mainly made by women, important people in the hamlet such as officials, assemblymen and representatives of certain Associations, or anybody who wishes to be recognised in the community such as anthropologists, shop keepers and so on, usually offer a bottle or two of rice wine. Except for those consumed in the course of the preparations, most of the wine bottles offered to the god will stand on the altar until the next day, with the offerer's name clearly written on the cover of the bottle so that anyone passing can see. Rice wine (*o-sake*) specifically offered to a god is called *o-miki,* and is supposed to have certain purificatory powers, and hence, it is drunk as a precaution against accidents which might occur during the festival the following day.

Probably because of the strength required to pull the huge floats around the village, the actual organisers of the festival are generally young people. In the course of the day, however, the whole village eventually becomes involved. Although in former times each hamlet made its own float, locally called *mando,* only two are made these days, one by the Friendship Society and the other by the Youth Group. Members of the two societies meet separately in the evenings for about a weeks before the festival and produce the images to be carried on the floats. In 1981 the Friendship Society created Momotaro, a character from a children's story, who, born from a peach (*momo*) floating in the river, grew into a conqueror of ogres. The Youth Group created a modern western-style cartoon figure resembling Spider Man. On the evening preceding the festival after the decoration of the *Tonnō-sama* in each hamlet, members of the two groups again gather together and make the floats. The village keeps two four-wheeled wooden carts to be used for the occasion, one in Noboto for the Friendship Society and another in Tochikubo for the Youth Group. The preparation of the floats is a far more elaborate job than simply fixing the images. The life-size figures have to be fastened on top of six or seven metre wooden poles, possibly the remains of the tradition of spears (*hoko*) in the original *Gion* festival in Kyoto. They are then raised at the centre of the carts (approx. 1.5 by 1.5m in size). Due to the height and weight of the poles, fixing them at the centre of the small carts without harming the shape of the images requires a great deal of co-ordination, and it is often carried out under electric lamps well into the night, the point being to hide the splendour of the completed floats from others in the village until the next day. When completed, people can only hope that it does not rain overnight.

Around 6:30 on the morning of the festival, members of the Youth Group first took their Spider Man float to Noboto to join up with the Momotaro float of the Friendship Society, before commencing the ritual journey around the village which goes from Hariyama to Kuryu, Hotaka shrine, Yamazaki, Kajiya, Tochikubo and Noboto. The floats are pulled by a group of young men holding short wooden poles which stick out from both sides of the carts. The carts are balanced by ropes at both the front and back which are held by groups of village school children. Both carts also carry a drummer and a number of still smaller children. Two tractors are mobilised to draw the carts up the hillside roads. At each hamlet, the floats stop for between thirty and sixty minutes, and those who have been pulling them are served food and drink and entertained with singing. It is one of the most bustling and festive occasions of the whole year; excited children run around, women busily serve food, and men constantly pour out *sake* and beer. Through a loudspeaker, the hamlet headman makes a speech, welcoming and thanking the young float bearers and encouraging them to drink to their heart's content and enjoy the hamlet's hospitality. Naturally the youngsters get more and more drunk as the journey proceeds. Towards the end, before the floats are dismantled and stored away for the next year, the bearers often violently rock them backwards and forwards in play. Due to the precarious balance between the height of the poles and the size of the supporting carts, the floats inevitably seem to fall over and someone gets hurt. Such events are part of the fun, however, and none of the onlookers seem to mind. The singing is described by villagers as *kagura*, sacred music and drama traditionally performed to please gods at Shinto festivals. The so-called *kagura* at the 1981 Gion festival in Hanasaku, however, mostly consisted of modern popular songs sung to the accompaniment of tapes played in the new *karaoke* music box.

Significantly, the Hanasaku *Gion* festival is said to have recently revived. During the years preceding the Second World War, it was one of the most flourishing festivals in the village, especially following an epidemic of dysentery which swept the village during the 1930s. After the war, however, it had to be dropped because of poor attendance, and was only revived in the mid-1970s, though on a reduced scale in terms of the number of floats. Although people claim that the festival was dropped through there not being enough young people in the village to organise it, it is impossible to confirm this statistically as the local government of Katashina *mura* does not keep records of different villages by age groups. My own statistics, however, show that those belonging to the twenty to thirty-five age-group account for nearly a quarter of the total village population (213 out of 888), slightly higher than for Katashina *mura* as a whole.[15]

Unlike the past, there is no competition among hamlets regarding the splendour of the floats produced. Nevertherless, the residents of different hamlets compete to a certain extent in their reception parties. Although the food served does not extend to raw fish (*o-sashimi*), it often includes western-style potato salad, a variety of pickles, fried bean curd stuffed with rice and mixed vegetable stew. On the whole, the festival provides an occasion to reinforce hamlet solidarity. The area covered along the floats' journey also shows the recognised territorial boundaries of the social, political and religious community. The recent revival of the festival and the relative continuity of the tradition manifest an interesting correlation with the general tendency described in preceding chapters of utilising traditional social and religious forms to express new prosperity and new interests.

Hamlet-level festivals

Unlike village festivals, some of which have enjoyed a recent revival, hamlet-level festivals and the activities of other religious associations known as *kō* are generally on the wane in Hanasaku. The amalgamation of local shrines during the Meiji period under the state Shinto system, which was in part aimed at the more effective functioning of the newly created larger political units such as *mura, ku,* etc. may in some ways be responsible for the decline of hamlet-level festivals. The hamlets in Hanasaku are, however, said to have held one kind of independent festival or another until some time after the Second World War. Now, only three survive, the *Anakannon* festival in Hariyama, the *Kompira-sama* festival in Tochikubo and the *Kokuzō-sama* festival in Noboto. Of these, I have already described the *Anakannon* festival in connection with sericulture and its recent decline. The hamlet festival in Tochikubo in 1982 was similarly a quiet occasion, involving only an offering of red rice to the god and later its distribution among hamlet residents. The *Kokuzō-sama* festival of Noboto, however, presented a somewhat different picture. On the previous day, a work party was organised to clear the footpaths leading to the shrine of the god, located on top of a small mountain at the rear of the hamlet.[16] Road marks and wooden lamps were then placed in trees to show the way to the shrine. On the festival day, the *yado* house, the household whose turn it was to arrange the festival that year, collected one measure of glutinous rice from each hamlet household and prepared *sekihan* rice with red beans it provided itself. Following lunch, everyone went to the shrine to offer the *sekihan* to the god and to distribute it to those who came to show respect. Although a few individuals stayed at the shrine, visits were sporadic and not all residents or representatives of resident households went. The most interesting aspect of this occasion was the sutra chanting meeting afterwards. In the old days, informants said, the sutra chanting was done in front of the shrine after the offering ceremony. Now, it takes place in the hamlet hall, where about twenty women gather and recite sutras to the usual accompaniment of metal sounds. The reciting soon ends, however, and the meeting develops into a dancing party which continues much longer than the recitation itself, and appears to be the main purpose of the gathering.

In this connection, it is worth noting certain differences between *minshuku* and agricultural hamlets in the character of women's gatherings. Women in the former always appear to be more out-going, cheerful and pleasure-seeking than those of the latter. I have already mentioned that the *wakazumakai* or Young Wives' Association, whose activities are mainly recreational, is much more active in *minshuku* hamlets. The same applies to the Friendship Society and the Youth Group. At the *karaoke* singing contest held in Hanasaku in the autumn of 1981, sponsored by the Tourism Development Society, the Friendship Society, the Youth Group

and the Housewives' Association, almost no women from the three agricultural hamlets were present. Although the event was held in the village
hall opened in Tochikubo about three years ago, and hence some distance
from the agricultural hamlets, especially Kuryu and Hariyama, many now
own cars and a number of men came from those hamlets. Most women
who came to see the contest were thus from *minshuku* hamlets and
included not only young women but also a large number of middle-aged
ones, enjoying an evening out. Many of the women from *minshuku* hamlets also frequently participate with the men in the trips organised by the
country inn association including those to Tokyo to advertise their inns.
The women's gatherings I attended in Yamazaki, one of the agricultural
hamlets, were mainly educational: a meeting to learn how to wear a
kimono properly, or how to put on make-up or about the 'proper position'
of a mother in the family and so forth. Many of these meetings are
arranged by factories and companies in Numata which wish to promote
their products (cosmetics, women's underwear, etc.) to village women.
Most of them are held in *minsuku* hamlets as well, but in the agricultural
hamlets, the hours after the meetings are usually spent generally gossiping,
while in the *minshuku* hamlets, they are more often spent dancing or
singing. In addition, groups of women in the *minshuku* hamlets often get
together simply to learn new songs or dances. The hamlet festival of
Noboto, which has the largest number of country inns, seems to have
provided a good occasion for such a women's social gathering, helped by
the fact that it falls in April, the least busy tourist season.

In comparison, the religious meetings for the agricultural god (*o-kōshin-
kō*) which used to fall in August and late November have completely
disappeared in Noboto and Tochikubo.[17] In Kajiya, a few old farm households still meet for a ceremony, while in agricultural hamlets nearly all the
households still participate.[18] Although a number of wayside stones in the
shape of upright slabs inscribed with two Chinese characters reading
Kōshin are found in the village, no rite is specifically performed in front of
them. The *Kōshin* festival in Hanasaku consists instead of a feast at the
yado household, the main dishes on this particular occasion being *udon*
and *soba*, two favourite types of noodle made from wheat and buckwheat
respectively. As in other festivals, one measure of wheat is contributed to
the *yado*, where in the evening one person from each member household
gathers. Most participants are male and it is said that in the old days there
used to be eating competitions on the *Kōshin* day. A few men in the village
are still talked about as old time champions, having eaten twenty or more
servings of *udon* and *soba* at one sitting. In 1981, however, three or four
was about the maximum.

Another two *kō* which have declined are those for the mountain god Jūni-sama and for the god of horses, Batokannon. When almost everyone in the village was engaged in charcoal-making, the *Jūnikō* was one of the most important religious meetings. The residents of each hamlet in Hanasaku formed one *Jūnikō* and used to perform a monthly rite on the eleventh night. Those who are engaged in forestry work still take propitiatory precaution against the mountain god when they become particularly impure, through say a birth or death in their house. In the past, such people were not allowed to enter the mountain for at least a week. Now when they are defiled people normally take a bottle of rice wine or *o-miki* to their work-place and share it with their colleagues after sprinkling it around as an offering to the god. None of the hamlets now hold the monthly rites for the mountain god although all except Yamazaki hold a small shrine ceremony for the officials concerned once a year. The *Jūni-sama* of Yamazaki was destroyed by a typhoon several years ago, after which even the simple annual rite was dropped. Similarly, since there are no longer any horse keepers in the village, there are no *kō* meetings for the horse god either. On the day of the god, 16 January, however, a few cattle raisers cooked some special food and offered it to the god who is represented in the shape of a small wayside stone found in several places around the village.

Unlike the *Jūnikō* or *Koshinkō* organised to worship local gods in relation to specific occupational groups, there are a few *kō* organised to sponsor pilgrimages to famous shrines or temples outside the village. Two of the most widespread of these *kō* were those for *Fudō-sama* in Hiragawa village, Tone *mura* and for the *Akagi-sama* in Oigami of the same *mura*. Although almost all villagers used to belong to these *kō* in the past, now only a few women married into Hanasaku from Hiragawa and Oigami occasionally make pilgrimages there and bring back *fuda*, amuletic papers, to distribute among their neighbours. In contrast to the decline of *kō* activities related to local gods, however, it is interesting to note that a new pilgrim club was recently formed by the entrepreneur family in Kajiya, the owner of the petrol station, to make an annual visit to the *Fudō* temple on Mt. Narita in Chiba prefecture, some forty miles from Tokyo. This is apparently the most famous temple dedicated to Fudō-sama, a deity of Buddhist origin and the same deity to whom the temple in Hiragawa is dedicated. The annual festival at the *Fudō* temple in Narita is so famous that it is often televised nationally and it counts many famous writers, musicians and businessmen among its devotees.[19] The pilgrimage trip to this festival was originally initiated by the entrepreneur as part of the annual bonus for those working for the family, but anyone in the village who pays the necessary expenses can join the trip if they wish.

This chapter has not attempted an exhaustive analysis of all the religious practices and their meanings as they are observed and understood by people in Hanasaku. Rather it has tried to indicate some of the more notable changes in the religious life of the people and place them in the broader context of the village as a whole. Generalisations are difficult to draw. Although some attempt has been made to contrast *minshuku* and agricultural hamlets, differences in the degree of the development of the toruism industry do not always explain the decline or persistence of certain religious activities in different hamlets. Nevertheless, where they have survived, such activities have remained more of a social than religious occasion, as in the cases of the *Gion-matsuri* and the *Kokuzō-sama* festival in Noboto or even with the newly formed pilgrimage club to Narita. This phenomenon indirectly suggests that economic changes or the development of a tourism industry in a village may not always lead to the disappearance of tradition, although the general attitudes of the participants might change. At the same time, it is clear that the persistence or revival of some of the festivals function to reinforce a sense of community membership; hence one could argue that economic changes have not necessarily weakened the community nature of the village even though its residents are no longer economically dependent on each other.

Notes

1 Beardsley, Hall and Ward 1959: 447.
2 Although the present resident priest claims to be the nineteenth descendant of its original priest, *Senfukuji* apparently has not always had a resident priest in the past. Until the Meiji period (1868–1912), the *Ryōgenji* in Numata used to send its priest to officiate at ceremonies for *Senfukuji* parishioners. Later on the *Ryōgenji* priest sent his younger brother to be the *Senfukuji* resident priest and the present one is an adopted son of this priest.
3 Earhart 1969: 14.
4 Dore 1958: 297–8.
5 Itabashi 1980: 94.
6 The same legend has also been reported for western Gunma prefecture in relation to a different god; cf. Sofue et al 1972.
7 Hariyama came into existence as a separate settlement only during the late Tokugawa period. Perhaps for this reason, the hamlet holds a ceremony separately beforehand and participates in the main part of the festival later on only as an observer; Moon Kim 1984: 61, 218.
8 Normally branches of a tree called *sasaki* (Cleyera Ochnacea) are used at Shinto ceremonies; Embree 1939: 43–4; Dore 1958: 303; Blacker 1975: 40; Hendry 1981: 85. I was unable to find out whether the tree referred to as *hinoki* in this area is identical with

sasaki, but the priest claimed that any kind of evergreen tree has a purificatory value at Shinto rituals.

9 Unknown grave stones and those of households which do not belong to any existing 'extended household group' are usually placed in the back garden of the village temple. Likewise, the house-gods (*yashiki-inari*) of discontinued households or those who left the village are usually brought to the shrine compound.

10 In the case of *fukusenji-gumi* of lower Yamazaki, the right to become the monkey has recently been limited to members of the extended household group who also belong to the same neighbourhood group although the same does not apply to the other three groups in Kajiya.

11 Satō 1980: 137.

12 In order to prove his descent from a feudal lord the head of one member household of the group produced a written genealogy on which the names of ancestors of the preceding nine generations were recorded, ending with the grandfather of the present head. Unfortunately, however, I was unable to confirm the authenticity of the document.

13 Oto 1983: 33–4.

14 *Ibid.*; Sakurai 1980: 95.

15 Katashina *mura* statistics:

	1965	1970	1975	1980
Total population	7,570	6,754	6,228	6,134
Twenty to thirty-five age group	1,433	1,191	1,101	1,262
Percent	18.9	17.6	17.7	20.6

16 Although Kokuzō-sama is referred to as a *Hotoke-sama* rather than *kami-sama*, signifying that it is deity of Buddhist origin, neither the rituals involved nor its general protective function in relation to the particular territorial group differ much from those held in honour of other guardian deities of Shinto origin.

17 A variety of associations described as *kō* have been reported throughout Japan; Embree 1939: 138–51; Nakane 1967: 146–8; Hori 1968: 66–8; Fukutake 1972: 106; Hendry 1981: 66–9. Many of these are religious groups, but some are a type of credit association created to meet unexpected expenses.

18 Even in agricultural hamlets, the August festival was dropped a few years ago as the month became one of the busiest seasons due to the introduction of various vegetable crops.

19 Dore 1958: 331.

Conclusion:
The revitalisation of tradition

In the preceding chapters I have shown how Hanasaku village in central Japan has changed over the past twenty-five years. In this final chapter I shall try to explain why it has altered the way it has by analysing the major features of economic and social change in Hanasaku and by examining how these features are interconnected. From this perspective we may be able to make a few statements with regard to the more general issue of the relation between economic development and social change.

As with all the other village communities in Japan, Hanasaku is also part of a nation and of the world, and the course of its recent history has thus been inevitably affected by forces external to the community. The decline of traditional supplementary occupations such as the charcoal industry, timbering and animal husbandry, the shift of crops from subsistence food crops to rice and vegatables grown for cash, the spread of agricultural machinery and decrease in the labour needs of farming can all be considered as changes directly and indirectly derived from changes at the national and international level, which have affected many other villages in a similar way.[1]

The impact of these developments on community organisation, however, does not seem to be identical everywhere. When non-farming jobs to which the population superfluous to agriculture can turn become available locally, for instance, the movement may not necessarily be disruptive to community organisation. This is perhaps the first point where Hanasaku diverges from other villages. As we have seen, the development of tourism as a local industry in Hanasaku more or less coincided with the gradual decline of other supplementary occupations. Although the capital to build the ski resort came from outside, the villagers as land owners were able to keep the jobs for themselves. The development of the tourism industry together with the increase in local construction work, therefore, has provided enough substitute jobs to prevent any large-scale emigration occurring in the village. Although the actual population has decreased, there has been little family-level emigration, and this is one of the crucial factors for understanding the process of social change in Hanasaku since it means that the basic framework of the village social organisation has remained unchanged.

Secondly, contrary to the general assumption, the greater involvement in wage-earning activities does not in itself undermine the traditional functioning of the household. To combine farming with other occupations has in fact been the general pattern of the household economy in mountain villages like Hanasaku. The nature of supplementary occupations has changed from charcoal-making and forestry work to construction labour and the like. Except for a few cases where the inn business has completely taken over from farming as a household occupation, farming still remains the 'main' enterprise for most households to which all the other economic activities are subordinated. The potential succession crisis that some farm households are now faced with mainly arises from the fact that this pattern may not continue if it no longer appeals to the young.

Here one may argue that the development of a tourism industry in the village and the closer contact with urban people that the industry involves have affected young people's attitude toward the 'traditional' way of life in a negative way. Such an explanation seems to me inadequate, however. The issue is much more complicated than that. As will be argued later, the contact with urban people does not necessarily foster a negative attitude toward traditional ways of life, nor is the latter in any way more notice-able in Hanasaku than in any other village. There is of course the general tendency of the young to turn away from farming and other physical work, but surely such a tendency is not a phenomenon unique to Hana-saku. What appears to be certain is that the continuity of some farm households is threatened not so much because the ideology concerning the household itself has changed as because jobs available for them are not satisfactory. The first sons and the first daughters when there is no son still think that they should remain and succeed to the household. It is largely because of this idea that most of them stay at home or return home, despite the fact that they are no longer interested in farming as an occupa-tion and despite the difficulties in finding a marriage partner mentioned previously. More often it is the parents who express the view that they do not necessarily want their children to remain in the countryside if farming and wage-labour are the only possibilities open for them. Such an opinion rarely leads to overt action. Few parents actively encourage their would-be successors to leave the community. It does not necessarily betray that they no longer care about the continuity of their households either. It simply expresses the priority given to the 'better' future of their children as compared to their belief that farming of the family estate should continue.

This brings us to the third element which we might consider unique to

Hanasaku. The advent of tourism in the village opened new opportunities for the parents faced with the above dilemma: namely starting an inn as a household enterprise. The business provided the young, both male and female, with an occupation more stable and attractive than farming and other wage-labour outside the household. Hence those who started the businesses were able to consolidate the continuity of their households as well as the traditional function of the household as an economic unit. While in a household which combines farming and wage-earning jobs there are now few occasions for its members to work together, a family-run inn by its nature requires a greater degree of co-operation among its members. The advent of a tourism industry in certain hamlets of Hanasaku has thus contributed towards strengthening rather than weakening the household organisation in its traditional form while in those hamlets that have remained predominantly agricultural both the continuity and functioning of traditional households, *ie,* are much more seriously threatened.

What is significant here is of course that it is the small-scale, family-run *minshuku* that are more widely developed than any other form of tourist catering businesses. This fact clearly indicates that the forces of tradition or certain elements of traditonal social organisation may positively determine the ways new economic opportunities are incorporated and thus challenges the view that social change accompanying economic development is always a one-way traffic from the 'traditional' to the 'modern'.

Fourthly, then, a question arises whether the pattern of economic diversification in Hanasaku has weakened the traditional solidarity of the village community. For example, may we assert that values are deteriorating and the community is less co-operative and less harmonious nowadays than in the past? I have shown in Chapters 4 and 7 that conflicts are appearing within the village as a result of recent economic diversification, for example, between the villagers who manage the ski resort and those who work for it, or between the inn operators and the farmers. On the whole, however, the dividing tendency is largely counter-balanced by the fact that Hanasaku is no longer a microcosm of its own, but part of a larger political system. Because Katashina *mura* lies in a region where ecological conditions are not altogether favourable for agriculture, the local government has, over the past decades, adopted a policy of local development which emphasises the tourism industry and agriculture to an equal extent. One consequence of this policy is that the tourist industry has developed not only in Hanasaku but also in many other villages in the *mura*. Hanasaku being one of the eight districts under the new administrative system of Katashina *mura*, its residents have to compete with those of other districts for government subsidies whether it be for agricultural development or for the development of the tourism industry. Despite the existing differences of individual interests, therefore, people often find it more advantageous for them to close ranks in the name of the village, an aspect expressed in the way that items for the 'citizens' requests' are selected (Chapter 7). The same also applies to the division of the village into hamlet units, in that the increase of political interaction with the outside often necessitates the subordination of loyalty to the hamlet to the unity of the village as a whole.

The 'village solidarity' in this modern context is therefore not something given but something achieved through a continuous process of negotiation in a similar sense to that in which Anthony Giddens once argued for social norms in general.[2] However, this does not necessarily mean that traditional community unity is now less emphasised. There may be more diverging elements nowadays than in the past since villages are on the whole less isolated and homogeneous than before and for this reason the process of negotiation may be more complicated and slow, but community solidarity and unity are still highly valued and considered worth striving for.[3]

The final and the most remarkable aspect of the ways in which the Hanasaku people have responded to the new economic prosperity is the proliferation of social and religious activities. The most notable part of the phenomenon is the increase in the number of ritual activities surrounding the household unit. People also often meet for sports, recreation, festivals and so on, and some of the religious festivals concerning the units of extended household groups, hamlets and the village have been revived to serve a social function. The revival of certain festivals may be partly interpreted as reflecting the nationwide phenomenon termed the 'tradition cult' (dentō sūhai).[4] The designation of the main village festival, Saruoi-matsuri, as a national cultural asset and the subsequent governmental support can also be seen as a part of the same phenomenon. Whatever the motivation behind these moves, it is clear that increased social interaction reinforces village solidarity, especially when it is in line with traditional practices.

Even when the new developments do not accord with traditional practices, however, they do not necessarily destroy the latter. Increased economic opportunities have reduced the status differentials between main and branch households, and the latter are no longer economically subordinate to the former. Nevertheless, we have seen in Chapter 6 that social and ritual ties are largely maintained between them on an equal basis in the form of the shinrui relationship. Similarly, different life styles and the mechanisation of cultivation have reduced or eliminated the need for large-scale co-operation in such activities as roof thatching, funerals, and rice transplanting. While the scale of co-operation has been accordingly reduced, however, the underlying principles. (e.g. those of reciprocity, participation by household, etc.) are still adhered to. In Chapter 7 we have also seen that, while the number of local associations has increased and their activities have diversified, the new associations are still formed and recognised under the traditional group organising principles, i.e. those based on the territorial divisions of the village.

The evidence from Hanasaku thus leads us to reconsider some of the theoretical assumptions regarding economic development and social change in general: especially those which suggest a kind of unilineal transformation of societies or those in a similar vein which suggest that economic development, by eliminating the economic necessity for co-operation, will eventually lead to a decline in community solidarity. One of the underlying assumptions of these views seems to be that 'tradition' is something static and passive in nature and thus more likely to be acted upon than the reverse. From what we have observed in Hanasaku, however, we may conclude to the contrary: tradition has a dynamic autonomy of its own to regenerate itself even in the midst of the most drastic economic change. As mentioned earlier, although social actions may not be repetitive, the basic principles not only continue but also can be reinforced and revitalised in their traditional form as a consequence of economic development.[5]

On the whole, the subjects dealt with in this book, namely the social and cultural consequences of economic development or more specifically those of tourism, have not so far attracted much of anthropologists' attention. Nash once pointed out that one reason for the relative lack of anthropologists study of tourism is the a priori view often held by anthropologists that tourism is something that has been 'imposed' upon the societies they study and is thus 'bad' for such societies.[6] A similar interpretation is perhaps possible for the relative lack of anthropological study of economic development in general. Economic development may not be altogether 'bad', but it is often thought to transform the basic social forms and hence it has been more of a sociologist's concern than an anthropologist's whose main interest lies with traditional social forms rather than their changes. One of the main purposes of this book is to show that such an assumption is not necessarily right. As previously shown, tourism has provided for the people in Hanasaku a kind of positive adaptive strategy with which they can manipulate the changing economic situation to their advantage.

Furthermore, it is also possible that the 'tradition' itself may provide the villagers with an important resource to be exploited in their attempt to shape the tourism they receive. Signs of this are already appearing. It was mentioned in Chapter 4 that the original attraction of small-scale family-run inns (*minshuku*) for city-dwellers was that they provide more opportunities for 'learning about the country life' and 'mixing with the people'. This reflects a general attitude prevalent among the tourists. Catching on to this, therefore, the villagers have not only built sports facilities to attract more tourists but also have reconstructed some of their traditional life style, such as open hearths burning charcoal, tools for hand-pounding rice cakes etc. although they themselves no longer use such facilities.

This phenomenon is clearly related to the nationwide trend of the 'traditional cult' mentioned earlier, and at both the local and national levels, the process involves certain elements of 'invention of tradition'.[7] It seems therefore that tradition is not only reinforced and revitalised in a certain context of economic development, but also continuously redefined and reformulated. It is only when this transactional aspect between the autonomous force of tradition and invention of tradition on the one hand and the overall modernising forces that are commonly supposed to accompany economic development on the other has been properly considered that we can fully comprehend the complexities involved in the dynamics of social and cultural change.

Notes

1 The extent and dramatic nature of the increase in agricultural productivity in Japan has been described by Dore 1978: 105–6. Cf. Moon Kim 1984: 370–1.
2 Giddens 1976.
3 Cf. Smith 1978. When discussing people's effort to patch up the split in community following the destructive Clover Incident in Kurusu, Smith also mentions an attitude to the similar effect.
4 Cf. Moeran 1981a: 36.
5 Epstein 1962 presents a case where economic devleopment accompanying the construction of an irrigation system in a south Indian village has resulted in the reinforcement of traditional social practices.
6 Nash 1981: 465.
7 Cf. Hobsbawm E. and T. Ranger eds. 1983.

Glossary

This glossary brings together, for reference, all the Japanese words which appear more than once in the text and are partially discussed in different places. Words already translated in the text are not included.

amazake	甘酒	sweet drink made of rice often used as a ceremonial drink in Hanasaku, especially for women
arabon	新盆	the first bon festival after a person's death
bon (O-bon)	盆	midsummer festival for the dead
bunke	分家	branch house
buraku	部落	hamlet (pp. 2–3)
butsudan	仏壇	Buddhist altar
chūsen	抽選	a lottery; balloting
daikoku bashira	大黒柱	the principal pillar of a house; the successor
dōzoku	同族	extended household group (pp. 118–21)
ē	ええ	a form of reciprocal labour exchange
ē-gaeshi	ええ返し	return of ē labour already received
fūfuyōshi	夫婦養子	adopted couple (p. 101)
fushinkaya	普請茅	reed for roof-thatching
gaiseki	外戚	literally out-relations; those related to the members of a household through a married-in member, male or female
gochō-gumi	伍長組	institutionalised neighbourhood group; sometimes referred to as *tonari-gumi* 隣組
gunsha	郡社	the main Shinto shrine in a county under the pre-war state Shinto system
gyoseimura	行政村	administrative village (p. 9, n. 3)
hitsuban	櫃番	a ritual role in the *Saruoi-matsuri* of Hanasaku
hiyatoi	日雇い	day labourer
hōkōnin	奉公人	resident servant
honke	本家	main house
hotokesama	仏様	buddha; also applied to anyone who has died recently
hyakushō	百姓	farmer
ie	家	house or household
ihai	位牌	ancestral tablet
ikke	一家	local term for dōzoku
inkyo	隠居	retirement from the main positions of a household such as Head
iwashi	いわし	sardine, a type of fish often used in religious ceremonies in Hanasaku

jōkai	常会	regular meetings of the hamlet assembly in Hanasaku
jun'yōshi	順養子	brother or sister adopted into the position of a son or a daughter (p. 101)
kaimyō	戒名	posthumous Buddhist name
kamidana	神棚	a Shinto god-shelf
kasogenshō	過疎現象	phenomenon of rural under-population
katoku	家督	the headship of a household
kaya	茅	miscanthus; a type of reed used for roof-thatching as well as for sacks
kayayama	茅山	a communally owned mountain which grows *kaya*
kō	講	a type of group or association, mostly religious in nature, but sometimes organised with a co-operative or recreational purpose
kōkeisha mondai	後継者問題	difficulties in finding a successor to a household
ku	区	a sub-unit of the new administrative village, *mura*, translated here as district
kumi	組	anything that comprises a part of the whole; sometimes a hamlet (*buraku*) is referred to as a *kumi* and hamlet representative as *kumichō*
kusayama	草山	a communally owned mountain which used to provide grass for household cattle, materials for manure fertiliser and firewood
mabiki	間引き	a type of infanticide (p. 20)
mago shintakku	孫新宅	literally a grandchild branch; a branch household of a branch household
meishin	迷信	superstition
michi-bushin	道普請	road repair
mimai	見舞	a sympathy call (p. 93, n. 7)
minshuku	民宿	a country inn
minshuku mura	民宿村	a village in a tourist resort where many small-scale country inns have developed
miokuri	見送り	a ceremony conducted as a part of a funeral in Hanasaku to send off the spirit of a dead person (p. 126)
miuchi	身内	personal kindred (pp. 125–30)
mujin	無尽	material help or labour service which is provided as part of community obligation and is expected to be reciprocated
mujinkō	無尽講	a mutual aid association
mukei bunkazai	無形文化財	Intangible Cultural Asset
mura	村	administrative village; see *gyoseimura*
mura hachibu	村八部	a mechanism for village ostracisation
nakōdo	仲人	go-between
nenbutsu	念仏	Buddhist sutra chanting
nenkan	年間	a term for full-time employees of the Olympia ski ground in Hanasaku
ninsoku	人足	community labour pool in Hanasaku
ōhonke	大本家	literally 'big main house', meaning main household of one's own main household
okyaku-sama	御客様	chief guests at a wedding ceremony
omiki	お神酒	rice wine (sake) offered to a god

Glossary

ōya	大屋	patron household in relation to a new-comer household (*waraji-nugi*) in the village
oyabun-kobun	親分 - 子分	a type of patron-client relation
sakaban	酒番	a ritual role *in Saruoi-matsuri*
Saruoi-matsuri	猿追い祭り	name of the main village festival in Hanasaku; see Chapter 8
seinendan	青年団	the Youth Group
sekihan	赤飯	rice cooked with red azuki beans, used on occasions of celebration
senzo	先祖	ancestors
shi-zunchū	シーヅン中	literally 'during the season'; those employed by the Olympia ski ground in Hanasaku during the skiing season only
shinbokukai	親睦会	the Friendship Society
shinchikuiwai	新築祝い	house-warming party
shinrui	親類	household which assumes a patron-like role in Hanasaku
shintaku	新宅	local term for branch household
shizenmura	自然村	'natural village' as opposed to the new administrative village (p. 9, n. 3)
sonsha (mura yashiro)	村社	the main village shrine under the pre-war state Shinto system
tensaku undō	転作運動	a nation-wide campaign to discourage rice production
tetsudaikō	手伝講	mutual-aid association
tokubaiyama	特賣山	mountain range whose right of use was leased out by the government, on a special application made communally, to the farmers in Hanasaku for charcoal-making
ujigami	氏神	a tutelary diety
ujikosōdai	氏子総代	association for the management of the village Shinto shrine and its property
wakazumakai	若妻会	the Young Wives' Association in Hanasaku
waraji-nugi	わらじ脱ぎ	an immigrant household
watamashi	渡まし	gift presented at a household ceremony by relatives
yakudoshi	厄年	inauspicious ages
yashiki inari	屋敷いなり	main guardian deity of a household
zashiki	座敷	the most formal room in a Japanese house

Bibliography

The following abbreviations have been adopted:

AA	American Anthropologist
AJS	American Journal of Sociology
APSR	American Political Science Review
ATR	Annals of Tourism Research
CA	Current Anthropology
CSSH	Comparative Studies in Society and History
FEQ	Far Eastern Quarterly
ITR	Interim Technical Report, Ohio State University Research Foundation, Columbus
JRAI	Journal of Royal Anthropological Institute
MD	*Minkan Denshō*
MFL	Marriage and Family Living
MK	*Minzokugaku Kenkyū*
MN	*Minzokugaku Nempō*
OPCJS	Occasional Papers, Center for Japanese Studies, University of Michigan
P8ICAES	Proceedings of the 8th International Congress of Anthropological and Ethnographical Sciences
PS	Population Studies
SSK	*Sonraku Shakai Kenkyū*
SWJA	Southwestern Journal of Anthropology
TASJ	Transactions of the Asiatic Society of Japan
Trns.	Translated by

Ariga, Kizaemon. 1943. *Nihon Kazoku Seido to Kosaku Seido (Japanese Family System and Tenant System)*. Tokyo: Kawade shobō
—— 1954. 'The Family in Japan'. *MFL* 16: 362–73
Asakawa, Kanichi. 1903. *The Early Institutional Life of Japan*. Tokyo: Waseda Univ. Press
Bachnik, Jane M. 1983. 'Recruitment Strategies for Household Succession: Rethinking Japanese Household Organisation'. *Man* (N.S.) 18: 160–82
Beardsley, Richard K. 1951. 'The Household in the Status System of Japanese Villages'. *OPCJS* 1: 62–74
Beardsley, Richard K. *et al.* 1959. *Village Japan*. Chicago: University of Chicago Press
Befu, Harumi. 1962. 'Corporate Emphasis and Patterns of Descent in Japanese Family'. In Smith & Beardsley, eds., *Japanese Culture: Its Development and Characteristics*. Viking Fund Publications in Anthropology 34. New York: Wenner Gren Foundation
—— 1963. 'Patrilineal Descent and Personal Kindred in Japan'. *AA* 65: 1328–41
—— 1971. *Japan, an Anthropological Introduction*. San Fransisco: Chandler

—— & Edward Norbeck. 1958. 'Japanese Usages of Terms of Relationship'. *SWJA* 14: 66–86

Bennett, John W. 1967. 'Japanese Economic Growth: Background for Social Change'. In R. P. Dore ed., *Aspects of Social Change in Modern Japan*: 411–53. Princeton, New Jersey: Princeton Univ. Press

—— & Iwao Ishino. 1963. *Paternalism in the Japanese Economy: Anthropological Studies of Oyabun-kobun Patterns*. Minneapolis: Univ. of Minneapolis Press

Bernstein, Gail. 1976. 'Women in Rural Japan'. In Lebra *et al.* eds., *Women in Changing Japan*: 25–49. Boulder, Colorado: Westview Press

Blacker, Carmen. 1975. *The Catalpa Bow*. London: Allen & Unwin

Braibanti, Ralph. 1948. 'Neighbourhood Associations in Japan and their Democratic Potentialities'. *FEQ* 7(2): 136–64

Brown, Keith. 1966. '*Dōzoku* and Ideology of Descent in Rural Japan'. *AA* 68: 1129–51

—— 1968. 'The Content of *Dōzoku* Relationships in Japan'. *Ethnography* 7: 204–14

—— & Michio Suenari. 1966. 'The Establishment of Branch Household – Examples from Farm Villages in the Environs of Misusawa City, Iwate Prefecture'. *MK* 31: 38–48

Chang, Kenne H-K. 1970. 'The *Inkyo* System in Southwestern Japan'. *Ethnography* 9: 342–57

Clement, John B. 1902. 'Japanese Calendars'. *TASJ* 30: 1–82

Cornell, John B, 1964. '*Dōzoku*: An Example of Evolution and Transition in Japanese Village Society'. *CSSH* 6(4): 449–80

—— & Robert J. Smith. 1956. *Two Japanese Villages*. Ann, Arbor: Univ. of Michigan Press

Dalton, George, ed. 1971. *Economic Development and Social Change: The Modernization of Village Communities*. New York: The Natural History Press

De Vos, George & Hiroshi Wagatsuma. 1966. *Japan's Invisible Race*. Berkeley: Univ. of California Press

Donohue, John D. 1957. 'An *Eta* Community of Japan: the Social Persistence of Outcast Groups'. *AA* 63: 1204–30

—— 1977. *Pariah Persistence in Changing Japan: A Case Study*. Washington: Univ. of America Press

Dore, Ronald P. 1953. 'Japanese Rural Fertility: Some Social and Economic Factors'. *PS* 7: 62–88

—— 1958. *City Life in Japan*. London: Routledge and Kegan Paul

—— 1959. *Land Reform in Japan*. London: Oxford Univ. Press

—— 1978. *Shinohata: A Portrait of a Japanese Village*. London: Allen Lane

——, ed. 1967. *Aspects of Social Change in Modern Japan*. Princeton, New Jersey: Princeton Univ. Press

Dorson, Richard M., ed. 1973. *Studies in Japanese Folklore*. New York: Kennikat Press

Dull, P. S. 1954. 'The Political Structure of a Japanese Village'. *FEQ* 13: 175–90

Earhart, H. Byron. 1969. *Japanese Religion: Unity and Diversity*. Belmont, California: Dickenson

—— 1974. *Religion in the Japanese Experience*. Belmont, California: Dickenson

Eisenstadt, S. N. 1966. *Modernization: Protest and Change*. Englewood Cliffs, New Jersey: Prentice-Hall

—— 1970. 'Social Change and Development'. In E. N. Eisenstadt, ed., *Readings in Social Evolution and Development*. Oxford and London: Pergamon Press

Embree, John F. 1939. *Suye Mura: A Japanese Village*. Chicago: Univ. of Chicago Press

—— 1941. 'Some Social Functions of Religion in Rural Japan'. *AJS* 47: 184–9

—— 1944. 'Japanese Administration at the Local Level'. *Applied Anthropology* 3: 11–18

Epstein, T. S. 1962. *Economic Development and Social Change in South India*. Manchester: Manchester Univ. Press

Erskine, William. 1933. *Japanese Festivals and Calendar Lore*. Tokyo: Kyō Bun Kwan

Evans-Pritchard, E. E. 1940. *The Nuer: A Description of the Modes of Livelihood and Political Institutions of a Nilotic People*. Oxford: Clarendon Press

Firth, Raymond. 1954. 'Social Organisation and Social Change' *JRAI* 84

Freeman, J. D. 1961. 'On the Concept of the Kindred'. *JRAI* 91: 192–220

Fujisaki, Hiroshi. 1957. *Kankonsōsai Jiten (Dictionary of Ceremonial)*. Tokyo: Tsuru Shobo

Fukutake, Tadashi. 1967. *Japanese Rural Society*. Trns. R.P. Dore. Tokyo: Oxford Univ. Press

—— 1981. *Japanese Society Today (2nd edition)*. Tokyo: Univ. of Tokyo Press

—— 1982. *The Japanese Social Structure: Its Evolution in the Modern Century*. Trns. R. P. Dore, Tokyo: Univ. of Tokyo Press

Giddens, A. 1976. *New Rules of Sociological Method*. London: Hutchinson

Gluckman, Max. 1958. *Analysis of a Social Situation in Modern Zululand*. Rhodes Livingstone Papers 28. Manchester: Manchester Univ. Press

Graburn, N. H. H. 1977. 'Tourism: The Sacred Journey'. In Valene Smith, ed.: 17–31

—— 1983. *To Pray, Pay and Play: The Cultural Structure of Japanese Tourism*. Aix-en-Provence: Centre des Hautes Etudes Touristiques. Serie B (26)

Hall, John W. & Marius B. Jansen. 1958. *Studies in the Institutional History of Early Modern Japan*. Princeton, New Jersey: Princeton Univ. Press

Hearn, Lafacadio. 1924. *Japan: An Attempt at Interpretation*. New York: Macmillan

Hendry, Joy. 1981. *Marriage in Changing Japan: Community and Society*. London: Croom Helm

Hirayama, Toshijiro. 1973. 'Seasonal Rituals Connected with Rice Culture'. In Dorson, ed.: 57–75

Hobsbawm E. & T. Ranger, eds. 1983. *The Invention of Tradition*. Cambridge: Cambridge Univ. Press

Hori, Ichiro. 1968. *Folk Religion in Japan*. Chicago: Univ. of Chicago Press

—— 1972. *Japanese Religion*. Trns. Yoshida Abe and David Reid. Tokyo: Kodansha International

Hoselitz, B. F. 1960. *Sociological Factors in Economic Development*. Chicago: Free Press

Ishino, Iwao. 1953. 'The *Oyabun-kobun*: A Japanese Ritual Kinship Institution'. *AA* 55: 695–707

—— 1962. 'Social and Technological Change in Rural Japan: Continuities and Discontinuities'. In Smith & Beardsley, eds.: 102–12

—— & John Bennett. 1953. *Types of Japanese Rural Community*. ITR 6. Columbus, Ohio

Isono, Fujiko. 1964. 'The Family and Women in Japan'. *The Sociological Review (Univ. of Keele)* 12(1): 39–54

Itabashi, Haruo. 1980. *Saruoi Matsuri no Chōsha Hōkoku (A Report of Saruoi Festival)*. Isezaki: Gunma Rekishi Minzoku Kenkyūkai

Itō, Abito. 1982. 'Shimogoto Sakiyama ni oite no Nōgyō to Shakai Henka (Agriculture and Social Change in Sakiyama, Shimogoto')'. *Bunka Jinruigaku Hōkoku 3: 31–54*. Tokyo: Univ. of Tokyo Press

Iwamoto, Mitsuya. 1978. 'Shinrui Soshiki to Sonraku Seikatsu (Kinship Organisation and Village Life')'. *Nihon Minzokugaku 118: 1–17*

Iwamoto, Yuderu. 1970a. *Kinsei Gyōsongyōdōtai no Hensen Katei (Changes of Fishing Communities in the Modern Period)*. Tokyo: Koshobo

—— 1970b. '1965 nen Iko no Gyōdōtai Kenkyū no Dōkō (Community Studies after 1965)'.

Gyōdōtai no Shiteki Kosatsu (2nd ed.) (*A History of Community Studies*). Tokyo: Nihon Hyōronsha

Izumi, Seiichi & Masao Gamō. 1952. 'Nihon Shakai no Chiikisei (Regional Character in Japanese Society)'. *Shin Nihon Chiri Taikei* 1: 37–73

Izumi, Seiichi & Nobuhiro Nagashima. 1963. 'Katoku Sōzoku kara mita Nihon no Higashi to Nishi (East and West Japan from the Viewpoint of Succession System)'. *Kokubungaku Kaishaku to Kanshō* 28(5): 121–6

Johnson, Erwin H. 1967. 'Status Changes in Hamlet Structure Accompanying Modernization'. In R. P. Dore, ed.: 153–83

—— 1976. *Nagura mura: An Ethnohistorical Analysis*. New York: Ithaca

Jōya, Mock. 1955. *Japanese Customs and Manners*. Tokyo: The Sakurai Shōten

Kanabe, T. 1967. 'Shinrui ni kansuru ichi kosatsu (A Study of Kindred)'. *Bunka Jinruigaku* 1(1): 3–40. Tokyo. Daigaku Bunka Jinruigakkai

Katashina no Minzoku. 1960. (Folkways of Katashina). Gunma Kyōiku Iinkai

Katashina Sonshi. 1963. (A History of Katashina). Katashina Sonshi Hensan Iinkai

Kawamoto, Akira. 1967. 'Kenkarison no Shakai Kōzō – Shimane Ken Sanson no Jirei (The Social Structure of Household Migration: A Case Study of Mountain Village, Shimane Prefecture)'. *Nōgyō Keizai Kenkyū* 38(1)

Kim, Ok-pyo Moon. 1979. *Outcaste Relations in Four Japanese Villages: A comparative Study*. Unpublished M. Litt. Thesis. Univ. of Oxford

—— 1984. *Economic Development and Social Change in a Japanese Village*. Unpublished D. Phil. Thesis. Univ. of Oxford

Kinoshita, K., Y. Yamamoto & M. Sasaki. 1978. '*Toshi Kinkō ni okeru Shūraku no Kinō* (The Functions of Suburban Villages)'. *SSK* 14: 3–40

Kitano, Seiichi. 1939. '*Kōshū Sanson no Dōzoku Soshiki to Oyakokata Kankō* (*Dōzoku* System and *Oyakokata* Custom in a Mountain Village in Yamanashi Prefecture)'. *MN* 2: 41–95

—— 1962. '*Dōzoku* and *Ie* in Japan? In Smith & Beardsley, eds.: 42–6

—— 1970. '*Dōzoku* and Kindred in a Japanese Rural Society'. In Reuben Hill & Rene König, eds. *Families in East and West*. 248–69. Paris and The Hague: Mouton

Kitaoji, Hironobu. 1971. 'The Structure of the Japanese Family'. *AA* 73: 1036–57

Koike, Zenkichi. 1981. *Gunma no Sonraku Kōzō* (*Village Structure of Gunma Prefecture*). Gunma: Maebashi

Koyama, Takashi. 1964. 'Changing Family Structure in Japan'. In Smith & Beardsley, eds.: 47–54

Kunimoto, Yoshiro. 1973. 'Deserted Mountain Villages of Western Japan'. *Japan Quarterly* 20(1): 87–96

Lebra, Joyce *et al*. eds. 1976. *Women in Changing Japan*. Boulder, Colorado: Westview Press

Lebra Takie S. & William Lebra. 1974. *Japanese Culture and Behaviour*. Honolulu: Univ. of Hawaii

Lewis, Davis C. 1986. '"Years of Calamity": *Yakudoshi* Observed in a City'. In J. Hendry & J. Webber, eds. *Interpreting Japanese Society*. Oxford: JASO Occasional Papers 5

Maeda, Takashi. 1976. *Summary of Ane Katoku (Elder Sister Inheritance)*. Osaka: Kansai Univ. Press

Malinowski, B. 1945. *The Dynamics of Culture Change*. Yale Univ. Press

Matsubara, Haruo. 1957. *Nōson Shakai no Kōzō (Village Social Structure)*. In Fukutake Tadashi, Hidaka Rokuro and Takahashi Akira, eds. *Kōza Shakaigaku* 4. Univ. of Tokyo Press

Matsumoto, Y. Scott. 1962. 'Notes on Primogeniture'. In Smith & Beardsley, eds.: 55–69

Matsunaga, Kazuto. 1981. '*Fukuoka Ken Yame Shi Kinkō Nōson no Henka Katei* (Economic and Social Change in a Farming Village near Yame City, Fukuoka Prefecture, Japan)'. *MK* 46(3): 249–74

Mead, Margaret. 1953. *Cultural Patterns and Technological Change.* UNESCO

—— 1956. *New Lives for Old.* New York: William Morrow & Co.

Meyer, Milton W. 1976. *Japan: A Concise History (revised edition).* Totowa, New Jersey: Littlefield, Adams & Co.

Morean, Brian. 1980. *Production, Marketing and Aesthetic Appraisal in a Japanese Pottery Community.* Unpublished Ph.D. Thesis. School of Oriental and African Studies, Univ. of London

—— 1981. 'Japanese Social Organization and the Mingei Movement'. *Pacific Affairs 54(1):* 42–56

—— 1981a. 'Tradition, The Past and The Ever-Changing Present in a Pottery Village'. In P.G. O'Neill, ed.: 32–6

—— 1983. 'The Language of Japanese Tourism'. *ATR* 10: 93–108

—— 1984. *Lost Innocence: Folk Craft Potters of Onta, Japan.* Berkeley: Univ. of California Press

Moore, Ray A. 1970. 'Adoption and Samurai Mobility in Tokugawa Japan'. *Journal of Asian Studies* 29(3): 617–32

Moore, W. E. 1963. *Social Change.* Englewood Cliffs, New Jersey: Prentice-Hall Inc.

Murdoch, James. 1926. *History of Japan Vol. 3.* New York: Greenberg

Naito, Kanji. 1970. 'Inheritance Practices on a Catholic Island: Youngest Son Inheritance'. *Social Compass* 17: 21–36

—— & Teigo Yoshida. 1965. 'A Social Anthropological Study on an Island Village – Komuta Community in Koshiki Island, Kagoshima Prefecture'. *MK* 30(3): 209–27

Nakamura, Yoshiji. 1971. *Nihon no Sonrakugyōdotai (Japanese Village Communities, new edition).* Tokyo: Nihon Hyōronsha

Nakane, Chie. 1967. *Kinship and Economic Organization in Rural Japan.* London: The Athlone Press

—— 1970. *Japanese Society.* London: Weidenfeld and Nicolson

—— 1980. '*Ie no Kōzō* (Houshold Structure)'. In *Ie, Tokyo Daigaku Kōkai Kōza* 11: 3–27

Nakano, Takashi. 1964. *Shōka Dōzokudan no Kenkyū (A Study of Merchant Dōzoku Groups).* Tokyo: Miraisha

—— 1967. '*Mura no Kaitai* (Disintegration of Village Community)'. *SSK* 2: 255–82

Nakayasu, Sadako. 1965. '*Kenkarison* (Household Migration)'. *Nihon Nōgyō Nenpo* 14: *Henbō suru Nōson.* Tokyo: Ochanomizu Shōbo

Nalson, John. 1982. 'Quiet Revolution in Traditional Society'. In Ronald Frankenberg, ed. *Custom and Conflict in British Society.* 70–93. Manchester: Manchester Univ. Press

Naoe, Hiroji. 1973. 'A Study of Yashikigami: The Deity of House and Ground'. In Dorson, ed.: 198–14

Nash, Dennison. 1981. Tourism as an Anthropological Subject'. *CA* 22(5): 461–81

Ninomiya, T. 1974. 'The Role of Sociologists in Social Development in Post War Japan'. In T. Fukutake and K. Moriyoka, eds. *Sociology and Social Development in Asia.* Tokyo: Univ. of Tokyo Press

Norbeck, Edward. 1953. 'Age-Grading in Japan'. *AA* 55: 373–84

—— 1954. *Takashima: A Japanese Fishing Community.* Salt Lake City: Univ. of Utah Press

—— 1955. '*Yakudoshi*, A Japanese Complex of Supernaturalistic Beliefs'. *SWJA* 11: 105–20

—— 1960. 'Economic Change and Japanese Social Organization'. In G. Dole and R. Carnerio, eds. *Essays in the Science of Culture.* New York: Thos. Y. Crowell

—— 1961. 'Postwar Cultural Change and Continuity in Northern Japan'. *AA* 63: 297–321

—— 1965. *Changing Japan.* New York: Holt, Rinehart and Winston

—— 1966. 'Little-known Minority Groups of Japan'. In De Vos and Wagatsuma, eds.: 183–99

—— 1977. 'Changing Association in a Recently Industrialized Community'. *Urban Anthropology* 6(1): 45–64

—— 1978. *County to City: the Urbanization of a Japanese Hamlet*. Salt Lake City: Univ. of Utah Press

Nōrinshō Nōseikyoku. 1967. *Kaso Chiiki Jittai Chōsha Hōkoku (A Report on the Underpopulated Areas)*. Nōrinshō

Ogburn, W. F. 1966 (1922). *Social Change with Respect to Cultural and Original Nature*. Delta Book, New York: Dell Publishing Co.

O'Neill, P. G., ed. 1981. *Tradition and Modern Japan*. Tenterden, Kent: Paul Norbury

Otō, Tokihiko. 1983. 'Gion Matsuri'. In *Kodansha Encyclopedia of Japan* 3: 34–5. Tokyo: Kodansha International Ltd.

Ouchi & Takada. 1979. '*Kinkō Nōson ni Okeru Chiiki Shakai no Henbō* (Changes in Suburban Villages)'. *SSK* 15: 163–89

Plath, David W. 1964. 'Where the Family of God is the Family'. *AA* 66: 300–17

Redfield, R., Fried & Beardsley. 1954. 'Community Studies in Japan and China: A Symposium'. *FEQ* 14: 37–53

Sakurai, Tokutaro. 1968. 'The Major Features and Characteristics of Japanese Folk Beliefs'. In Morioka and Newell, eds. *Sociology of Japanese Religion*. Leiden: Brill

Sakurai, Tokutaro, ed. 1980. *Minkan Shinkō Jiten. (Dictionary of Folk Beliefs)*. Tokyo: Tokyodo

Sansom, Sir George. 1943. *Japan: A Short Cultural History (revised edition)*. New York: Appleton-Century-Crofts, Inc.

Satō, Kōji. 1980. *Hanasaku Mura ni Okeru Sonraku Soshiki no Tokushitsu (Characteristic of Village Organization in Hanasaku)*. Isezaki: Gunma Rekishi Minzoku Kenkyūkai

Seki, Keigo. 1962. '*Nenrei Shūdan* (Age-Groups)'. In Omachi *et al.*, eds., *Nihon Minzokugaku Taikei (An Outline of Japanese Folklore)*: 127–74. Tokyo: Heibonsha

Shimazaki, Minoru. 1967. '*Mura no Kaitai* (Disintegration of Village Community)'. *SSK* 2: 249–55

Shimizu, Akitoshi. 1970. '*Ie no Naiteki no Kōzō to Sonraku Kyōdōtai* (The Inner Structure of *Ie* and the Village Community)'. *MK* 35(3): 177–215

Smelser, Neil J. 1966. 'Mechanisms of Change and Adjustment to Change'. In Hoselitz & Moore, eds. *Industrialization and Society*: 32–56. UNESCO: Mouton

Smith, Robert J. 1952. 'Cooperative Forms in a Japanese Agricultural Community'. *OPCJS* 3: 59–70. Ann Arbor.

—— 1961. 'The Japanese Rural Community: Norms, Sanctions and Ostracism'. *AA* 63: 522–33

—— 1974. *Ancestor Worship in Contemporary Japan*. Stanford: Standford Univ. Press

—— 1978. *Kurusu: The Price of Progress in a Japanese Village, 1951–1975*. Stanford: Stanford Univ. Press

—— & Richard K. Beardsley. 1962. *Japanese Culture: Its Development and Characteristics*. Viking Fund Publications in Anthropology 34. New York: Wenner Gren Foundation

—— & E. P. Reyes. 1957. 'Community Interrelations with the Outside World: The Case of a Japanese Agricultural Community'. *AA* 59:463–72

—— & E. L. Wiswell. 1982. *The Women of Suye Mura*. Chicago: The Univ. of Chicago Press

Smith, Thomas C. 1952. 'The Japanese Village in the Seventeenth Century'. *Journal of Economic History* 12:1–20

—— 1959. *The Agrarian Origins of Modern Japan*. Stanford: Stanford Univ. Press

Smith, T. C., ed. 1960. *City and Village in Japan: Economic Development and Cultural Change* IX(1): Part II

Smith, T. C. *et al.* 1968. *Nakahara.* Stanford: Stanford Univ. Press

Smith, Valene. 1977. *Hosts and Guests: The Anthropology of Tourism.* Philadelphia: Univ. of Pennsylvania Press

Sofue, Takao *et al.* 1972. *Jōshū Fukurokura: A Study of Fukurokura Village in Koi Mura, Agazuma County, Gunma Prefecture.* Meiji Univ.: Politics and Economics Faculty Report 8

Sonraku Shakai Kenkyūkai. 1954. *Sonraku Kenkyū no Seika to Kadai (Results and Problems of Village Study).* Sonraku Shakai Kenkyūkai Nempo I

—— 1959. *Sonraku Kyōdōtairon no Tenkai (Development of Theories on the Village Community)* Sonraku Shakai Nempo VI

Steiner, Kurt. 1956. 'The Japanese Village and Its Government'. *FEQ* 15: 185–99

—— 1968. 'Popular Political Participation and Political Development in Japan: The Rural Level', In R. Ward, ed. *Political Development in Modern Japan.* Princeton: Princeton Univ. Press

Suenari, Michio. 1972. 'First Child Inheritance in Japan'. *Ethnology* 11(2): 122–6

Sugano, Toshishaku. 1976. '*Sanson Keizai Shakai no Kaitei to Saihensei no Ruikei* (The Patterns of Integration and Disintegration of the Economy and Society of Mountain Villages)'. *SSK* 12: 1–66

Sutton, Joseph L. 1953. *Rural Politics in Japan.* OPCJS 4: 40–50. Ann Arbor.

Suzuki, Eitaro. 1940. *Nihon Nōson Shakaigaku Genri (Principles of Japanese Rural Sociology).* Tokyo: Jichosha

Takeda, A. 1951. '*Anekatoku to Yoshisei* (Elder Sister Inheritance and Adoption)'. *MD* 15(3): 12–16

Takeda, Choshu. 1968. '"Ancestor Worship", An Important Historic and Social Factor in Japanese Folk Buddhism'. *P8ICAES* 3: 123–5

Takeuchi, Toshimi. 1938. '*Mura no Seisai* (Village Sanctions)'. *Shakai Keizai Shigaku* 8(6): 1–31

—— 1954. '*Satogaeri* (Homecomings)'. *Nihon Shakai Minzoku Jiten* 502–3

—— 1976. *Shinshū no Sonraku Seikatsu (Village Life in Nagano Prefecture)* Vols I, II, III. Tokyo: Myocho Shuppan

Takikawa, Masajiro. 1933. 'Law'. *Japanese Encyclopedia of the Social Sciences* IX: 254–7. New York: Macmillan

Tamao, Tokushisa. 1980. 'Tourism within, from and to Japan'. *International Social Science Journal* 32: 128–50

Tauber, Irene. 1951. 'Family, Migration and Industrialization in Japan'. *American Sociological Review* 16(2): 149–57

—— 1960. 'Urbanization and Population Change in the Development of Modern Japan'. In T. Smith, ed.: 1–28

Titiev, Mischa, 1953. 'Changing Patterns of *Kumiai* Structure'. *OPCJS* 4: 1–28. Ann Arbor.

Trewartha, Glenn T. 1965. *Japan: A Geography.* Madison, Wisconsin: Univ. of Wisconsin Press

Tsurumi, Kasuko. 1970. *Social Change and the Individual.* Princeton, New Jessey: Princeton Univ. Press

Ushijima, Morimitsu. 1971. *Henbōsuru Suemura (Suye Mura in Transition).* Kyoto: Minerva Shobo

Ushiomi, Toshitaka. 1968. *Forestry and Mountain Village Communities in Japan: A Study of Human Relations.* Tokyo: Kokusai Bunka Shinkōkai (Japan Cultural Society)

Varner, Richard E. 1977. 'The Organized Peasant: The *Wakamonogumi* in the Edo Period'. *MK* 32:459–83

Vogel, Ezra. 1963. *Japan's New Middle Class*. Berkeley & Los Angeles: Univ. of California Press

—— 1967. 'Kinship Structure, Migration to the City and Modernization'. In R. P. Dore, ed. 91–111

Wakamori, Taro. 1963. 'Initiation Rites and Young Men's Organization'. In Dorson, ed.: 291–304

Ward, R. E. 1951. 'The Socio-Political Role of the *Buraku* (Hamlet) in Japan'. *APSR* XLV: 1025–40

—— 1953. 'Some Observations on Local Autonomy at the Village Level in Present-day Japan'. *FEQ* 12(2): 183–202

—— 1960. 'Urban-rural Differences and the Process of Political Modernization in Japan: A Case Study'. In T. Smith, ed.: 135–65

Watanabe, Yozo, 1963. 'The Family and the Law: The Individual Premise and Modern Japanese Family Law'. In von Mehren, ed. *Law in Japan: The Legal Order in a Changing Society*. Cambridge: Harvard Univ. Press

Yanagita, Kunio, ed. 1938. *Sanson Seikatsu no Kenkyū (Studies of Life in Mountain Villages)*. Tokyo: Minkan Denshō no Kai

—— 1957. *Japanese Manners and Customs in the Meiji Era*. Trns. and adopted by Charles S. Terry. Tokyo: Obunsha

—— 1970. *About Our Ancestors: The Japanese Family System*. Trns. by Fanny Mayer & Yasuyo Ishiwara. Tokyo: Japanese National Commission for UNESCO

Yoden, Hiromitsu & Haruo Matsubara. 1968. *Nōson Shakaigaku (Rural Sociology)*. Tokyo: Kawashima Shoten

Yoshida, Teigo. 1963. 'Cultural Integration and Change in Japanese Villages'. *AA* 65: 102–16

—— 1964. 'Social Conflict and Cohesion in a Japanese Rural Community'. *Ethnology* 3: 219–31

Yoshino, Roger & Sueo Murakoshi. 1977. *The Invisible Visible Minority: Japan's Buraku-min*. Osaka: Buraku Kaihō Kenkyūsho

Index